Zeus on the Loose

Unlock Your Child's Cosmic Superpower

Alex Trenoweth

The Wessex Astrologer

Published in 2025 by
The Wessex Astrologer Ltd
PO Box 9307
Swanage
BH19 9BF
England

For a full list of our titles go to www.wessexastrologer.com

Copyright © 2025 Alex Trenoweth

Alex Trenoweth asserts the moral right to be
identified as the author of this work.

Cover design by Fiona Bowring at Bowring Creative

Typeset by Kevin Moore

ISBN 9781916625310

A catalogue record for this book is available at The British Library

No part of this book may be reproduced or used in any form or
by any means without the written permission of the publisher.
A reviewer may quote brief passages.

For my daughter Jess

Just like me but a billion times better

Contents

A Note from the Author	vii
Foreword	xi
Introduction	xiii
Jupiter in Aries	1
Jupiter in Taurus	18
Jupiter in Gemini	34
Jupiter in Cancer	50
Jupiter in Leo	65
Jupiter in Virgo	81
Jupiter in Libra	97
Jupiter in Scorpio	115
Jupiter in Sagittarius	132
Jupiter in Capricorn	147
Jupiter in Aquarius	164
Jupiter in Pisces	182
Conclusion	199
Jupiter Sign Changes (Ingresses) from 1900 to 2050	200
Summary of the Adolescence of Case Studies	208
How to calculate the Jupiter and Uranus Sextiles	210

A Note from the Author

I've known I was going to be a schoolteacher since I was six years old (those who already understand the Jupiter cycle will know this was during my transiting Jupiter-natal Jupiter opposition). My parents tried to talk me out of it but my mother still has the little card that says: "When I grow up I want to be a teacher," written by me as a six-year-old. I didn't just want to be a teacher. I wanted to teach high school. Everyone warned me that it didn't pay very well, that the behaviour of children was getting worse and that conditions were poor but the thought of having my own classroom, with my own extended family of 30 children was irresistible for someone with Jupiter in Cancer.

Just before my second Jupiter return, I graduated from Western Michigan University in the summer of 1990. I decided I needed a little break before doing my teachers' training in the US so off I went to England for a six-month sabbatical to see the world. I got as far as the British Isles before getting married and having my own children. When my children were school age, I finally had my chance to do my re-training in the UK. I figured there was no career like teaching to work in child care for my children and working at the same time (of course I now realise how insane this was). I officially qualified as a school teacher in the spring of 2002 when I finally finished my Post Graduate Certificate in Education. It was my third Jupiter return.

After a full Jupiter cycle of teaching and observing how my pupils learn, I felt ready to show how astrology could enhance education. So I gathered up my notes and I began writing the first edition of *Growing Pains: Astrology in Adolescence* as transiting Jupiter moved through the sign of Gemini. I then launched the book on my fourth Jupiter return. Shortly after this, life quite literally took off. I spoke at astrology conferences all over the world and I had little choice but to leave full time teaching: the only option to juggle teaching and travelling was to become a day-to-day supply teacher. Then, I was asked if I would like to try teaching primary school. Completely by accident, I became not only a teacher who lasted past the five-year limit of the average teaching career, I also became one of the few teachers with ample experience in teaching children from age of three years old all the way up to eighteen years old. If I could summarise the teaching profession, I would say it is "hills and troughs". Ups and downs, highs and lows, telling everyone it was the best profession in the world and then making plans for early retirement. And, if anyone were to ask me how I managed to stay in this profession for so long, I could only say it was understanding astrology—particularly the cycles of Saturn and Jupiter - that helped me internalise the cycles of growth and development.

However, despite the success of *Growing Pains,* I still felt there was much more to say about both Jupiter and Saturn and so I decided to focus first on Jupiter with *Zeus on the Loose* and then a future book exclusively on the cycles of Saturn which hones and practises the lessons of Jupiter.

It is in the spirit of working with Jupiter cycles (you will notice we are not working with Sun signs here) that I launch *Zeus on the Loose,* written during Jupiter's transit through Gemini and launched just in time for the start of my fifth Jupiter return.

It is my greatest hope that astrology can help heal the massive problems we face in the educational field (such as the mass teacher exodus into better paid and less stressful professions) and collectively work to improve making better investments in education. We need to concentrate on preparing children to be productive, keep them from offending at young ages and ending up in prison and encouraging adults to keep refining and building on their learning to create a better society. After all, we've tried Myers-Briggs, the Big Five, DISC Assessment, Enneagram of personality, 16 PF, MMPI, CliftonStrengths and VIA Character Strengths (and probably a lot of other means that have never seen the light of day). Why not a little astrology?

And, by the way astrology is not about pigeonholing pupils into a one-size fits all learning container. Jupiter is about finding ways of pushing our limits and reaching for the sky. The suggestions listed in this book are just that. Suggestions. To help you, please refer to the Jupiter Ephemeris and the Case Studies.

Before you go any further, a little task for you to complete

1) Find Jupiter in your own chart (never mind anyone else for the moment) and take a note of the sign and the degree of Jupiter in that sign.

2) Identify your Jupiter returns for the rest of your life (there is an ephemeris at the end of the book to help you).

3) Go through the guidance notes in this book for your Jupiter sign before you try to help your child with theirs.

4) Find that pulse of Jupiter, make some plans. The world is full of opportunities to learn, no matter how old you are. Take Zeus by the hand and never buckle that seatbelt. After all, Zeus demands the faith that everything will turn out better than you expected.

Happy Travels,

Alex

Foreword

Steve Judd

Astrology was once a cornerstone of education in many ancient cultures, studied alongside medicine, astronomy, and philosophy. In fact, the development of astronomy was largely driven by the need for precise planetary data to support astrological predictions. For centuries, schools of astrology thrived across civilizations, each with its own traditions. But by the early to mid-17th century, the invention and widespread use of the telescope ushered in a more mechanistic view of the cosmos—one that emphasized observation over interpretation. Since the scientific revolutions of Descartes, Galileo, and Newton, astrology has been largely excluded from mainstream academic discourse.

In recent decades, however, there's been a growing call to reconsider astrology's place in education. Interest in astrology is rising worldwide, driven by a collective desire for more holistic, impersonal tools for self-understanding. Today, numerous schools and online communities are embracing astrology anew—not as superstition, but as a timeless system that has endured beyond empires, ideologies, and even religions. Some educational institutions are now cautiously exploring astrology's role in personal development. Rudolf Steiner's work on Astrosophy, for example, deepens the conversation about human-cosmic connection. Astrology can be a powerful tool for psychological insight, helping individuals understand their unique "user manual". It provides a structured, objective framework for self-discovery and personal growth—something increasingly valuable in our fragmented, fast-changing world.

Alex Trenoweth brings a rare combination of experience to this conversation. A lifelong educator and astrologer, she has dedicated herself to integrating these two worlds in meaningful, practical ways. I've known Alex for over thirty years and have personally witnessed her use astrology to support children, particularly those struggling within conventional educational systems. I've also seen her inspire adults to reflect on their own childhoods and rethink how they educate the next generation.

Zeus on the Loose is a major contribution to this movement. It offers a fresh, insightful exploration of child development through the lens of astrology—specifically, through the cycle of Jupiter. This book reveals how Jupiter's placement in the natal chart can illuminate a person's learning style, motivation, and educational needs. With practical guidance, symbolic depth, and case studies of well-known individuals, it bridges astrology and education in a way that is both accessible and profound. Readers are guided through every Jupiter placement, learning how each sign shapes early development, major life transitions, and philosophical growth. Alex provides a wealth of practical advice and suggested classroom activities, making this an invaluable resource not only for astrologers and parents, but for teachers seeking new tools for understanding their students.

When I first picked up an astrology book in 1977, I often said that if astrology were taught in schools, we could—within two generations—see an end to racism, misogyny, warfare, and other divisive patterns. That might sound idealistic, but astrology offers a framework for understanding the self that transcends stereotypes and promotes empathy. Nearly 50 years later, I'm proud to see Alex leading the way in bringing this deeper understanding into the classroom.

This book is not just a manual—it's a revolution. Alex, you rock—thank you for being its champion.

Steve Judd
1st June 2025, 21.45 pm.

Introduction

Astrology has long been a tool for exploring the human journey—its patterns, potential, and purpose. This book dives into a particular astrological treasure chest: the placement of Jupiter, the planet of growth, wisdom, and expansion. Each Jupiter sign represents a unique learning style, a distinct way of approaching life's challenges, and a special capacity for growth and understanding. By examining Jupiter's position in the natal chart, we uncover a roadmap for navigating life's opportunities and overcoming its hurdles.

This is not merely a book of interpretations. It is a practical guide for educators, parents, and anyone seeking to support personal development. Through examining Jupiter's role in education, growth stages, and key astrological transits, we can gain deeper insights into the ways individuals learn, think, and evolve. Each chapter provides a detailed exploration of one Jupiter sign, including developmental milestones, key transits, practical strategies for fostering growth, and case studies of well-known individuals with that Jupiter placement. Additionally, there is an exploration on the Jupiter and Uranus sextiles which occur during adolescence. This is unique and brand new research.

Whether you are a seasoned astrologer, a curious parent, or a lifelong student of personal growth, this book offers a comprehensive framework for understanding Jupiter's influence on education, self-discovery, and the unfolding of potential. By focusing on the planet of expansion, we open the door to endless possibilities—not just for knowledge, but for wisdom, understanding, and a fuller, more meaningful life.

Jupiter in Aries

Aries is a fire sign by element and a cardinal sign by modality. Transiting squares and oppositions to its natal position will occur in the other cardinal signs—Cancer, Libra, and Capricorn. This pattern repeats throughout the native's life, shaping how they learn, grow, and develop a personal philosophy. Cardinal signs are independent, self-sufficient, and enterprising. However, they must learn to work with others by exercising patience, caution, and tolerance.

Jupiter transits through each sign at a pace of about one year. Since children are typically grouped by academic year, those with Jupiter in Aries will learn alongside peers with the same placement. However, there may also be students with Jupiter in Pisces or Jupiter in Taurus in the same cohort.

Children with Jupiter in Aries thrive on competition and fast-paced activities. Broadly speaking, they must practise patience and tolerance for those who struggle to keep up with their pace. They should also learn to check their work for mistakes and develop the habit of extending their efforts to ensure thoroughness. Since Mars rules Aries, the way they gather and process information is further influenced by Mars' sign, house, and aspects.

The First Jupiter Square

All babies need the basics of adequate nutrition, a safe place to sleep, cleanliness and a comfortable environment. They also need the human touch in order to build trust and to feel their caregiver is responding to their signals for these necessities. Eye contact, talking/singing to the baby and providing a daily rhythm of sleep, cleaning, feeding and playing with age appropriate toys are essential for all babies, irrespective of the Jupiter signs. As the baby grows into a toddler, it is important caregivers have adequately "baby-proofed" the child's environment. These essential needs are important all the way into old age. Once these needs are met consistently, a bit of astrology can help the caregivers find the learner's internal "beat" for development.

Here are just a few suggestions for Jupiter in Aries learners:

During the first year of life, the Jupiter in Aries learner will experience Jupiter transiting through Taurus. At this stage, the world is a vast landscape of learning opportunities. Natally, they may prefer bold flavours like spicy or garlicky foods, but during this transit, they might gravitate toward sweeter or heartier options.

During the second year, transiting Jupiter will begin moving through the sign of Gemini. Helping them to develop fine motor skills by painting or colouring (hand over hand guidance) is a wonderful way to help them develop their vocabulary if specific adjectives are used. "Play dates" are usually a good idea as the baby approaches the "babbling" stage. Parents and carers may notice the child chatters to their toys, their imaginary companions or the pets if there is no one else to talk to. During this time, the learner will be perfecting the skills of the key tasks of this age group: walking unaided, speaking more clearly and being able to ask when they have to go to the potty. They will begin to understand how conversations work and will want to try out new words and turns of phrase, and will search for new people to try out these skills with.

During the third year, transiting Jupiter will begin moving through the sign of Cancer and the Jupiter in Aries will enter the world of developing emotions. There may be particular triggers that set off quite spectacular tantrums and these bouts of excessive emotions are perfect times for parents and carers to teach these learners the value of self-control, patience with others and being truly sorry if they hurt someone. Physical expressions of anger can be redirected in more positive directions such as by learning a simple skill like kicking a ball at a specified target. Because they are intuitive, and with the verbal lessons they have learned the previous year when Jupiter was transiting through Gemini, they may have to be encouraged to understand that verbal expressions of anger can hurt worse than lashing out with hitting and/or kicking. If they are taught the value of family and friends and the importance of asking for help and support in completing the key tasks when needed, they can learn to express their emotions appropriately and in the manner that allows them to have what they need.

The first Jupiter square is about developing the basic motor skills of walking, talking and toilet training. Jupiter in Aries children tend to be fast learners but they also need to be encouraged to slow down and listen to their bodies.

The First Jupiter Opposition

Between the ages of about three to six years old, most young children are preparing for formal education and socialisation. These are just some ideas to help Jupiter in Aries learners prepare for their first adventures away from their immediate care givers.

During the fourth year, transiting Jupiter will begin to move through the sign of Leo and the learner will begin to demonstrate their confidence in showing others what they can do. They can put on a good performance but, equally, they can become annoyed if they feel someone else is stealing their thunder. Helping them to understand that they are loved equally to their siblings or other relatives is the basis of this transit. Praise and genuine admiration for doing the right thing by sharing, complimenting others or helping with the chores are all ways to help the Aries learner at this stage as they begin to mature and socialise more.

Activities for enjoyment and learning outside of school: stage play (let them be the star but encourage them to share the stage too), making and wearing costumes and masks, dressing up to go to an event.

By their fifth year, transiting Jupiter will begin to move through the sign of Virgo as Jupiter in Aries learners begin to prepare for the start of their formal education. The shuffle of new people may bring about some anxiety about orderliness and hygiene. These learners may dislike the messes others leave behind, and tut and complain loudly to anyone who is listening. This is another opportunity for parents and carers to encourage patience and tolerance. The new-found interest in keeping things—and their bodies—clean is a good time to introduce more complicated chores. Helping them to create a grounded and organised schedule may help them to understand that there are times for being messy but if everyone helps with tidying up, the task is a whole lot more enjoyable. Jupiter in Aries learners may benefit from being given opportunities to practise patience and precision at this stage with projects that require hand-eye coordination such as simple sewing, stringing beads or similar tasks.

Activities for enjoyment and learning outside of school: learning about the physical bodies of people or animals, learning about sickness and how to take care of someone (or a pet) who is not feeling well, understanding the basics of medicine. Learning to identify plants and different species of animals, learning to measure accurately with simple tools such as rulers.

By their sixth year, the year of the first Jupiter opposition, transiting Jupiter in Libra may bring a tighter focus on their relationships. At this stage, many schools begin preparations for formal testing. These learners may need support in forming more meaningful relationships with their school friends. Drama, as friendship groups tend to change often at this age, could become an issue if the learners are not given the social tools to cope with working with others. Encouraging these learners to understand that making up with people they fall out with is an important part of how human relationships are managed. They may not like everyone in a classroom or in a family, but conflicts and how to resolve them (without resorting to getting physical) are a part of life. These learners eventually figure out how to charm others and to use better (and less aggressive) word choices to get what they want. As these skills may not be what they are naturally good at, it may take some gentle reminders as well as practise to get it right. As they tend to be fast learners, it generally doesn't take them long.

Activities for enjoyment and learning outside of school: planning a themed party with a few friends (try themes based around *Horrible Histories* or their favourite kids' movies) and have "preparation parties" where all the invitees have to make their own party favours and costumes, plan their food and activities, etc.

As the first Jupiter opposition comes to an end, Jupiter in Aries learners begin to understand other people better. They see their own needs are different to others, particularly as they begin school and start to meet more people.

The Closing Jupiter Square

By this stage, children will have settled into a home/school routine and it is likely schools will begin to prepare students for the Scholastic Achievement Tests (or their equivalents). Debate rages as to whether these tests cause stress for the children but, drawing from personal experiences, students tend not to get too upset if the adults around them don't behave as if the world is coming to an end. The purpose of these tests is to help identify strengths and weaknesses in the child's development. The results establish a baseline, not a final outcome. Here are some ways to help support the learners during these formative times:

As Jupiter transits through Scorpio during their seventh year, Jupiter in Aries pupils begin to understand how to use their own personal power. "Power" can mean different things to different people (such as physical strength, mental fortitude or emotional intelligence) but Jupiter in Aries tends to be bold and up front with what they know or want to know. They may become curious about the nuances that they pick up from media influences or overheard adult conversations. Rather than shying away from such discussions, isn't it better that they hear the answers from trusted adults rather than misinformation from unreliable sources such as their peers?

Activities for enjoyment and learning outside of school: mysteries and puzzles, being *gently* frightened (Halloween or cold, dark autumn nights are a good time to share simple ghost stories), nature walks so they can observe the cycle of life in plants and animals (NB: pupils at this stage may take an interest in death and pregnancies so be prepared to explain). They may also take an interest in the financial side of managing a home (never too early to introduce a child to the real world of finance).

In terms of learning, the eighth year is when transiting Jupiter moves through Sagittarius. The child may find faith that the world is indeed a good place. They find the confidence to explore new places, may become curious about other religions and will want to write or talk about them. This is an energetic year for learning and they need parents and teachers who can keep up with their needs or they will become resentful that they have missed out on something as Jupiter transits through Capricorn. As this is usually the year of SATs, this group tends to need a lot of breaks to work off physical energy and to give their brains much-needed blood flow.

Activities for enjoyment and learning outside of school: taking part in charity work, visiting places of worship, learning to discuss politics and identifying political leaders, learning about different countries (their map, geographical features, language, etc.).

The ninth year is when a child begins to be able to distinguish between what is real and what is make believe as transiting Jupiter makes its way through the sign of Capricorn. They have learned how to be honest with themselves about their progress and may become fretful about the future if they feel they are behind when compared to their classmates. This is a serious year for development and they may start taking their education seriously because they see it as a way to become successful. There tends to be a deep-seated fear about being good enough or fast enough or smart enough. Sometimes all that is needed is just a side hobby that allows them to be unique. Jupiter in Aries pupils tend to make fast progress when the only competitor is themselves.

Activities for enjoyment and learning outside of school: hobbies that encourage one step at a time, like wool crafts, learning to do simple carpentry skills, learning to do "handyman/woman" jobs around the house, they may also like to take part in "business games" or even having a small, self-run business.

As these pupils complete the closing Jupiter square, they begin to see the value of learning, of meeting new people and seeing new places. They should be encouraged to pause and reflect on what they have learned rather than just jumping to the next task. They are on the edge of beginning puberty and they may need to find the pulse of exertion and rest.

The First Jupiter Return

As the learner heads towards their final years of primary school, they should be able to work more independently, understand the general rules of the classroom/playground and see home and school as two separate environments.

In their tenth year, Jupiter will transit through the sign of Aquarius and the Jupiter in Aries learner becomes acutely aware of the strength of friendships and wider social circles. It may be a year when long term loyalties come to an end because these connections have become ineffective or even hostile. Connections become lost or broken as families move out of town. New families move in and these children discover people aren't just "replaced". Relationships take care and work. During this year, Jupiter in Aries learners discover strength in numbers and become adept at understanding how others can be useful to them and vice versa. They may wish to form clubs to share common interests or become interested in politics because they have discovered they have a voice that others want to listen to.

Generally speaking, there may be a tendency to bend the rules just to see what will happen (be sure they understand consequences).

Activities for enjoyment and learning outside of school: leading/forming a new club and setting rules and expectations, simple science experiments (YouTube is full of ideas of home science experiments—ensure they have permission and understand they have to clean up), learning how to do simple tasks like changing light bulbs, fuses and understanding electrical circuits, recording and monitoring data accurately as part of an experiment.

In their eleventh year, Jupiter transits through the sign of Pisces and the child may find it difficult to focus on academic tasks if they are not permitted to use their imagination. They realise that in their haste to be successful, they have not had the opportunity to explore their creative side. An interest in music, poetry or other avenues of creative expression may become apparent. This is the year that puberty begins to really kick in and the child may find ways to explore their sexual side via light-hearted romances. However these Aries in learners at this stage need to have a routine that includes looking after their bodies and keeping their work space in reasonable order.

Activities for enjoyment and learning outside of school: Music lessons, art projects not found in school like pottery courses that allow the learner to complete a project all the way to a satisfactory completion, studying a particular artist and their work medium (painting, sculpture, carving, etc).

When we return to a place have visited before, it is our nature to make comparisons to what has changed since the first time we were there. We may want to seek out the things we did before or perhaps try something completely different. As almost all students will have had their first Jupiter returns by the end of their eleventh year, schools could hold an end of year festival that would allow pupils to demonstrate their individual skills. Schools tend to hold sporting events during this time but how about a not-the-sporting-event competition? Students could try to (safely) break World Records and then re-visit their record during later Jupiter returns.

To Jupiter in Aries, the type of children who are impatient to move as quickly as they can, school can be something they see as a blockage to their next big excitement—unless they have been taught the values of patience, tolerance and managing their intellectual energy so they can deepen their knowledge. Poor habits such as rushing through their work (complete with illegible handwriting), being overly competitive with their grades or even showing aggression through "play fighting" when they don't get their way are now just a few of the problems their new secondary teachers must face. Of course, secondary school teachers have higher expectations for these early adolescents and the consequences for these poor choices are likely to end up with the loss of opportunities for the activities they enjoy such as attending sporting events or enjoying the relative freedom of being outside with their friends playing games.

The stages of development during their first twelve years will repeat in the same sequence, for roughly the same amount of time, for the rest of their lives. A wide variety of activities in the home will support the school in giving learners a well rounded education.

The Jupiter and Uranus Sextiles: In the Thick of Puberty

As noted in the Introduction, the thirteenth year of a child's life is usually when rebellion and defiance start to become noticeable. Astrologically, transiting Jupiter forms a sextile aspect to its natal position at the same time Uranus, the planet of rebellion, will also make its first Ptolemaic aspect to its own natal position (also by sextile aspect). This combination quite literally means "big rebellion" and marks the time when adolescents (and their parents) begin the struggle to make that separation into adulthood.

Identifying when and how a young adolescent may struggle with the changing social rules they must face could be helpful for parents. For example, if an adolescent experiences the Uranus sextile before the Jupiter sextile, parents may view their child as needing more guidance for following the expectations of the home environment (which would include expectations in school). In the Case Studies section, subjects with this tendency are noted as "rebels". If an adolescent experiences the Jupiter sextile before the Uranus sextile, parents may view their child as needing more encouragement for academic work and possibly with social skills. In the Case Studies section, subjects with this tendency are noted as "truth seekers". There is no "good" or "bad" with these notations and they are only presented as starting points for understanding the life-long impact this stage of development has on learners as they continue their journey all the way into old age. To demonstrate how this particular stage of development can vary from person to person, there is a summary of the time frame for the subjects of the case studies on page 208.

Furthermore, an adolescent's developing body means they may be interested in forming intimate relationships but their brain needs time to catch up with all the new situations it finds itself in. For children born with Jupiter in Aries, Jupiter will be transiting through the sign of Gemini as it had been during their second year. It can be helpful for parents to recall the lessons of the second year as difficulties with relationships and learning can typically come down to choices of words. And children at this stage of development can have a very interesting choice of words which they'll enjoying using if they see it makes others flinch.

The Saturn Opposition

The Saturn opposition begins some time during the fourteenth or fifteenth year (possibly earlier or later depending on individual cases) and marks the end of astrological adolescence. Parents and teachers usually notice that the adolescent begins to calm down and take a more mature approach to their academic progress. In the UK, this coincides with choosing academic subjects (as opposed to trying a little bit of everything), formal exam preparation and a marked change in mood. Depression, anxiety and their symptoms must be monitored and taken seriously. Schools will have access to support mechanisms for parents and carers, teachers will have been trained in how to identify potential difficulties and for parents who are home schooling, social services can be a sound source for help.

As they head towards their transiting Saturn opposition, Jupiter in Aries children will also re-visit what they learned as transiting Jupiter usually (it can vary from person to person) passes through the signs of Cancer and Leo. They will develop sensitivity as well as have a strong desire to be respected for who they are. Re-visiting the appropriate stage of astrological development can be helpful to provide the right sort of help and support.

The Second Jupiter Opposition

By the time a young adult finishes mandatory education, they will have a good idea of what they want to do with their lives and yet they still have time to re-take exams or re-train if they discover they want to do something else. The second Jupiter opposition is a time of making serious decisions: the young adult is no longer a child. The learner now knows there are consequences for undesirable behaviour and can no longer blame "the system" for their poor choice. Sadly, our prison services are filled with young people who have slipped through the net. As a collective whole, society could do with using a little astrology to help these young people get back on track. A more comprehensive mentoring service could be helpful.

Here are some ideas to help young adults focus on the rest of their adult lives:

For the Jupiter in Aries learner, transiting Jupiter will be in Libra as the young adult finishes their formal education at around the age of eighteen. Because Libra is associated with relationships, Jupiter in Aries learners may be in committed relationships and wish to marry before they are financially or emotionally ready. Obviously this tendency varies wildly between individuals but it is a wise parent or authority figure who helps a young couple prepare for married life and all its responsibilities.

The Second and Subsequent Jupiter Returns

As a person continues to develop emotionally, physically and spiritually they will build on the lessons they learned in the formative years. Jupiter returns occur (roughly) at the ages of 24, 36, 48 and 60 (and beyond). The suggestions for activities can be modified to suit the developmental cycle for each Jupiter cycle. For example, a Jupiter in Aries learner experiencing a Jupiter in Gemini transit during their third year of life can be encouraged to practise their fine motor skills by practising the alphabet; during their fifteenth year, they may wish to try calligraphy; during their twenty-seventh year, they may want to perfect their *Shodo*) and so on. The key for all Jupiter returns is to choose a skill (or even one per year) and exercise the brain, all the way to the final years of life. As always, with Jupiter, the sky is the limit.

Jupiter returns at all ages should be celebrated and an experienced astrologer can help locate the exact moment of the return. New clothes to reflect a changing style, a good meal (with a magnificent dessert) with influential friends and maybe even a holiday to some exotic place are just a few ideas. To celebrate the ingress (entry) of Jupiter in a new sign, consult the table in the appendix. The Chinese culture does a wonderful job with celebrating, "The Year of the…". While theirs may be a different culture and system, the similarity of intention is still there.

Fine tuning the role of Jupiter

Jupiter in Aries is ruled by the planet Mars. Mars is the planet of action, energy and initiative. The influence of Jupiter expands and teaches through the efforts of Mars. As Mars is a much faster planet than Jupiter, it is very likely that, even in classes with children in the same year group, they would have different Mars placements.

Mars in Aries: This is fast energy! It may seem like these pupils are born ready to give anything a try. The words "take it easy" will have no effect whatsoever. Hobbies and interests are taken up and abandoned with lightning speed and so need to be paced. For teachers, keep lessons at a fast pace and change activities quickly but make sure they finish to the required expectations.

Mars in Taurus: These pupils may tend to take their time to enjoy the fine things of life but they may need to be reminded of the importance of education in order to have jobs that will allow them to afford such goods. They like to collect nice things and may be very slow to accept change. These are highly sensory motivated students.

Mars in Gemini: These pupils generally need time to talk or write about their experiences. They are naturally curious about the world, have endless questions and will read anything and love games of any sort but especially ones that indulge their need for trivia. They can lose focus easily so objectives in learning must be clear.

Mars in Cancer: These pupils tend to cling, and find it difficult to leave familiar places and people. They may show signs of being frightened of the unknown. Starting school can often be the first taste they have of leaving home. Little reminders of home (maybe something small they can put in their coat pockets) can be comforting to them.

Mars in Leo: These pupils like to be centre stage in learning and they will only learn if they think you are watching so praise is absolutely essential.

Do be genuine: a Jupiter in Aries learner can spot a fake from a long way away and won't be afraid to let anyone know.

Mars in Virgo: The key word for these pupils is "efficiency". They have a discerning eye and high standards that can mean they avoid traditional childhood activities because they don't want to see their carefully ordered world turned upside down. Encourage them to not get overly hung up on small details.

Mars in Libra: Group activities come naturally to these pupils but they must be trained for exam conditions too. They tend to be cautious about expressing their opinions because they don't want to offend anyone but role playing arguments can help them develop the confidence to stand up for what they believe in.

Mars in Scorpio: These pupils like to study independently so tend to surprise others with what they know—and there are usually one or two topics that they know inside out. For parents, keeping the lines of communication open about socially taboo subjects will help them to know who to go to with any awkward questions.

Mars in Sagittarius: These pupils love adventure and thrive on activities which pose an element of risk. Quests, treasure hunts and anything that allows the *bon vivant* in them to come alive will appeal to them. However, they must also be taught the importance of safety and risk assessment.

Mars in Capricorn: These pupils have a mature attitude towards their education—but beneath that maturity is a fear of failure. Learning objectives should be very clear and plain.

Mars in Aquarius: These pupils thrive on being allowed to experiment. However, they also need to embrace the more mundane things such as tidying up and making sure they have permission to conduct their experiments.

Mars in Pisces: These pupils understand and have compassion for all living creatures and will pour all their energy into saving the life of anything that shows the slightest sign of illness. The death of a butterfly will have these learners composing poems or requiems. They will need help prioritising their work.

Jupiter in Aries: Case Studies

Sting (Gordon Sumner)

Gordon Sumner, best known as Sting, was born on October 2, 1951, at 1:30 AM in Wallsend, UK (RR: A; Collector: March) with Jupiter in Aries, ruled by Mars in Leo.

In the early 1960s, around the time of his first Jupiter return, a relative took young Gordon to a ship launch, where he saw the Queen Mother waving. From that moment, he knew he wanted a better life. While he didn't make it into the Royal Family, he became music royalty instead, becoming one of the most famous singers in pop music and beyond.

During adolescence, transiting Uranus in Virgo was sextile to its natal position about eight months before transiting Jupiter in Gemini sextiled his natal Jupiter in Aries—indicating a rebellious streak.

When transiting Jupiter opposed his natal Jupiter, he left Warwick University after just one term. He drifted between jobs as a bus conductor and tax officer before returning to university and qualifying as a teacher in 1974. At the time, transiting Jupiter was making a series of oppositions to his natal planets in Leo.

By April 1975, as Jupiter completed its second return, Sumner was finishing his first year as a teacher. By then, he was an accomplished jazz musician, performing with the Phoenix Jazzmen on weekends and during breaks. According to legend, he wore a black-and-yellow striped jumper during performances, leading his bandmates to nickname him Sting. In 2011, as Jupiter made its fifth return, Sumner recalled that he had stopped thinking of himself as Gordon.

In 1976, his teaching career ended as transiting Jupiter squared his Mars in Leo three times. That year, he married his first wife just before transiting Jupiter squared his Ascendant/Descendant axis; their separation came six years later when transiting Jupiter squared that position again.

In January 1977, Sting moved to London and formed The Police with Stewart Copeland and Henry Padovani (later replaced by Andy Summers). Just weeks after transiting Jupiter in Cancer squared his natal Saturn in Libra, the band released their first hit single, 'Roxanne', ahead of their debut album *Outlandos d'Amour*. The song later made *Rolling Stone's 400 Greatest Songs of All Time*.

For half a Jupiter cycle, The Police continued their meteoric rise. Their final album, *Synchronicity* (August 1983), was released as Sting's transiting Jupiter in Sagittarius was squaring his natal Venus in Virgo. During a performance at Shea Stadium, he decided to leave the band, later describing the show as "like playing on top of Everest".

Though the band never officially disbanded, the members pursued solo projects. In 1984, as transiting Jupiter in Capricorn squared his Libran Sun three times, major life events unfolded: his first child with Trudie Styler was born in January, he divorced his first wife, and by the end of the year, Styler was pregnant with their second child. Somehow, he still found time to perform with Band Aid.

Sting released *The Dream of the Blue Turtles* in June 1985, as transiting Jupiter in Aquarius was conjunct his Descendant. The album had a strong jazz influence, reminiscent of his early performances a half Jupiter cycle

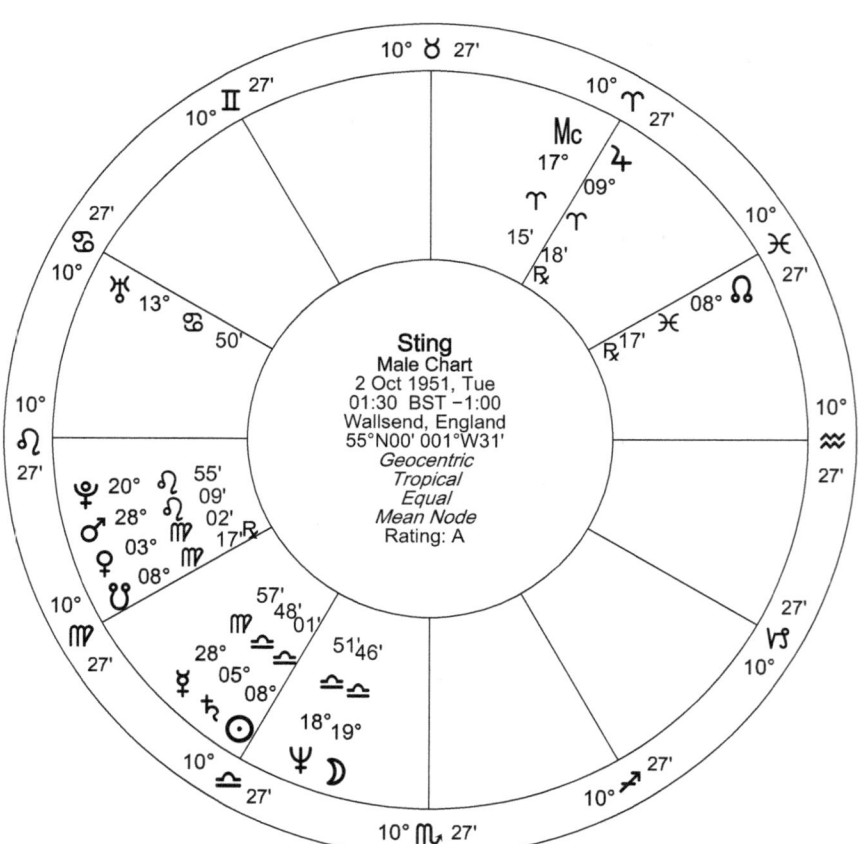

earlier. He also contributed to the soundtrack for *Leaving Las Vegas*, starring Nicolas Cage—who, interestingly, was born almost exactly a full Jupiter cycle after him.

Sting has remained one of the world's top performers, frequently collaborating with other musicians. In April 2009, as transiting Jupiter in Aquarius opposed his natal Pluto, it was revealed that he was one of the UK's wealthiest people.

Mars, the ruler of his Jupiter in Aries, is often linked to one's sex drive. With Jupiter in Leo, it's an amusing astrological footnote that his widely publicised tantric sex sessions with Trudie Styler have almost overshadowed his long and successful music career.

Nicolas Cage

Nicolas Cage was born on January 7, 1964, at 5:30 AM in Harbor City, CA (RR: AA; Collector: Clifford) with Jupiter in Aries, ruled by Mars in Capricorn.

Born Nicolas Coppola, he has an extra dose of Jupiter influence with a Sagittarius Ascendant. His father was a literature professor and his mother was a dancer, but he honed his acting skills by watching his famous uncle—none other than Francis Ford Coppola.

Around the time of his first Jupiter opposition his mother struggled with mental health issues, and by Cage's first Jupiter return, his parents had divorced. He was sent to live with his uncle in Northern California.

During adolescence, transiting Uranus in Scorpio sextiled its natal position about six months before transiting Jupiter in Gemini sextiled his natal Jupiter, reinforcing his rebellious nature.

With such strong Jupiter influences, it's no surprise that Cage struggled to find meaning in life and often saw himself as an outsider. At 15, during his second waning Jupiter square, he was acting in local theatres, playing punks, crazy guys, and outsiders. Confident in his abilities, he tried to convince his uncle to give him a screen test. However, he was met with silence.

Cage's first role was a minor one in *Fast Times at Ridgemont High* (1982), the only time he was credited as Nicolas Coppola. After this, he changed his name to Cage to avoid accusations of nepotism. The following year, as transiting Jupiter crossed his Ascendant, he appeared in his uncle's film *Rumble Fish*.

In October 1986, transiting Jupiter opposed his natal Pluto in Virgo three times. That year, Cage starred in another of his uncle's films, *Peggy Sue Got Married*, though his performance was criticised. In 2008, as transiting Jupiter in Capricorn was conjunct his natal Sun three times (extending the effects of the transit for the entire year), co-star Kathleen Turner released a memoir claiming Cage had driven drunk multiple times. He filed for defamation and won.

Cage's second Jupiter return in 1987 marked a turning point. He struck gold with *Moonstruck*, which earned six Academy Award nominations (including Best Actress for Cher). That same year, *Raising Arizona*—another cult classic—was released.

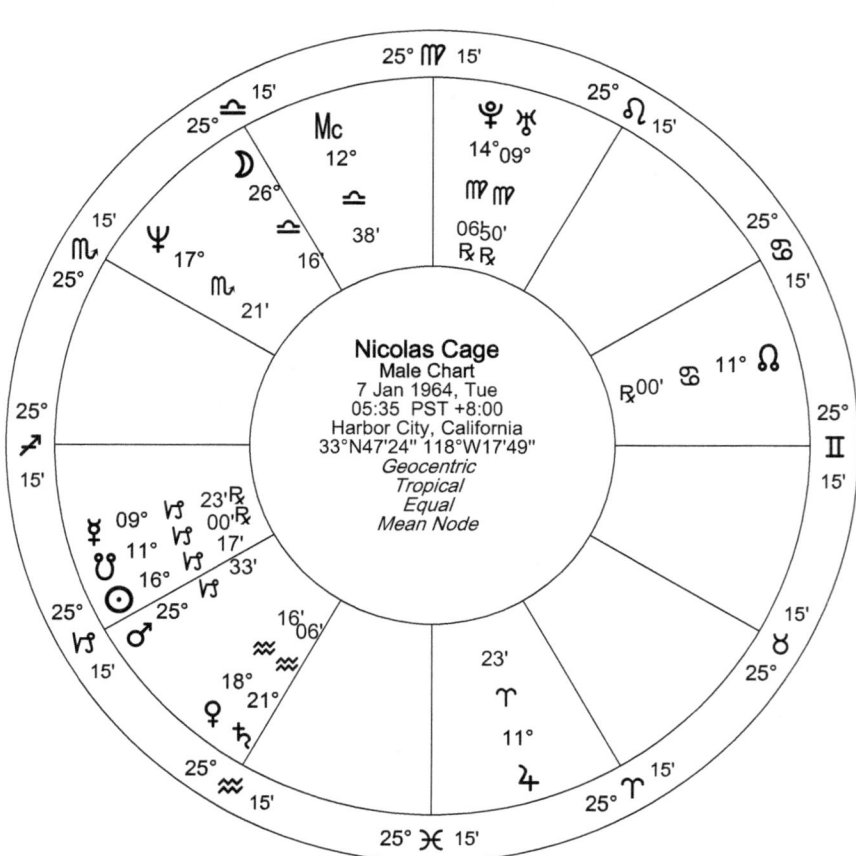

Transiting Jupiter squared its natal position when *Wild at Heart* premiered in May 1990, and Cage revealed that he had always been drawn to roles of unbridled passion.

In late 1995, as transiting Jupiter crossed his Ascendant again, *Leaving Las Vegas* was released. He received his first Academy Award nomination for playing the suicidal Ben. He also married for the first time during filming. He followed this success with *Face/Off* (1997), released as transiting Jupiter was conjunct his natal Saturn three times.

For his third Jupiter return in 1999, Cage starred in *8MM*. Though panned by critics, the film was a box office success and later became a cult classic. In 2001, *Captain Corelli's Mandolin* was released just as transiting Jupiter squared his natal Pluto. That same year, he received his second Academy Award nomination for *Adaptation* (2002), a film released during another Jupiter square. That was also the year he married (and divorced) Lisa Marie Presley.

Cage made his directorial debut with *Sonny* in 2002, as transiting Jupiter squared his natal Neptune three times. His career began to slip, despite the commercial success of *National Treasure* (2004), released during a Jupiter opposition. That same year, he married again—this time for a full Jupiter cycle.

The Wicker Man remake (2006) was released just before transiting Jupiter was conjunct his Neptune, earning him criticism for being "entertainingly bad". Around this time, Cage also made a series of risky property purchases and extravagant spending decisions that led to lawsuits and financial instability.

Jupiter in Taurus

Taurus is an earth sign by element and a fixed sign by modality. Transiting squares and oppositions to its natal position will take place about every three years in the other fixed signs, Leo, Scorpio and Aquarius. This pattern will repeat for the rest of the native's life, defining how a person learns, grows and develops a personal philosophy. Generally speaking, the fixed signs are collectors and for Taurus, this usually manifests itself in physical collections such as stamps, coins or even more specialised items for hobbies such as kitchen gadgets. One of the big lessons Jupiter in Taurus learners have to understand is that not all valuables have a monetary price tag. Understanding their Venus sign can help identify this tendency.

Jupiter transits through signs at a pace of about one sign per year. It is important to note that as children are taught by year group, they will learn alongside other children with Jupiter in Taurus. Depending on the time of year they were born, they will be educated along with classmates with either Jupiter in Aries or Jupiter in Gemini. This topic has been explored in depth in *Growing Pains: Astrology in Adolescence.*

In terms of learning, Jupiter in Taurus children need to have time to take in information, digest it and eliminate the information they no longer need. It can be very difficult to persuade Jupiter in Taurus to move classroom seats and they will need fair warning for any upcoming changes to their schedules. To encourage positive behaviour, it can help if parents/carers or teachers use physical objects such as marbles (or other items) as rewards for good behaviour that the learner can put into a jar. As these learners enjoy collecting, it can be motivating to them to try to collect more marbles. The marbles can then be exchanged for other rewards. At home, money can be a good reinforcer but for obvious reasons this will not work at school. Edible reinforcers are usually forbidden in schools and parents/carers should be equally cautious in using food items to reward positive behaviour or withholding it to punish poor behaviour.

The First Jupiter Square

All babies need the basics of adequate nutrition, a safe place to sleep, cleanliness and a comfortable environment. They also need the human touch in order to build trust and to feel the caregiver is responding to their signals for these necessities. Eye contact, talking/singing to the baby and providing a daily rhythm of sleep, cleaning, feeding and playing with age appropriate toys are essential for all babies, irrespective of the Jupiter signs. As the baby grows into a toddler, it is important caregivers have adequately "baby proofed" the child's environment. These essential needs are important all the way into old age. Once these needs are met consistently, a bit of astrology can help the caregivers find the learner's internal "beat" for development.

Here are just a few suggestions for Jupiter in Taurus learners:

At some point during the first year of life, transiting Jupiter will move into the sign of Gemini. This corresponds to the time of life when all children begin to develop their speech patterns. At some point during the first year of their life, the Jupiter in Aries learner will experience Jupiter transiting through the sign of Gemini. As the learner is a baby, the world is simply full of learning opportunities. Natally, the Jupiter in Taurus learners may lean towards sour food (such as yoghurt, apples, pomegranate or sprouts) but, like a lot of children, they also may have a sweet tooth.

During the second year of life, transiting Jupiter enters the sign of Cancer and the Jupiter in Taurus learner may show signs of clinginess to their mother or other major care givers. They may begin showing signs of stress if they haven't become acclimatised to change and they may need plenty of preparation beforehand and even the comfort of favourite toys to ease their anxieties when faced with new surroundings.

Jupiter will reach its first transiting square during Jupiter's transit into Leo in the third year. As with all harsh aspects, this can be a challenging time. However, the Jupiter in Taurus learner may be keen to show off new skills. By this time, their vocabulary is developing at a rapid pace and they would have mastered basic skills such as walking, talking and toilet training. The only drawback is that parents and carers should be aware of the "shock factor" when the child says or does something socially inappropriate. Laughing, taking embarrassing photos or videos or making a big deal out of such incidences only reinforces the likelihood of the Jupiter in Taurus learner doing it again—and usually in public at the most inconvenient opportunity. Aim to praise good behaviour which increases the likelihood that the child will repeat this behaviour and ignore poor behaviour (even punishing poor behaviour could be reinforcing it for all the wrong reasons). The child can gain a good sense of their self worth, work out what they are respected for and may even begin to develop a talent that will eventually lead them to a high level of expertise.

The First Jupiter Opposition

Between the ages of about three and six years old, most young children are preparing for formal education and socialisation. These are just some ideas to help Jupiter in Taurus learners prepare for their first adventures away from their immediate care givers.

During the fourth year, Jupiter will transit the sign of Virgo and the child will begin applying skills that will allow them to self-moderate more efficiently. There may also be opportunities for the child to teach others the skills they have learned or become a source of encouragement for their peers as well as significant others.

Activities for enjoyment and learning outside of school: learning about the physical body of people or animals, learning about sickness and how to take care of someone (or a pet) who is not feeling well, understanding the basics of medicine. Learning to identify plants and different species of animals, learning to measure accurately with simple tools such as rulers.

As Jupiter transits through the sign of Libra during their fifth year, children with Jupiter in Taurus are most likely preparing to enter mainstream education. This seems rather fortuitous as both Taurus and Libra are ruled by the planet of diplomacy and charm, Venus. If manners have been encouraged from an early age, Jupiter and Taurus learners will be putting them to good use to charm their teachers and fellow students. If Jupiter in Taurus learners have not been taught good decorum, it may lead to them feeling ostracised not only by teachers, but their fellow students. Remember, these are likely to be stubborn learners who do not take well to changes in rules.

Activities for enjoyment and learning outside of school: planning a themed party with a few friends (try themes based around *Horrible Histories* or their favourite kids' movies) and have "preparation parties" where all the invitees have to make their own party favours and costumes, plan their food and activities, etc.

From the sixth year, as Jupiter transits through Scorpio, the Jupiter in Taurus child may become aware of their own power as well as their vulnerabilities. They may learn to become "masters of disguise" by hiding away when doing something they know is wrong such as taking advantage of other pupils—even the older ones. Bear in mind a playground has many hiding places and even the most vigilant teacher cannot keep his/her eyes on every movement of every child every second of the day. Secrets—even the perceived ones that no one else takes very seriously--coming into the light could be what Jupiter in Taurus learners fear the most as Jupiter transits the sign of Scorpio. Encouraging the Jupiter in Taurus learner to use their sensitivity and perception to understand other people's feeling is the main lesson as Jupiter reaches its opposition in Scorpio.

Activities for enjoyment and learning outside of school: mysteries and puzzles, being *gently* frightened (Halloween or cold, dark autumn nights are a good time to share simple ghost stories), nature walks so they can observe the cycle of life in plants and animals (NB: learners at this stage may take an interest in death and pregnancies so be prepared to explain). By this age, children can become more involved with how family finance works and a chore schedule can help them understand how their contributions help the family unit.

The Closing Jupiter Square

By this stage, children will have settled into a home/school routine and it is likely schools will begin to prepare students for the Scholastic Achievement Tests (or their equivalents). Debate rages as to whether these tests cause stress for the children but, drawing from personal experiences, students tend not to get too upset if the adults around them don't behave as if the world is coming to an end. The purpose of these tests is to help identify strengths and weaknesses in the child's development. The results establish a baseline, not a final outcome. Here are some ways to help support the learners during these formative times:

The seventh year is when Jupiter transits through the sign of Sagittarius. For Jupiter in Taurus learners, this is a time of inspiration, acquiring knowledge and perhaps thinking they don't really need an education because they have already learned so much. As with most things, once an idea enters their heads, it can be hard to convince them to change their minds. A new religion or an urge to visit a different culture are but two possible alternatives. This is a wonderful opportunity for teachers to take advantage of these new interests by encouraging the Jupiter in Taurus learner to begin armchair exploring. For parents, also taking an interest by investing in these side steps from the national curriculum will become times that the Jupiter in Taurus learner will absolutely treasure.

Activities for enjoyment and learning outside of school: taking part in charity work, visiting places of worship, learning to discuss politics and identifying political leaders, learning about different countries (their map, geographical features, language, etc.).

During the eighth year, as Jupiter transits through Capricorn, the Jupiter in Taurus pupil may begin to really knuckle down on their education. Whilst this may be great news for teachers and parents (who are probably tired of endless phone calls and conferences), the learner's sudden commitment may be down to fearing for their future. Both Taurus and Capricorn are earth signs: Taurus is primarily interested in basic luxuries but Capricorn provides a good bite of ambition. The Jupiter in Taurus learner's various collections may go into overdrive as the child begins to stockpile for the impending apocalypse of future failure. Reassuring the child of family and educational commitments to their well being may be the most important step in relieving potentially built up stress.

Activities for enjoyment and learning outside of school: hobbies that encourage one step at a time, like wool crafts, learning to do simple carpentry skills, learning to do "handyman/woman" jobs around the house, activities that encourage business skills.

During the ninth year, Jupiter transits through the sign of Aquarius. Whilst both Capricorn and Aquarius are ruled by Saturn, Aquarius tends to have a way of working around the rules through innovation, being unafraid to experiment with the structures that are tried and trusted and, generally, just enjoying not doing as they are told. Obviously, outright defiance is not always a safe avenue to travel across but there are ways of allowing these learners to express their need to "see what happens if". Encouraging an interest in Science, a subject essentially based on experimentation, allows the Jupiter in Taurus child to understand that even the most outrageous experiments have ethical regulations. Failing that, an abridged version of *Frankenstein* might get the point across. During this time, Jupiter will complete its closing square and the Jupiter in Taurus learner can begin to understand the importance of taking tried and trusted advice from adults who simply have more experience and knowledge. It's even better if the child can come away knowing that they are cared for, supported and protected by those around them so they can continue to develop their sense of self-worth.

Activities for enjoyment and learning outside of school: leading/forming a new club and setting rules and expectations, simple science experiments (YouTube is full of ideas of home science experiments—ensure they have permission and understand they have to clean up), learning how to do simple tasks like changing light bulbs, fuses and understanding electrical circuits, recording and monitoring data accurately as part of an experiment, campaigning to run for a student office such as Student Council.

The Jupiter Return

As the learner heads towards their final years of primary school, they should be able to work more independently, understand the general rules of the classroom/playground and see home and school as two separate environments.

As Jupiter in Taurus children head into the unknown (or perhaps too well known) corridors of adolescence during their tenth year, they will experience transiting Jupiter in Pisces. Instead of dreaming of blowing things up just to see what would happen, they turn into cute, fluffy little bunnies that are so comfortable in their environment that they find it difficult to stay awake. As tempting as it may be to jolt them to consciousness, allow their dreams to inspire them (and you). Get out the new watercolours, dust off the poetry books and ask the Music teacher (as if they weren't busy enough) to start up a new band. Allow Jupiter in Taurus learners the space and opportunity to tweak their appreciation for the finer things in life. At home they may take an interest in cooking, and even at school there may be opportunities to enjoy being in a kitchen.

Activities for enjoyment and learning outside of school: Music lessons, art projects not found in school like pottery courses that allow the learner to complete a project all the way to proficiency, studying a particular artist and their work medium (painting, sculpture, carving, etc.).

The eleventh year marks Jupiter's transit into Aries. Having been given a taste of the high life, they now start to get impatient for more, more, more, now, now, now. Where did the cute, fluffy little bunnies go? At this stage of life, their brains are growing rapidly so they are developing new habits that will serve them for the rest of their lives. Sure, their demands can set nerves on edge, but this is a wonderful opportunity to take advantage of all that energy. Teachers, who have been telling Jupiter in Taurus to get a move on for what seems like forever, can get them doing speed rounds, participating in competitions and displaying their newfound skills to amazed family, friends and teachers. As they move on into their Jupiter returns, they may begin to understand the importance of gathering the energy to go for what they want, when they want and in the manner they want to do it.

Activities for enjoyment and learning outside of school: any activities that involve racing, focusing on perfecting a singular skill, physical exercise, activities that help them understand their own strengths and limits.

During the twelfth year, transiting Jupiter will return to its natal position. When we return to a place we have visited before, it is our nature to make comparisons to what has changed since the first time we were there. We may want to seek out the things we did before or perhaps try something completely different.

As almost all students will have had their first Jupiter returns by the end of their eleventh year, schools could hold an end of year festival that would allow pupils to demonstrate their individual skills. Schools tend to hold sporting events during this time but how about a business fair to raise money for charity? As Venus is their ruling planet, pupils could be placed into teams with awards going to the Best Business Plan (for example) as well as other categories.

The stages of development during their first twelve years will repeat in the same sequence, for roughly the same amount of time, for the rest of their lives. A wide variety of activities in the home will support the school in providing learners with a well-rounded education.

The Jupiter and Uranus Sextiles: In the Thick of Puberty

As noted in the Introduction, the thirteenth year of a child's life is usually when rebellion and defiance begin to become noticeable. Astrologically, transiting Jupiter forms a sextile aspect to its natal position at the same time Uranus, the planet of rebellion, will also make its first Ptolemaic aspect to its own natal position (also by sextile aspect). This combination quite literally means "big rebellion" and marks the time when adolescents (and their parents) begin the struggle to make that separation into adulthood.

Identifying when and how a young adolescent may struggle with the changing social rules they must face could be helpful for parents. For example, if an adolescent experiences the Uranus sextile before the Jupiter sextile, parents may view their child as needing more guidance for following the expectations of the home environment (which would include expectations in school). In the Case Studies section, subjects with this tendency are noted as "rebels". If an adolescent experiences the Jupiter sextile before the Uranus sextile, parents may view their child as needing more encouragement for academic work and possibly with social skills. In the Case Studies section, subjects with this tendency are noted as "truth seekers". There is no "good" or "bad" with these notations and they are only presented as starting points for understanding the life-long impact this stage of development has on learners as they continue their journey all the way into old age. To demonstrate how this particular stage of development can vary from person to person, there is a summary of the time frame for the subjects of the case studies on page 208.

Furthermore, an adolescent's developing body means they may be interested in building intimate relationships but their brain needs time to catch up with all the new situations it finds itself in. For Jupiter in Taurus learners, transiting Jupiter in Cancer will sextile its natal position, often making it difficult for this type of learner to break away from old habits. Moving home or school (or even seats in the classroom) can be quite devastating for them as, quite frankly, they have gotten very comfortable. At this stage of development, it may be important for parents to keep these young teenagers moving: don't let them sleep too late at the weekends and make sure they keep their bedrooms tidy (encourage this from an early age). It may not be a good idea to let them eat their meals in their bedroom.

Try to encourage them to open the curtains, go for long walks and just get some fresh air.

The Saturn Opposition

The Saturn opposition begins some time during the fourteenth or fifteenth year (possibly earlier or later depending on individual cases) and marks the end of astrological adolescence. Parents and teachers usually notice that the adolescent begins to calm down and take a more mature approach to their academic progress. In the UK, this coincides with choosing academic subjects (as opposed to trying a little bit of everything), formal exam preparation and a marked change in mood. Depression, anxiety and their symptoms must be monitored and taken seriously. Schools will have access to support mechanisms for parents and carers, teachers will have been trained in how to identify potential difficulties and for parents who are home schooling, social services can be a sound source for help.

As they head towards their transiting Saturn opposition, Jupiter in Taurus pupils will also re-visit what they had learned as transiting Jupiter usually (it can vary from person to person) passes through the signs of Leo and Virgo. They will develop sensitivity to be respected for who they are as well as a discerning eye for making improvements. Re-visiting the appropriate stage of astrological development can be helpful to provide the right sort of help and support.

The Second Jupiter Opposition

By the time a young adult finishes mandatory education, they will have a good idea of what they want to do with their lives and yet they still have time to re-take exams or re-train if they discover they want to do something else. The second Jupiter opposition is a time of making serious decisions: the young adult is no longer a child. The learner now knows there are consequences for undesirable behaviour and can no longer blame "the system" for their poor choices. Sadly, our prison services are filled with young people who have slipped through the net. As a collective whole, society could do with using a little astrology to help these young people get back on track. A more comprehensive mentoring service could be helpful.

Here are some ideas to help young adults focus on the rest of their adult lives:

Transiting Jupiter will be in Scorpio as the young Jupiter in Taurus adult finishes their formal education at around the age of eighteen. Because Scorpio is associated with sensitivity and power, Jupiter in Taurus learners may feel a committed relationship is too "deep" for them. Conversely, they may avoid emotional intimacy by overcompensating with physical intimacy. Obviously this tendency varies wildly between individuals but it is a wise parent or authority figure who helps the Jupiter in Taurus young adult into understanding their responsibilities.

The Second Jupiter Return and Beyond

As a person continues to develop emotionally, physically and spiritually they will build on the lessons they learned in the formative years. These return (roughly) at the ages of 24, 36, 48 and 60 (and beyond). The suggestions for activities can be modified to suit the developmental cycle for each Jupiter cycle. For example, a Jupiter in Taurus learner experiencing a Jupiter in Cancer transit during their third year of life can be encouraged to practise their memory skills by practising the alphabet; during their fifteenth year, they may wish to try memorising longer texts, such as those found in Holy books*; during their twenty-seventh year, they may want to want to participate in specialised game shows that rely on memory. The key for all Jupiter returns is to choose a skill (or even one per year) and exercise the brain, all the way to the final years of life. As always with Jupiter, the sky is the limit.

Jupiter returns at all ages should be celebrated and an experienced astrologer can help locate the exact moment of the return. New clothes to reflect a changing style, a good meal (with a magnificent dessert) with influential friends and maybe even a holiday to some exotic place are just a few ideas. To celebrate the ingress (entry) of Jupiter in a new sign, consult the table in the appendix. The Chinese culture does a wonderful job with celebrating "The Year of the...". While theirs may be a different culture and system, the similarity of intention is still there.

---

*   The Holy Books are religious - which is associated with Jupiter.

Fine Tuning Jupiter in Taurus

Jupiter in Taurus is ruled by Venus, the planet of sensuality, beauty and tempting men to war to fight over beautiful things.

Venus in Aries: These pupils generally like to be teased or antagonised into learning: an intriguing starter on the board can get them thinking about where the lesson might be heading. "Target questioning" could be the next step.

Venus in Taurus: These pupils like to learn by building on knowledge which has already been acquired. Helping them keep their learning resources organised can appeal to their need to collect things.

Venus in Gemini: "Carousel learning" is having lots of short activities in about 5-6 stations related to the main topic. Children move from one station to the next, trying out the activities. This can be modified for any age or any subject.

Venus in Cancer: These pupils tend to have a good sense of history. They tend to develop "roots" everywhere they go and may feel threatened if they have to move away from the familiar.

Venus in Leo: Teachers usually find that any opportunity to show off brings out the best in these pupils. They are proud of their work. However, they can dominate quieter, more accommodating children if not monitored.

Venus in Virgo: These pupils like routine and organisation and tend to eschew activities that get them dirty. However, they like to actively find ways to be helpful. If they are given tasks to be responsible for, they will always ensure they do a good job if shown the expectations.

Venus in Libra: These pupils enjoy socialising so much that they can forget what school is about—learning to read and write. Teachers should encourage independent learning but may discover more work gets done if these learners are allowed to work in pairs.

Venus in Scorpio: These pupils relish topics that are considered out of bounds in a regular lesson and they will make it abundantly clear what they like and what they don't. These learners are quite happy with independent research (although boundaries need to be firmly established and maintained).

Venus in Sagittarius: These pupils understand the meaning of "a long journey" and will happily go along with anything provided there is an explanation of what is in it for them.

Venus in Capricorn: These pupils tend to take learning seriously, hand their homework in on time and submit solid but yet unadventurous work. They need to be encouraged to set challenging targets for themselves.

Venus in Aquarius: These pupils may find it difficult to accept conventional ways of doing things: they tend to have an innate need to 'twist' things slightly so whatever it is they are doing is unique to themselves.

Venus in Pisces: These pupils may need some time to absorb instructions before getting on with tasks. They may need to ask lots of questions before they understand what they need to do. It may help to have lots of reminders on classroom displays until they get used to expectations.

Case Studies

Liam Neeson

Born 7 June 1952 (no time) Ballymena, UK with Jupiter in Taurus and its ruler, Venus in Gemini.

Although Taurus is a fixed sign, the stubbornness often associated with it is tempered in Neeson's case by its ruler, Venus, positioned in the versatile sign of Gemini, conjunct his Mercury and Sun. His long and varied film career includes starring in thrillers such as the *Taken* series as well as romances like *Nell* (where he met his future wife, Natasha Richardson) and *Love Actually*.

Neeson describes his upbringing as a typical working-class childhood in Northern Ireland. Boxing became an interest at age nine, during his first waning square of Jupiter to its natal position. He also recalls fond memories of baling hay and milking cows on his uncle's farm during the summers. His passion for drama developed in his teenage years—an important period in adolescent brain development.

During this time, transiting Uranus in Virgo was sextile to its natal position in Cancer, about six months before transiting Jupiter in Gemini formed a sextile to his natal Jupiter—suggesting a rebellious streak.

After university and a series of casual jobs, Neeson joined the Lyric Players' Theatre in Belfast just as he experienced his second Jupiter return in 1976. By 1980–81, transiting Jupiter was in the midst of a series of conjunctions to his natal Saturn as he filmed his first major role in *Excalibur*, where he met Helen Mirren, who is said to have helped him secure an agent.

Though he played many roles, it was *Schindler's List* that brought him his greatest critical success (if Academy Award nominations are a measure). Filming took place in 1993, as Jupiter completed a series of three conjunctions to his natal Saturn. The film's release coincided almost exactly with transiting Jupiter's conjunction to his natal Mars in Scorpio.

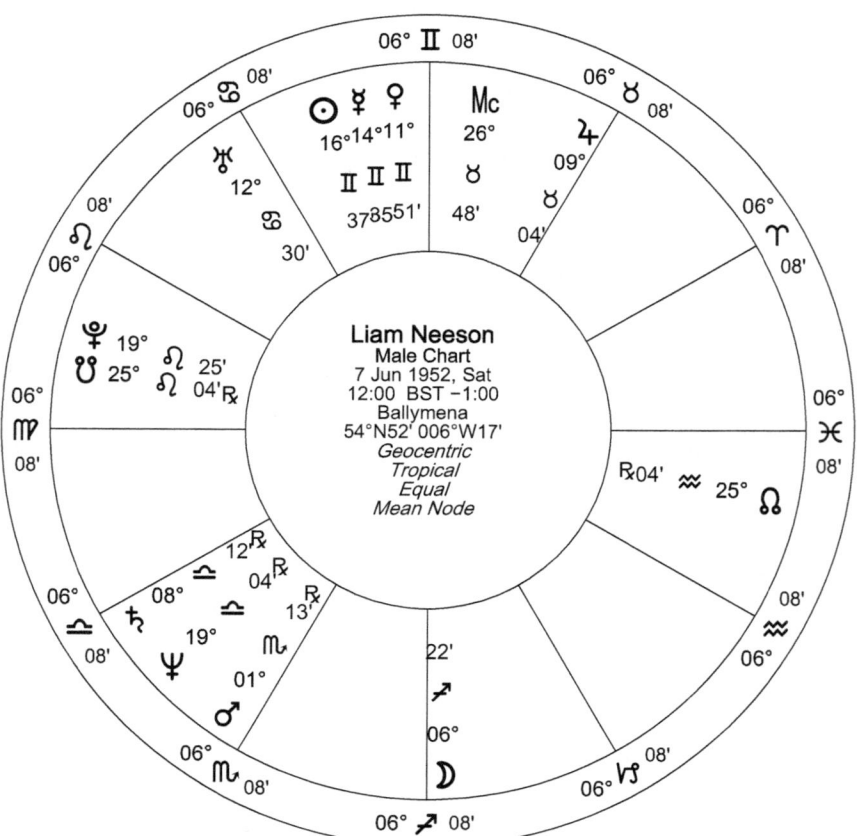

Neeson continued to star in numerous films, but perhaps it was *Love Actually,* a romantic comedy so unlike his typical tough-guy roles, that truly endeared him to audiences. Released in 2003, during a Jupiter conjunction to his natal Pluto in Leo, the film resonated deeply. In an eerie twist of fate, his beloved wife Natasha was tragically killed in a ski accident six years later, as transiting Jupiter in Aquarius opposed the same degree. The conjunction repeated twice more, a painfully public marker of grief.

With a career spanning nearly 40 years and an impressive résumé, Neeson has secured his place as one of Hollywood's greatest actors. But from an early age, he knew that love was his greatest gift. Such is the success of Jupiter in Taurus.

Dana Plato

Born 7 November 1964 at 12:24 PM, Huntington Park, California (RR: AA; Collector: Noel) with Jupiter in Taurus ruled by Venus in Libra.

For someone with Jupiter in Taurus, the opportunity to build strong, immovable foundations is vital. A lack of stability early on can lead to a weak foundation and, ultimately, a collapse of whatever security they manage to construct. Plato's natal Jupiter in Taurus opposed her natal Neptune in Scorpio, creating potentially shaky groundwork. While more research is needed to determine whether this aspect is a hallmark of addiction or simply an unfortunate fluke, her chart suggests the former.

Plato was given up for adoption at 17 months by her teenage mother, who already had another infant. However, her adoptive parents' marriage was unstable, and they divorced around her first Jupiter square. She returned to her adoptive mother, who took her to auditions. By the time of her first Jupiter opposition, Plato had appeared in over 100 commercials and was an accomplished figure skater.

She experienced a series of three Jupiter returns beginning in late June 1976. By then, she had made brief TV appearances. During adolescence, transiting Uranus in Scorpio was sextile to its natal position, about seven months before transiting Jupiter in Cancer was sextile to her natal Jupiter in Gemini, suggesting a rebellious nature.

Notably, in late 1978, transiting Uranus was conjunct her natal Sun, and later, Uranus opposed her Neptune. It was during this period that she landed the role that made her a household name - Kimberly Drummond in

Diff'rent Strokes. The character, a wholesome, wealthy American girl from Park Avenue, was a stark contrast to Plato's real-life struggles. The show's immense success, coupled with a Uranus-Neptune aspect, foreshadowed her later difficulties with addiction.

During 1978-79, Plato experienced her first Saturn opposition, with transiting Jupiter opposing Saturn the following year - indicating cracks in her metaphorical foundation. She later admitted to using drugs and alcohol at this time and even suffered an overdose.

In 1984, at age 19, she became pregnant and married her child's father. She was written out of *Diff'rent Strokes*, as producers feared her pregnancy and personal struggles would negatively impact the show's image. That year, transiting Jupiter squared her natal Venus three times, while Saturn opposed her natal Jupiter from late 1984-85.

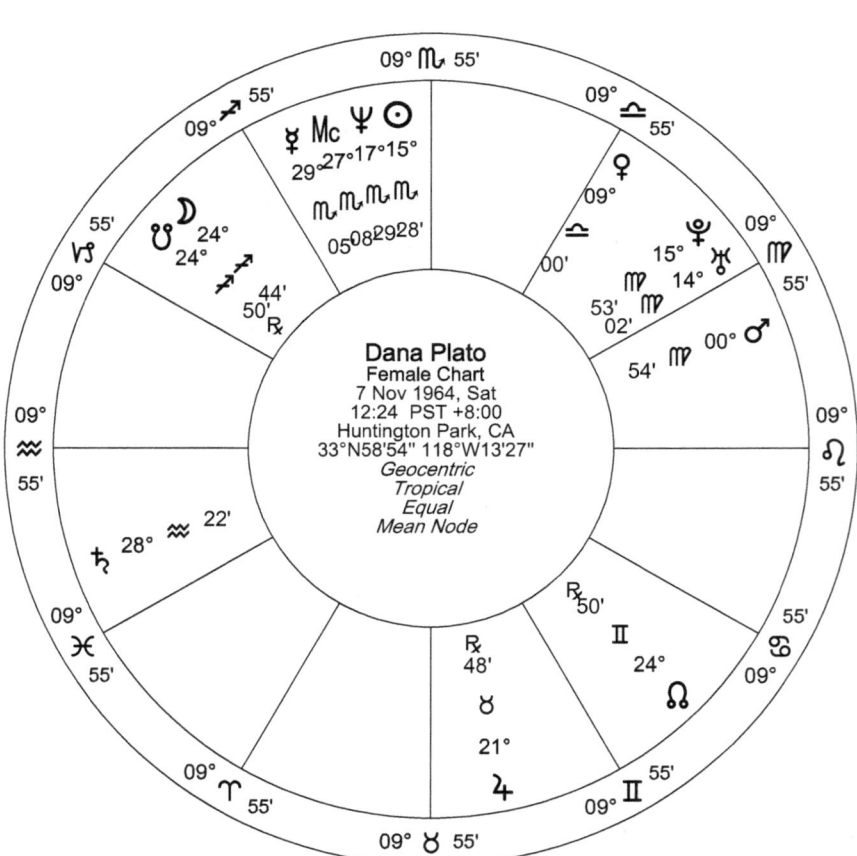

After *Diff'rent Strokes*, she took on minor roles before leaving acting. In 1989, she had breast implant surgery and posed for Playboy—a period marked by transiting Saturn in Capricorn squaring her natal Venus in Libra three times. With both planets in their dignity, this represented a major challenge to her self-image. It was also a difficult period for relationships—Plato divorced and lost custody of her son.

In 1991, as transiting Jupiter squared its natal position, she robbed a video store and was sentenced to five years' probation. The following year, she was jailed for forging a prescription for diazepam. She entered rehab but struggled to find work and financial stability.

The last seven years of her life were marked by hardship, beginning with a transiting Saturn square to her natal Jupiter in early 1993. She largely stayed out of the limelight, and her second Jupiter opposition passed without public incident. However, she made a final public appearance on *The Howard Stern Show* the day before her death. A few months prior, Jupiter had opposed her natal Venus. Perhaps she was feeling confident, with a strong need to be open about her struggles. On the show, she spoke candidly about her addictions and insisted she had been sober for 10 years. Callers accused her of lying, prompting her to offer an on-air drug test, which she later retracted.

The next day, she overdosed—her death ruled a suicide.

Plato is a tragic example of what can happen when Jupiter in Taurus builds its values on the shaky ground of fame, fortune and beauty.

Jupiter in Gemini

Gemini is an air sign by element and a mutable sign by modality. Transiting squares and oppositions to its natal position will take place in the other mutable signs, Virgo, Sagittarius and Pisces. This pattern will repeat for the rest of the native's life, defining how a person learns, grows and develops a personal philosophy. Mutable signs are flexible, co-operative and interested in what goes on around them. They are usually very curious and collect and distribute information that passes their way.

Jupiter transits through signs at a pace of about one sign per year. It is important to note that as children are taught by year group, they will learn alongside other children with Jupiter in Gemini or, depending on when they were born within the academic year, alongside classmates with either Jupiter in Taurus or Jupiter in Cancer. This topic has been explored in depth in *Growing Pains: Astrology in Adolescence.*

Children with Jupiter in Gemini tend to be intellectually active and may have difficulty focusing on one thing at a time because they want to try a little bit of everything. It could be quite difficult to nail down their preferences because they seem to like everything or they like something one minute and don't like it the next. This may become most obvious with their taste in literature or music. It may be best just to let them get on with anything that keeps them quiet or keeps their hands busy for a few minutes. Tongue in cheek aside, this is how the Jupiter in Gemini learner expands their horizons.

Let's look at Jupiter as it transits through the other signs of the zodiac for the Jupiter in Gemini child.

The First Jupiter Square

All babies need the basics of adequate nutrition, a safe place to sleep, cleanliness and a comfortable environment. They also need the human touch in order to build trust and to feel their caregiver is responding to their signals for these necessities. Eye contact, talking/singing to the baby

and providing a daily rhythm of sleep, cleaning, feeding and playing with age appropriate toys are essential for all babies, irrespective of the Jupiter signs. As the baby grows into a toddler, it is important caregivers have adequately "baby proofed" the child's environment. These essential needs are important all the way into old age. Once these needs are met consistently, a bit of astrology can help the caregivers find the learner's internal "beat" for development.

Here are just a few suggestions for Jupiter in Gemini learners:

At some point during the first year of their life, the Jupiter in Gemini learner will experience Jupiter transiting through the sign of Cancer. As the learner is a baby, the world is simply full of learning opportunities. Natally, the Jupiter in Gemini learner may enjoy trying different tastes and textures rather than just a singular dish.

During the second year, transiting Jupiter will move onto Leo. The Jupiter in Gemini learner is playful by nature and probably won't mind who is watching as long as there's an appreciative audience. Spending extra time nurturing the child with new songs or vocabulary is a wonderful way of stimulating their imagination as well as giving them ammunition to show off at the first opportunity. Joking aside (Jupiter in Gemini won't mind keeping things light-hearted), the antics of these children will keep everyone entertained. Keep the camera ready (but off social media).

Jupiter will transit into Virgo during the third year. Although both Gemini and Virgo are both ruled by Mercury, they have very different manifestations. Gemini skims over the surface of its interest; Virgo wants to hang back and tidy up. At this stage, the idea of maintaining a strict routine may become important as may the notion that it's better to be clean than messy. With the right encouragement, the Jupiter in Gemini child can gain a good understanding of what is valuable and useful against what is transient or without value. They start to work out what is good for their body and, if encouraged, will develop dietary habits that will serve them for the rest of their lives.

The First Jupiter Opposition

Between the ages of about three to six years old, most young children are preparing for formal education and socialisation. These are just some ideas to help Jupiter in Gemini learners prepare for their first adventures away from their immediate care givers.

During the fourth year, Jupiter will transit into the sign of Libra and the child will begin applying skills that will allow them to develop a sense of diplomacy. They may become aware that if they want to make friends, they need to be more aware of how to behave in different environments. For example, it the Jupiter in Gemini learner once thought it entertaining to say (or do) anything for a laugh, they may start to respond differently when they start to realise not everyone finds them funny. This is the time for reinforcing (assuming good manners have been embedded from a young age) the art of being polite. Whilst no one is recommending that this would be a good time to take such a young child to the opera, treating them to more grown up ideas of dressing for the occasion may be something a Jupiter in Gemini learner would appreciate at this stage.

Activities for enjoyment and learning outside of school: planning a themed party with a few friends (try themes based around *Horrible Histories* or their favourite kids' movies) and have "preparation parties" where all the invitees have to make their own party favours and costumes, plan their food and activities, etc.

As Jupiter transits through sign of Scorpio during their fifth year, children with Jupiter in Gemini begin to develop curiosity for learning that will define them as they continue to grow. A comfortable, monitored studying space will help encourage them to do their school work to a good standard. They may develop an interest in mysteries and puzzles. Perhaps most important is that Jupiter in Gemini learners begin to take a bigger bite of the experiences that are offered to them. They want look a little closer and dive a little deeper.

Activities for enjoyment and learning outside of school: mysteries and puzzles, being *gently* frightened (Halloween or cold, dark autumn nights are a good time to share simple ghost stories), nature walks so they can observe the cycle of life in plants and animals (NB: learners at this stage may take an interest in death and pregnancies so be prepared to explain). They may also show an interest in how the family finances are managed.

From the sixth year, as Jupiter transits through Sagittarius, the Jupiter in Gemini learner may express an interest in adventures that happen in faraway places or may even study different faiths. In most school curriculums, there are many opportunities for school day trips (which can be as exhausting for little legs as a full on adventure holiday for adults) that include different places of worship or the admiration of sacred objects. Their curious and eager minds will naturally have the opportunity to expand just through admiring the world around them. Just be aware: Jupiter in Gemini children tend to repeat everything they hear.

Activities for enjoyment and learning outside of school: taking part in charity work, visiting places of worship, learning to discuss politics and identifying political leaders, learning about different countries (their map, geographical features, language, etc).

This stage, at the end of the first Jupiter square, should serve the child well as they begin to move through the school system if they have had the right encouragement.

The Closing Jupiter Square

By this stage, children will have settled into a home/school routine and it is likely schools will begin to prepare students for the Scholastic Achievement Tests (or their equivalents). Debate rages as to whether these tests cause stress for the children but, drawing from personal experiences, students tend not to get too upset if the adults around them don't behave as if the world is coming to an end. The purpose of these tests is to help identify strengths and weaknesses in the child's development. The results establish a baseline, not a final outcome.

Here are some ways to help support the learners during these formative times:

As Jupiter transits through Capricorn during the seventh year, Jupiter in Gemini learners begin to develop the grit their teachers have probably been waiting for: they begin to take their studies a bit more seriously. This is quite fortuitous as it coincides with the UK's Standard Assessment Tests (SATs) taken in the summer term when most children will be seven years old. These tests, based on good old reading, writing and arithmetic (it's a bit more complicated than this) help identify the areas that schools need to improve on. Whilst much debate rages on whether or not it is a good idea to put such young children through such stress (in the author's experience many children are oblivious to their importance), these tests can help identify if the pupil has any special needs. And here is an important point: Jupiter in Gemini learners tend to be very good at hiding any academic weaknesses. They tend to be such good talkers that they can fool anyone into believing they can do anything—so the teachers keep piling on more difficult tasks, oblivious to the fact the Jupiter in Gemini learner is secretly crashing under academic pressure.

Activities for enjoyment and learning outside of school: hobbies that encourage one step at a time, like wool crafts, learning to do simple carpentry skills, learning to do "handyman/woman" jobs around the house, activities that encourage business skills.

Formal testing during primary school will be a thing of the past as the Jupiter in Gemini learner enters their eighth year and Jupiter transits through Aquarius. When Jupiter transits through Aquarius it usually means there are major shifts in social groups which, for children, translates as friendship groups. Whilst it is inevitable that everyone has issues with friends at some point, for children it can be devastating. Parents can help by introducing their children to other children outside of school and teachers can support this year group with special lessons on kindness and inclusion (already a feature in UK schools). As always, awareness is the key to helping Jupiter in Gemini as they navigate this tricky year.

Activities for enjoyment and learning outside of school: leading/forming a new club and setting rules and expectations, simple science experiments (YouTube is full of ideas for home science experiments—ensure they have permission and understand they have to clean up), learning how to do simple tasks like changing light bulbs, fuses and understanding electrical circuits, recording and monitoring data accurately as part of an experiment, campaigning for a student office.

By the time Jupiter in Gemini learners reach their ninth year, they've probably had such a drama-filled few years that they need a nap. So that's what they do: they switch off. However, rather than cracking the whip, this is actually a very good time to take the pressure off and just let them express themselves through Art and Music. For parents, if your child's school lacks the awareness to stop the academic pressure, you can help create a more relaxing atmosphere at home. Jupiter in Gemini will still love to learn but they probably need to learn about the things they can't learn at school. Jupiter in Gemini learners might love to help with the cooking or maybe take on an extracurricular class at the weekends. Or maybe they just want some chill space. If in doubt, ask them what they want to do. They'll let you know.

Activities for enjoyment and learning outside of school: music lessons, art projects not found in school like pottery courses that allow the learner to complete a project all the way to the proficiency, studying a particular artist and their work medium (painting, sculpture, carving, etc.).

The Jupiter Return

Transiting Jupiter will enter Aries in the Jupiter in Gemini learner's tenth year. This is pure intellectual energy that needs to be tempered with a good deal of physical release. If the Jupiter in Gemini learner asks to learn a new sport, take them up on it. The interesting thing about this fire-air combination is that whilst the physical side is certainly gathering strength, the intellectual side won't be taking it easy. Jupiter in Gemini learners are usually very good at understanding obscure rules, statistics and advance plays. They are sportspeople who play with their heads. The problem is that the majority of their classmates probably also have Jupiter in Gemini so the competitiveness comes out full force. Be prepared for sweaty socks and head injuries. Teach these guys how to look after their bodies (they will need to be reminded to take regular showers and wash their clothes) and protect themselves from injuries.

Activities for enjoyment and learning outside of school: any activities that involve racing, focusing on perfecting a singular skill, physical exercise, activities that help them understand their own strengths and limits.

The penultimate year of primary school, during their eleventh year as Jupiter transits through the sign of Taurus, could be one marked by physical growth and they will need to slow down to become acclimatised to their growing bodies. This is, of course, the onset of puberty and a Jupiter in Gemini learner may need to be reminded that nothing stays the same. Intellectually they may understand this but they may need a little reminding that they are just getting a bit too big for certain activities. Much of this is to do with their tendency to be youthful and energetic, even well into adulthood. There are activities that children never outgrow: camping, the treat of short term travel (as luxurious as possible if you please) and of course, the encouragement to stay still long enough to expand on one (maybe two) of their favourite interests during this year of their lives.

Activities for enjoyment and learning outside of school: outdoor walks, animal watching, tasting different foods, gardening, simple physical strength exercises, collecting interesting things (and keeping them organised). If it's possible the family could adopt an animal to look after. If there is room in the garden, looking after a chicken or two might be something they are old enough for.

At some point during their twelfth year, Jupiter in Gemini learners will experience their first Jupiter return. As for all situations we return to, there is a need to compare the most recent visit to the last. Jupiter in Gemini pupils may look back on their progress only to realise how much more they need to know. For some, this can serve as an intellectual kick in the pants. For others, it can be an intimidating time of fearing they will never catch up. Such is the way of the mutable signs: they tend to polarise into super speedy learners and those who are terrified someone will rumble them and expose that they don't know as much as they "should". For the former, school will be seen as a giant playground. For the latter, school will be seen as a haunted house, full of reminders that they will never be adequate enough. It is so important to tackle these issues before these children enter secondary school, before they become swallowed up by the big school where there are simply too many pupils and not enough resources to help them develop the confidence to overcome these (imaginary) feelings of incompetence.

When we return to a place we have visited before, it is our nature to make comparisons to what has changed since the first time we were there. We may want to seek out the things we did before or perhaps try something completely different.

As almost all students will have had their first Jupiter return by the end of their eleventh year, schools could hold an end of year festival that would allow pupils to demonstrate their individual skills. Schools tend to hold sporting events during this time but how about a writing contest for the year group? There could be categories for different styles such as fiction, poetry or non-fiction categories such as oral histories or more journalistic categories for interviewing Year 10s on work experience.

The stages of development during their first twelve years will repeat in the same sequence, for roughly the same amount of time, for the rest of their lives, irrespective of which side of the intellectual fence they sit.

The Jupiter and Uranus Sextiles: In the Thick of Puberty

As noted in the Introduction, the thirteenth year of a child's life is usually when rebellion and defiance begin to become noticeable. Astrologically, transiting Jupiter forms a sextile aspect to its natal position at the same time Uranus, the planet of rebellion, will also make its first Ptolemaic aspect to its own natal position (also by sextile aspect). This combination quite literally means "big rebellion" and marks the time when adolescents (and their parents) begin the struggle to make that separation into adulthood.

Identifying when and how a young adolescent may struggle with the changing social rules they must face could be helpful for parents. For example, if an adolescent experiences the Uranus sextile before the Jupiter sextile, parents may view their child as needing more guidance for following the expectations of the home environment (which would include expectations in school). In the Case Studies section, subjects with this tendency are noted as "rebels". If an adolescent experiences the Jupiter sextile before the Uranus sextile, parents may view their child as needing more encouragement with academic work and possibly with social skills. In the Case Studies section, subjects with this tendency are noted as "truth seekers". There is no "good" or "bad" with these notations and they are only presented as starting points for understanding the life-long impact this stage of development has on learners as they continue their journey all the way into old age. To demonstrate how this particular stage of development can vary from person to person, there is a summary of the time frame for the subjects of the case studies on page 208.

Furthermore, an adolescent's developing body means they may be interested in forming intimate relationships but their brain needs time to catch up with all the new situations it finds itself in. For children born with Jupiter in Gemini, Jupiter will be transiting through the sign of Leo as it had been during their second year. It can be helpful for parents to recall the lessons of this year as difficulties with relationships and learning can typically come down to the choice of hogging the spotlight for themselves or stepping aside and letting someone else have the opportunity to shine.

And children at this stage of development can have very interesting opinions on who deserves the spotlight the most.

The Saturn Opposition

The Saturn opposition begins some time during the fourteenth or fifteenth year (possibly earlier or later depending on individual cases) and marks the end of astrological adolescence. Parents and teachers usually notice that the adolescent begins to calm down and take a more mature approach to their academic progress. In the UK, this coincides with choosing academic subjects (as opposed to trying a little bit of everything), formal exam preparation and a marked change in mood. Depression, anxiety and their symptoms must be monitored and taken seriously. Schools will have access to support mechanisms for parents and carers, teachers will have been trained in how to identify potential difficulties and for parents who are home schooling, social services can be a sound source for help.

As they head towards their transiting Saturn opposition, Jupiter in Gemini learners will also re-visit what they had learned as transiting Jupiter once again passes through the signs of Virgo and Libra. They will develop sensitivity as well as have a strong desire to be respected for who they are. Forming appropriate social groups may need encouragement from caregivers. Re-visiting the appropriate stage of astrological development can be helpful to provide the right sort of help and support.

The Second Jupiter Opposition

By the time a young adult finishes mandatory education, they will have a good idea of what they want to do with their lives and yet they still have time to re-take exams or re-train if they discover they want to do something else. The second Jupiter opposition is a time of making serious decisions: the young adult is no longer a child. The learner now knows there are consequences for undesirable behaviour and can no longer blame "the system" for their poor choices. Sadly, our prison services are filled with young people who have slipped through the net. As a collective whole, society could do with using a little astrology to help these young people get back on track. A more comprehensive mentoring service could be helpful.

Here are some ideas to help young adults focus on the rest of their adult lives:

Transiting Jupiter will be in Sagittarius as the young adult finishes their formal education at around the age of eighteen. Both Gemini and Sagittarius are signs of intellect so chances are, the young adult will choose further education IF nurtured and given every opportunity to develop their confidence in learning. As both signs are mutable, the pendulum could also swing the other way towards a person who uses their intellect for more nefarious purposes to get them into trouble but yet be able to talk their way out of it.

The Second and Subsequent Jupiter Returns

As a person continues to develop emotionally, physically and spiritually they will build on the lessons they learned in the formative years. Jupiter returns (roughly) at the ages of 24, 36, 48 and 60 (and beyond). The suggestions for activities can be modified to suit the developmental cycle for each Jupiter cycle. For example, a Jupiter in Gemini learner experiencing a Jupiter in Leo transit during their third year of life can be encouraged to practise their fine motor skills by reciting simple tongue twisters or; during their fifteenth year, they may wish to try a debating club; during their twenty-seventh year, they may want to perfect their lecturing skills and so on. The key for all Jupiter returns is to choose a skill (or even one per year) and exercise the brain, all the way to the final years of life. As always, with Jupiter, the sky is the limit.

Jupiter returns at all ages should be celebrated and an experienced astrologer can help locate the exact moment of the return. New clothes to reflect a changing style, a good meal (with a magnificent dessert) with influential friends and maybe even a holiday to some exotic place are just a few ideas. To celebrate the ingress (entry) of Jupiter in a new sign, consult the table in the appendix. The Chinese culture does a wonderful job with celebrating "The Year of the…". While theirs may be a different culture and system, the similarity of intention is still there.

Fine Tuning Jupiter in Gemini

Jupiter in Gemini is ruled by the planet Mercury, the planet of communication and travel. To get a more specific idea of how a person with Jupiter in Mercury grows, look to the sign Mercury occupies.

Mercury in Aries: These pupils normally speak their mind impulsively and without considering how someone else might feel. Witty but not always charmingly so, carers and teachers will have to make these learners aware that not everyone finds them funny.

Mercury in Taurus: These pupils enjoy talking so much that their speech is boiled down to carefully chosen words and phonetic nuances. Sometimes these pupils will even decide there is nothing important to say and will therefore remain quiet until called upon.

Mercury in Gemini: These pupils see the world as one big opportunity to learn and they will seize every chance they get to add to their vast library of knowledge. Although they come across as knowing something about everything, teachers usually discover they lack depth and very often bore too easily.

Mercury in Cancer: These pupils are creatures of habit and memory and tend to avoid unfamiliar territory if at all possible. They have learned that the unfamiliar is where the hurt is. Because they take everything to heart, they have a difficult time in sorting fact from opinion.

Mercury in Leo: These pupils never tire of being admired for their quick wit, passion and eloquence. Unfortunately they seldom give others a chance to speak and they usually need to be taught to take their turn.

Mercury in Virgo: These pupils consume a mental diet of the finest organic ingredients. Detesting the trivial, they soon earn a reputation for being hardnosed critics. With their discerning minds, these learners can almost always come up with more efficient ways of doing things.

Mercury in Libra: These pupils need another person to not only keep them company but to gauge their reactions. Sensitive to the needs of others, they are quick to balance out any inequalities and smoothly hammer out differences amongst their friends.

Mercury in Scorpio: These pupils seem to be able to look straight through the insignificant stuff and head directly to the jugular vein of knowledge. Their acidic remarks in class often make their teachers think their personal papers have been snooped through.

Mercury in Sagittarius: These pupils don't so much talk as preach. Although they seem to possess a curious mind, they can sometimes seem to lack discretion in their choice of conversation. Someone always gets offended and does exactly what these learners like best: engage in a hot debate.

Mercury in Capricorn: These pupils understand the importance of earning an education. They sneer at experimentation and eagerly embrace the tried and trusted. However, they learn at a steady rate and often just need a bit more confidence so they can bring their ideas out into the open.

Mercury in Aquarius: These pupils like to do things differently to the rest of the class and they will do anything to avoid the conventional way of doing things. They do most of their learning outside of the classroom but will occasionally deign to demonstrate their knowledge if the teacher sits down with everyone else.

Mercury in Pisces: These pupils may seem as if they are not paying attention but they are soaking everything in. The challenge is to get them to put down what they have learned onto paper. They often need a bit of help organising their notes.

Case Studies

Emma Stone

Emma Stone was born on 6 November 1988 (no recorded time) in Scottsdale, Arizona, with Jupiter in Gemini and Mercury in Scorpio.

Stone is an award-winning actress and producer. Fittingly for someone with Jupiter in Gemini, her major accolades tend to come in pairs: two Academy Awards, two BAFTAs, and two Golden Globes. True to her sign, she's multi-talented—demonstrating Jupiter in Gemini's hallmark versatility. In 2017, she was one of the world's highest-paid actresses.

As a child, during her eighth year (age seven), Stone experienced anxiety attacks. As an adult, she has said that acting helps her cope. Her acting debut came around the time of her first Jupiter return, during which she had several small but well-received roles in teen comedies.

During adolescence, transiting Uranus in Aquarius was sextile her natal Uranus in Sagittarius about three months before transiting Jupiter in Gemini was sextile her natal Jupiter—indicating a rebellious streak.

Stone's breakthrough came with her portrayal of Miss Skeeter in *The Help* (2011), a film that grossed over $220 million worldwide—her highest-grossing film to that date. She played a young journalist, a role likely enhanced by transiting Jupiter opposing her natal Mercury shortly before the film's release.

However, her biggest role was in *La La Land* (2016) in which she not only acted but sang and danced as well. Stone won the Academy Award for Best Actress. A few days after the release of the film, transiting Jupiter was exactly opposite her natal Mars in Aries and as the film built momentum, transiting Jupiter was conjunct her natal Venus in Libra. The film is

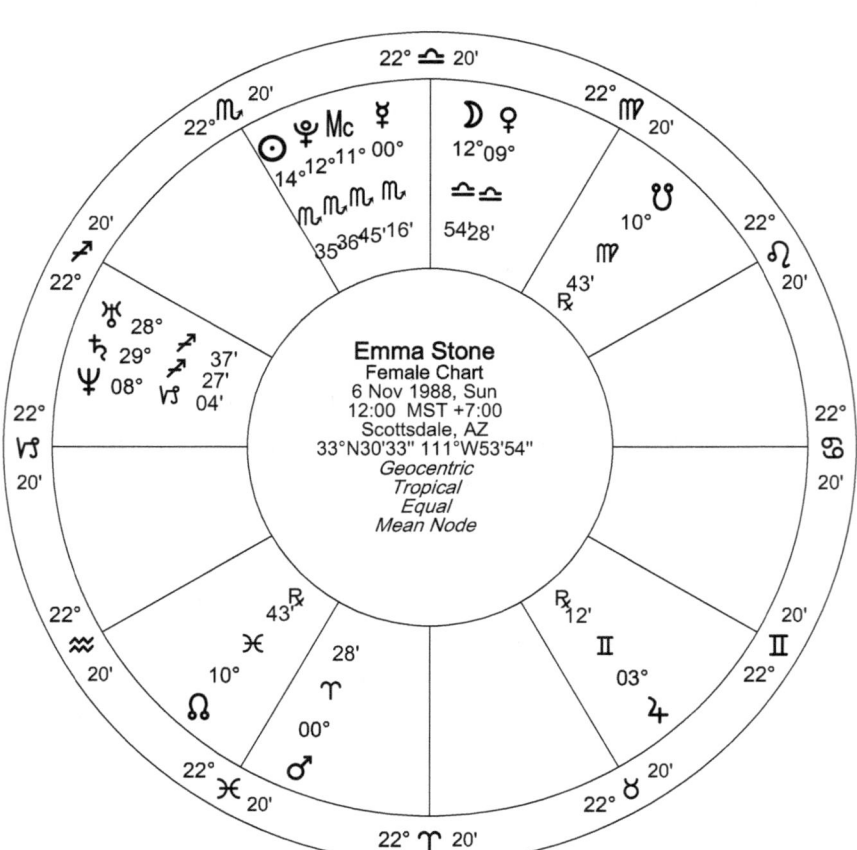

essentially about an aspiring actress and musician whose perfect love life was a near miss.

In *Poor Things* (2023), Stone portrayed a woman brought back to life by a mad scientist—a performance that earned her a second Academy Award. Interestingly, the Jupiter transits during the filming mirrored those during *La La Land's* release.

In 2020, she and her husband founded the production company Fruit Tree, which released five films, with more in development at the time of writing. Astrologically, the timing was ideal: at the start of 2020, transiting Jupiter in Capricorn was conjunct her natal Neptune.

Charlie Sheen

Charlie Sheen was born on 3 September 1965 at 10:48 PM in New York, NY (RR: A; Collector: Rodden), with Jupiter in Gemini and Mercury in Leo.

Sheen had the potential to follow in his father Martin Sheen's footsteps as a respected veteran actor. However, substance abuse, scandal, and a taste for excess derailed his trajectory—from meteoric rise to spectacular fall. With Jupiter in Gemini, there's often no middle ground.

During adolescence, transiting Uranus in Scorpio was sextile its natal position in Virgo about eight months before Jupiter in Leo was sextile his natal Jupiter—indicating a rebellious nature. Interestingly, these sextiles occurred just after his first Saturn opposition.

Sheen's early success coincided with Jupiter transiting his Gemini Ascendant three times—the final pass occurring in late 1983, around the likely time casting began for *Red Dawn*, his breakout role. His next major film, *Platoon*, aligned with Jupiter conjunct his Sun in Pisces and opposite his natal Uranus/Pluto. With natal Mars loosely conjunct Neptune in Scorpio, it's no surprise his fame would come through war movies, sexual escapades, and battles with addiction.

In 1987, he starred in *Wall Street* during a Jupiter in Aries opposition to his natal Venus in Libra—an astrologically fitting moment, as the film's infamous line was "Greed is good."

Eight Men Out (1988) and *Young Guns* (later that year) were released as Jupiter once again crossed his Ascendant. In 1989, Sheen showcased his versatility with the comedy *Major League*. Just weeks before its April release, Jupiter in Gemini conjoined his North Node. Around the time of his second Jupiter return, *Never on Tuesday* was released—another commercial success.

Although he remained steadily employed, the popularity of his films declined. He made occasional television appearances in *Friends*, *Spin City*, and *Saturday Night Live*. In 2003, fortune returned with his casting in *Two and a Half Men*, as Jupiter in Virgo conjoined his Sun.

However, in March 2011—shortly before transiting Jupiter in Aries again opposed his natal Venus (almost exactly two Jupiter cycles after *Platoon*)—he was fired from *Two and a Half Men* due to substance abuse. His wife's public concerns about his mental health led to their twin sons being removed by social services.

In November 2015, just after Jupiter in Leo conjoined his Mercury, Sheen revealed that he had been HIV-positive for at least four years. This disclosure led to the so-called "Charlie Sheen Effect", which caused a

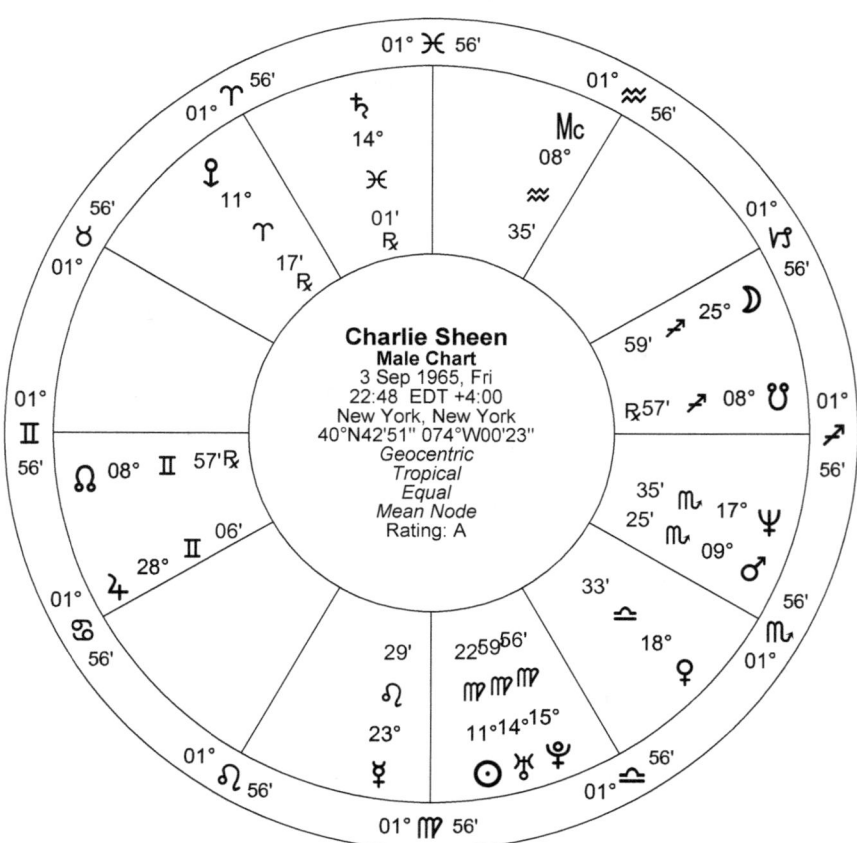

95% spike in over-the-counter HIV test kit purchases. Some argued that his admission did more for HIV awareness than any UN campaign had managed.

As transiting Jupiter in Libra conjoined his natal Venus, Sheen was accused of sexually assaulting a minor actor—a case later settled out of court. Three years later, as Jupiter squared his natal Venus three times, another actor made a similar allegation.

Charlie Sheen is a stark example of Jupiter in Gemini's dual potential: touching greatness one year, and courting destruction the next.

Jupiter in Cancer

Cancer is a water sign by element and a cardinal sign by modality. Transiting squares and oppositions to its natal position will take place in the other cardinal signs, Libra, Capricorn and Aries. This pattern will repeat for the rest of the native's life, defining how a person learns, grows and develops a personal philosophy. Cardinal signs are independent, self-sufficient and enterprising and they need to be led towards learning how to work with others.

Jupiter transits through signs at a pace of about one sign per year. It is important to note that as children are taught by year group, they will learn alongside other children with Jupiter in Cancer. Depending on the time of year they were born, they will also have classmates with Jupiter either in Gemini or Leo. This topic has been explored in depth in *Growing Pains: Astrology in Adolescence*.

Children born with Jupiter in Cancer rely on their instincts and memories, rather than books, to learn. Like the other water signs, a Jupiter in Cancer learner uses their intuition in order to decide if a person is friend or foe, if a situation is beneficial or harmful or if the timing is right or not. But as Jupiter in Cancer is ruled by the Moon, their feelings can always change given the right amount of nurturing and support. So they could say they hate Algebra one day and the next day, they are happily balancing equations just because they want to make their favourite teacher happy. Caring about the way others learn are the simplest terms to describe how Jupiter in Cancer learns. They tend to put others first, to their own detriment, perhaps because deep down they may feel guilty if they don't. Having pets, taking care of the garden, doing voluntary work or learning caring skills are all tasks that can fulfil their need to fuss and worry over others so they can get back to looking after themselves.

Let's have a look at some of the possible ways Jupiter in Cancer expands as a child grows and develops.

The First Jupiter Square

All babies need the basics of adequate nutrition, a safe place to sleep, cleanliness and a comfortable environment. They also need the human touch in order to build trust and to feel the caregiver is responding to their signals for these necessities. Eye contact, talking/singing to the baby and providing a daily rhythm of sleep, cleaning, feeding and playing with age appropriate toys are essential for all babies, irrespective of the Jupiter sign. As the baby grows into a toddler, it is important caregivers have adequately "baby proofed" the child's environment. These essential needs are important all the way into old age. Once these needs are met consistently, a bit of astrology can help the caregivers find the learner's internal "beat" for development.

Here are just a few suggestions for Jupiter in Cancer learners:

At some point during the first year of their life, the Jupiter in Cancer child will experience Jupiter transiting through the sign of Leo. As the learner is a baby, the world is simply full of learning opportunities. Natally, the Jupiter in Cancer learners may lean towards salty, milk-based foods (or milk substitutes) during this stage.

By the second year of life, transiting Jupiter will be in Virgo, a sign known for its discernment. A Jupiter in Cancer learner may begin to show signs of fussy eating or other ways of showing they have definite preferences. At such a young age, they cannot verbally indicate that they are carefully analysing everyone or everything but given encouragement and support, a family language of sorts can be developed. If the main carers listen and imitate what the Jupiter in Cancer is saying at this stage (without resorting to baby talk), it can be seen that the child is definitely letting folks know what s/he thinks.

Jupiter will transit into Libra during the third year of a Jupiter in Cancer learner's life. During this time relationships, particularly the relationships of the immediate family, will become something the Jupiter in Cancer learner will be very sensitive to. An argument will cause the child to fuss or, perhaps even more concerning, withdraw. Raised voices may cause particular alarm for the perceptive Jupiter in Cancer. The child is learning about diplomacy and its uses, and although still a toddler, will learn peace-making skills that will serve them well as they move through the education system.

The First Jupiter Opposition

Between the ages of about three to six years old, most young children are preparing for formal education and socialisation. These are just some ideas to help them prepare for their first adventures away from their immediate care givers.

In the fourth year, Jupiter will transit into Scorpio and if parents and other members of the family thought nothing escaped the scrutiny of Jupiter in Cancer, then just wait for this stage. The Jupiter in Cancer learner may start to understand what other people want. They start to get that there are bargaining chips involved and they usually intuit how to use them. Everything might involve a bit of wheeling and dealing. Want them to pick up their toys? It might cost you. But the thing is, at this stage, Jupiter in Cancer understands that they are a part of a household and by that logic, they can understand that they are able to make a contribution. It might help to make family tidy-up time a lot more enjoyable if everyone feels obligated to join in just because they are a part of the team.

Activities for enjoyment and learning outside of school: mysteries and puzzles, being *gently* frightened (Halloween or cold, dark autumn nights are a good time to share simple ghost stories), nature walks so they can observe the cycle of life in plants and animals (NB: children at this stage may take an interest in death and pregnancies so be prepared to explain). They may take an interest in money and how it works.

By the fifth year, Jupiter will transit into Sagittarius around the time the Jupiter in Cancer child will begin formal schooling. Jupiter in Cancer usually loves familiar places and school for these learners may as well be outer space. However, the Jupiter transit may give a sudden burst of adventurousness that just may shock everyone. Nap time? Forget about it. There's too much to see and do and learn. They still may take too much interest in the child that scrapes his/her knee in the playground (with this group of learners, an injury tends to draw a crowd) but teachers could use this as an information point on how to take care of an injury (starting with washing hands first). Learning about the healing process could even segue into a quick religious education lesson on how different cultures through history dealt with their injured.* Activities for enjoyment and learning outside of

---

* The Jupiter in Cancer learner is naturally curious about history.

school: taking part in charity work, visiting places of worship, learning to discuss politics and identifying political leaders, learning about different countries (their map, geographical features, language, etc.).

The sixth year marks the beginning of the first Jupiter opposition as Jupiter transits into Capricorn. Usually children of this age (in the UK) have had some experience in practising letters and their sounds. However, now comes the real work with fluency and by the time children are this age, they are ready to really begin expanding their basic knowledge. It is likely they will be more motivated if they can meet real career people (in their uniforms) to talk to them about what reading means to them and how it helped them in their careers. Special bonus points to these guests if they can actually read an ability-suited book to the class. Imagine and a real postman (in uniform) reading *Postman Pat*.

Activities for enjoyment and learning outside of school: hobbies that encourage one step at a time, like wool crafts, learning to do simple carpentry skills, learning to do "handyman/woman" jobs around the house, activities that encourage business skills.

By the time of their first Jupiter opposition, they will begin to understand that life isn't just about family but the thrill of exploring the world and working towards a career that really interests them.

The Closing Jupiter Square

By this stage, children will have settled into a home/school routine and it is likely schools will begin to prepare students for the Scholastic Achievement Tests (or their equivalents). Debate rages as to whether these tests cause stress for the children but, drawing from personal experience, students tend not to get too upset if the adults around them don't behave as if the world is coming to an end. The purpose of these tests is to help identify strengths and weaknesses in the child's development. The results establish a baseline, not a final outcome. Here are some ways to help support the learners during these formative times:

Science may be of a particular interest as they typically enjoy exploring (ever speak to a child of this age about outer space?) and performing experiments. Under tight supervision, this is likely to be something that will make a strong impression on them. At home, again under tight parental supervision, simple experiments can be conducted. Most parents should be able to recall the basic science they learned from home (and if they can't, there's always YouTube). Elder siblings can contribute and, if there are younger siblings, the Jupiter in Cancer learner should be only too happy to take a little brother or sister under their wing and impress them with what has been learned in school. The more the family can come together to support Jupiter in Cancer learners for their SATs, the happier and more secure the learner will be.

Activities for enjoyment and learning outside of school: leading/forming a new club and setting rules and expectations, simple science experiments (YouTube is full of ideas of home science experiments—ensure they have permission and understand they have to clean up), learning how to do simple tasks like changing light bulbs, fuses and understanding electrical circuits, recording and monitoring data accurately as part of an experiment.

As Jupiter moves into the sign of Pisces in the Jupiter in Cancer's eighth year, it could seem learning has come to a halt. Children might seem a little sleepy - and they may well be. School can be a hectic time for these learners and they may need a break from all the considerations about possible future careers, the intrigue of science experiments and all the high-octane revision they have been doing. It stands to reason that they may need a bit of time to process all that information. Everyone needs a little poetry break and for Jupiter in Cancer, this is the year for it. For teachers, organising a class "Poetry Slam" could give the learners a bit of time out from what may seem like the relentless drive of education. This fun activity can be for the whole class to participate in so everyone has the opportunity to use their imaginations. Taking in a bit of extra art or music could also help soothe their aching and over-worked minds whilst exercising their wonderful sense creativity.

Activities for enjoyment and learning outside of school: Music lessons, art projects not found in school like pottery courses that allow the learner to complete a project all the way to the end, studying a particular artist and their work medium (painting, sculpture, carving, etc.).

It should feel like things are picking up again during the Jupiter in Cancer child's ninth year. Transiting Jupiter in Aries should see them rested from the poetry break when Jupiter was transiting through Pisces and ready for action. Despite their many differences, both Cancer and Aries are cardinal signs. Both academic groups should thrive on action and competition (though Jupiter in Cancer can be quite protective of classmates who are less able). This probably seems like a very challenging time for Jupiter in Cancer but the important lesson they will learn from this period is that they can rely on the family for support. Less supported Jupiter in Cancer children may feel resentful and that more could have been done for them. It truly doesn't take much more to make a Jupiter in Cancer learner happy than to simply show up for them.

Activities for enjoyment and learning outside of school: any activities that involve racing, focusing on perfecting a singular skill, physical exercise, activities that help them understand their own strengths and limits.

The Jupiter Return

When we return to a place have visited before, it is our nature to make comparisons to what has changed since the first time we were there. We may want to seek out the things we did before or perhaps try something completely different.

As the learner heads towards their final years of primary school, they should be able to work more independently, understand the general rules of the classroom/playground and see home and school as two separate environments.

In their tenth year, Jupiter in Cancer learners may feel as if they can put down roots and relax as Jupiter transits the sign of Taurus. This isn't the same as when Jupiter was transiting through Pisces but more a case of just feeling they are not constantly being driven. Nature walks or tending to the home or school's garden can give a great sense of tranquillity whilst also allowing teachers the chance to teach living science (part of the national curriculum). These learners just need a bit of time to take in the beauty around them, to contemplate the wonders of nature. "Natural" crafting (using nature's bounties to create art) may also be appreciated. At home, parents could go on family camping trips or hiking expeditions. These learners may not say it but the great outdoors beckons to them.

Activities for enjoyment and learning outside of school: outdoor walks, animal watching, tasting different foods, sensory activities and toys, simple physical strength exercises, collecting interesting things (and keeping them organised), money games or managing a small business.

The eleventh year is the year before the first Jupiter return and Jupiter in Cancer learners may have a sense that things are coming to an end. As they finish their last year of primary school, Jupiter will be transiting the sign of Gemini. Moving on to new things (a new home away from home) can mean the friends they've had all their lives could be going to a different school. One would think the Jupiter in Cancer learner, one so rooted to the family, would struggle with this but they may surprise you with how ready they are if they know there are ways of keeping in touch. In this day and age, there are so many ways of keeping track of our social groups (even if we know we should move on). Intellectually the Jupiter in Cancer learners will understand this but they may need the support of family to tell it to their hearts.

Activities for enjoyment and learning outside of school: singing, synonyms for common words, giving names to unfamiliar items, becoming familiar with numbers and letters through developing an interest in calligraphy, a completely different skill to their old handwriting lessons, learning marketing and networking skills.

In their twelfth year, Jupiter in Cancer learners will have their first Jupiter return. For all the signs of Jupiter, it is a wonderful time to take a long holiday with family but it is especially important for Jupiter in Cancer. Jupiter in Cancer learners need to be able to explore the world alongside the people they are familiar with. They need cheerleaders, familiar food and loving faces around them as they prepare for the big step into secondary school. They knew that this day was coming but there still may be tears as they say goodbye to their childhood. For Jupiter in Cancer learners who are supported by their families, they will learn that saying goodbye is a rite of passage, something they will have to do over and over for the rest of their lives. For those Jupiter in Cancer learners who are left to fend for themselves, saying goodbye—however this will be translated by the learner - will be something they will avoid doing whenever they can.

As almost all students will have had their first Jupiter returns by the end of their eleventh year, schools could hold an end of year festival that would allow pupils to demonstrate their individual skills. Schools tend to hold sporting events during this time but how about a not-the-sporting-event competition? Jupiter in Cancer learners could gain some experience doing some work for charities or local care homes (with supervision of course).

The stages of development during their first twelve years will repeat in the same sequence, for roughly the same amount of time, for the rest of their lives.

The Jupiter and Uranus Sextiles: In the Thick of Puberty

As noted in the Introduction, the thirteenth year of a child's life is usually when rebellion and defiance begin to become noticeable. Astrologically, transiting Jupiter forms a sextile aspect to its natal position at the same time Uranus, the planet of rebellion, will also make its first Ptolemaic aspect to its own natal position (also by sextile aspect). This combination quite literally means "big rebellion" and marks the time when adolescents (and their parents) begin the struggle to make that separation into adulthood.

Identifying when and how a young adolescent may struggle with the changing social rules they must face could be helpful for parents. For example, if an adolescent experiences the Uranus sextile before the Jupiter sextile, parents may view their child as needing more guidance for following the expectations of the home environment (which would include expectations in school). In the Case Studies section, subjects with this tendency are noted as "rebels". If an adolescent experiences the Jupiter sextile before the Uranus sextile, parents may view their child as needing more encouragement for academic work and possibly with social skills. In the Case Studies section, subjects with this tendency are noted as "truth seekers". There is no "good" or "bad" with these notations and they are only presented as starting points for understanding the life-long impact this stage of development has on learners as they continue their journey all the way into old age. To demonstrate how this particular stage of development can vary from person to person, there is a summary of the time frame for the subjects of the case studies on page 208.

Furthermore, an adolescent's developing body means they may be interested in forming intimate relationships but their brain needs time to catch up with all the new situations it finds itself in. For children born with Jupiter in Cancer, Jupiter will be transiting through the sign of Virgo as it had been during their second year. It can be helpful for parents to recall the lessons of the second year as difficulties may arise with organising their personal spaces or learning where to draw the line between caring for themselves and caring for others.

The Saturn Opposition

The Saturn opposition begins some time during the fourteenth or fifteenth year (possibly earlier or later depending on individual cases) and marks the end of astrological adolescence. Parents and teachers usually notice that the adolescent begins to calm down and take a more mature approach to their academic progress. In the UK, this coincides with choosing academic subjects (as opposed to trying a little bit of everything), formal exam preparation and a marked change in mood. Depression, anxiety and their symptoms must be monitored and taken seriously. Schools will have access to support mechanisms for parents and carers, teachers will have been trained in how to identify potential difficulties and for parents who are home schooling, social services can be a sound source for help.

As they head towards their transiting Saturn opposition, in Cancer learners will also re-visit what they had learned as transiting Jupiter usually (it can vary from person to person) passes through the signs of Libra and Scorpio. They may need support managing changing friendship groups and/or utilising their personal power in appropriate ways. Re-visiting the appropriate stage of astrological development can be helpful to provide the right sort of help and support.

The Second Jupiter Opposition

By the time a young adult finishes mandatory education, they will have a good idea of what they want to do with their lives and yet they still have time to re-take exams or re-train if they discover they want to do something else. The second Jupiter opposition is a time of making serious decisions: the young adult is no longer a child. The learner now knows there are consequences for undesirable behaviour and can no longer blame "the system" for their poor choices. Sadly, our prison services are filled with young people who have slipped through the net. As a collective whole, society could do with using a little astrology to help these young people get back on track. A more comprehensive mentoring service could be helpful.

Here are some ideas to help young adults focus on the rest of their adult lives:

For the Jupiter in Cancer learner, transiting Jupiter will be in Capricorn as the young adult finishes their formal education at around the age of eighteen. Because the sign of Cancer tends to focus on the past, there may be a need to re-calibrate their direction by focusing on (but not worrying about) the future.

The Second and Subsequent Jupiter Returns

As a person continues to develop emotionally, physically and spiritually they will build on the lessons they learned in their formative years. Jupiter returns (roughly) at the ages of 24, 36, 48 and 60 (and beyond). The suggestions for activities can be modified to suit the developmental cycle for each Jupiter cycle. For example, a Jupiter in Cancer learner experiencing a Jupiter in Virgo transit during their third year of life can be encouraged to create a personal "cubby hole" where they can retreat to (and keep tidy); during their fifteenth year, they may wish to try extend this skill into something like basic carpentry; during their twenty-seventh year, they may wish to extend these skills further by redecorating their own homes or even adding an extension. The key for all Jupiter returns is to choose a skill (or even one per year) and exercise the brain, all the way to the final years of life. As always, with Jupiter, the sky is the limit.

Jupiter returns at all ages should be celebrated and an experienced astrologer can help locate the exact moment of the return. New clothes to reflect a changing style, a good meal (with a magnificent dessert) with influential friends and maybe even a holiday to some exotic place are just a few ideas. To celebrate the ingress (entry) of Jupiter in a new sign, consult the table in the appendix. The Chinese culture does a wonderful job with celebrating "The Year of the…". While theirs may be a different culture and system, the similarity of intention is still there.

Fine Tuning Jupiter in Cancer

Jupiter in Cancer is ruled by the Moon. The speed of the Moon's movement through the zodiac is about 14 degrees per day. Thus a chart set for noon may not accurately signify which sign the Moon is in (unless the noon chart shows the Moon's degree to be between 7 degrees and 23 degrees). If the Moon is in the early degrees of a sign, there is a possibility that the Moon may be in the previous sign. If it is in the later degrees, it may be in the next sign.

Understanding the Moon's sign in a natal chart provides extra insight into how Jupiter in Cancer expresses itself—especially in learning, emotional processing, and social environments. Here's a breakdown of Moon sign behaviour when paired with Jupiter in Cancer:

Moon in Aries: These pupils often rush ahead before fully mastering a task. They can become frustrated when asked to show their working or explain how they reached a conclusion. Impatience is common—but so is passion.

Moon in Taurus: These pupils resist change. Any shift in schedule or classroom routine can be met with stalling or subtle sabotage. Their slow pace may delay group progress, but their steadiness pays off in retention and consistency.

Moon in Gemini: These pupils want to sample everything. They treat learning like a buffet—trying a bit of this, a dash of that. They'll need encouragement to go deeper with subjects instead of hopping from topic to topic.

Moon in Cancer: Highly emotional and deeply nostalgic, these pupils store every lesson in a memory vault. But how they feel on a given day often determines which "files" they're willing to access. Their learning is filtered through mood and attachment.

Moon in Leo: Even sitting quietly is a performance. These pupils crave validation and tend to overreact when they feel ignored. Give them their moment in the spotlight, and they'll often settle down—at least for a little while.

Moon in Virgo: Natural organisers, they prefer structure and neatness—even in learning. They may resist messy or open-ended tasks unless reassured there's a process (and cleanup time!). These pupils thrive with clear steps and timelines.

Moon in Libra: These pupils are at their best in pairs or small groups. Socially graceful, they prioritise harmony but may need support in developing independent work habits. They naturally mediate classroom tension.

Moon in Scorpio: Deep and penetrating, these pupils sense undercurrents in every room. They're emotionally intense and often preoccupied with themes of power, loyalty, and transformation—even if they can't yet articulate it.

Moon in Sagittarius: Freedom-lovers, these pupils ask big questions early—especially around politics, religion, and ethics. They're bold but may speak before thinking. Adults can guide them by helping refine their opinions into informed beliefs.

Moon in Capricorn: They crave stability and respect. They want to be seen as reliable and competent, which may cause them to avoid risks. Help them understand that failure is a step towards mastery—not a sign of weakness.

Moon in Aquarius: Born rebels, they want to do things differently - just because. These pupils resist being boxed in and often thrive in independent learning environments. Clear rules are still necessary, but give them room to innovate.

Moon in Pisces: These dreamy pupils absorb everything around them, though they may struggle to organise it all. They may often need help translating their ideas into tangible output. Be patient—they're swimming in a sea of feelings and impressions.

Case Studies

Margot Robbie

Born: 2 July 1990, 7:45 AM, Dalby, Australia (RR: A; Craft) with Jupiter in Cancer ruled by Moon in Scorpio.

Margot Robbie is an Australian actress and producer, known for her versatility, critical acclaim, and commanding presence in Hollywood. She has earned three Academy Award nominations and, in 2017, was named one of *Time Magazine's* 100 most influential people in the world.

During adolescence, transiting Jupiter in Virgo was sextile her natal Jupiter in Cancer about eight months before the first transiting Uranus in Pisces sextile to her natal Jupiter—suggesting the classic truth seeker signature.

As a child in her ninth year, as Jupiter transited through the sign of Pisces, she did indeed take a break from academic work, enrolled in a circus school and won a certificate for her trapeze skills. As a teenager, she performed the types of jobs most inexperienced young people find themselves doing: she cleaned houses, tended a bar and worked a fast food restaurant.

Her acting career began with a flourish: at age 18, during her first Jupiter opposition (transiting Jupiter in Capricorn), Robbie landed a role on the Australian soap *Neighbours*. A few years later, during her second Jupiter return (Jupiter back in Cancer), she starred in *The Wolf of Wall Street* (2013), launching her into international stardom.

Like many Jupiter in Cancer natives, Robbie has navigated both traditional and groundbreaking roles with emotional depth. In 2016, during Jupiter's series of squares to her natal Jupiter, she played major parts in *The Legend of Tarzan* and *The Suicide Squad*. Around the same time, Jupiter squared her natal Neptune—a classic aspect of visibility and

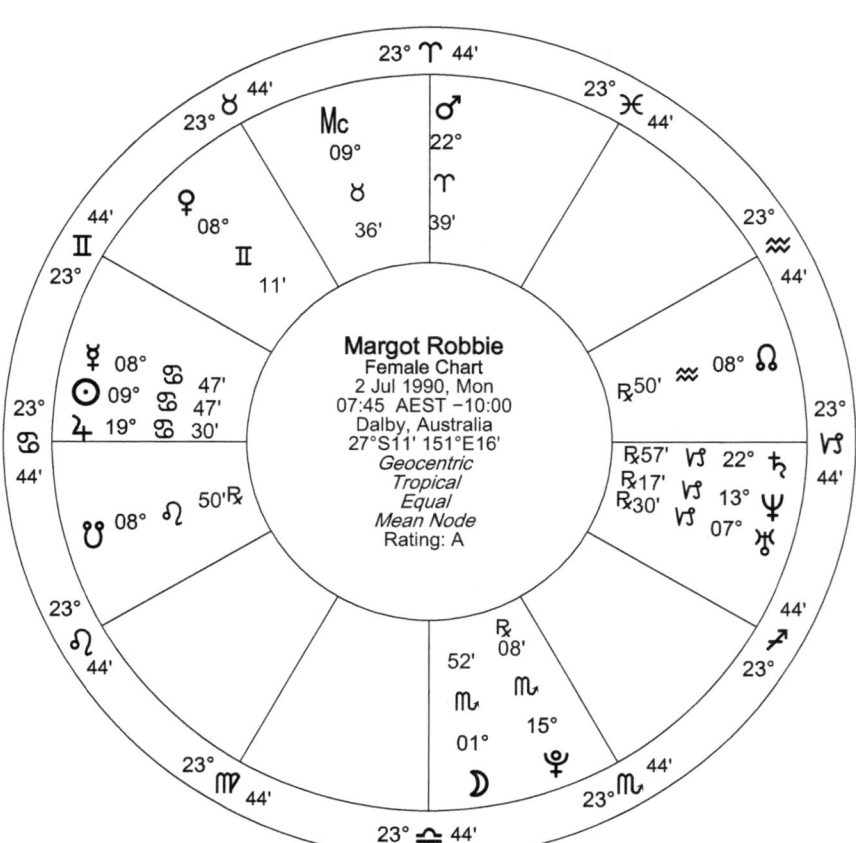

projection. Her portrayal of Tonya Harding in *I, Tonya* (2017) earned her critical acclaim during the tail end of those transits.

Her most iconic role may be *Barbie* (2023), released as Jupiter in Aries made a series of closing squares to her natal Jupiter. The film's themes—female empowerment, identity, and transformation—mirror the expansive, emotionally reflective nature of Jupiter in Cancer. In a surreal twist, Barbie's journey in the film mirrors Jupiter in Cancer's life path: starting in a cosy, idealised home and venturing into the complex, emotionally messy real world.

Mike Tyson

Born: 30 June 1966 (no birth time), New York, NY with Jupiter in Cancer ruled by the Moon in Sagittarius.

Mike Tyson is regarded as one of the most formidable heavyweight boxers in history. He was the undisputed world champion from 1987–1990 but his legacy is complicated by legal issues, addiction, and infamous incidents.

Jupiter in Cancer craves safety and secure emotional roots—something Tyson lacked. His mother died when he was 16, and his early years were marked by instability. Raised in high-crime neighbourhoods, he was arrested dozens of times before the age of 13. His Moon in Sagittarius likely gave him a survivalist's need for freedom, escape, and autonomy, while Jupiter in Cancer longed for emotional grounding. During adolescence, transiting Uranus in Scorpio was sextile to its natal position about eighteen months before the first transiting Jupiter in Virgo was sextile to his natal Jupiter in Gemini, indicating he is a rebel. Very unusually, he had his transiting Uranus sextiles before his first Jupiter return.

At a youth detention centre, he was introduced to boxing—his saving grace. Shortly before his professional debut at 19, transiting Jupiter opposed his natal Jupiter: a classic launch moment. He became world champion at 20.

In 1987, transiting Jupiter squared his natal Jupiter. Around this time, he became a household name and was immortalised as the face of Mike Tyson's *Punch Out!!*, a wildly popular Nintendo game. But trouble soon followed: in 1992, as Jupiter in Libra squared his natal Jupiter in Cancer, he was convicted of sexual assault and sentenced to six years in prison. He served three.

In 1997, as Jupiter in Aquarius made harsh squares to his natal Neptune, Tyson's infamous ear-biting incident occurred during a fight with Evander Holyfield. This shocking event remains one of modern sports' most controversial moments.

Tyson later expressed remorse and began rebuilding his career. In 2012, as Jupiter returned to his North Node in Taurus, he launched the Mike Tyson Cares Foundation, aiming to give disadvantaged youth the "fighting chance" he never had.

His adult life is a Jupiter in Cancer odyssey: a powerful rise, deep emotional wounds, and an eventual return home—literally and figuratively. He now finds peace raising pigeons, an interest that began in his boyhood. No matter how far Jupiter in Cancer travels, it always circles back to where the heart is.

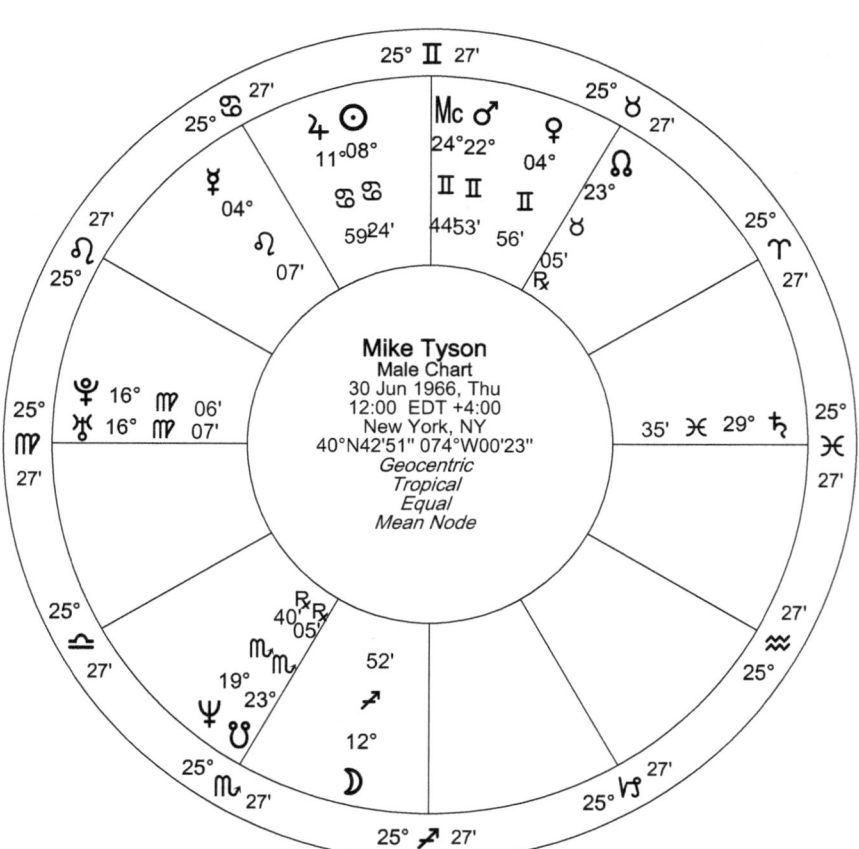

Jupiter in Leo

Leo is a fire sign by element and a fixed sign by modality. Transiting squares and oppositions to its natal position will take place about every three years in the other fixed signs Scorpio, Aquarius and Taurus. This pattern will repeat for the rest of the native's life, defining how a person learns, grows and develops a personal philosophy. Generally speaking, the fixed signs are noted for their persistence and for Leo, this usually manifests itself in dramatic performances both off and on the stage: it can seem like these learners would do anything for attention. Natural entertainers, their creativity and generosity can sometimes be excessive but nothing beats the warmth of their friendship. It can be very difficult to persuade Jupiter in Leo to move away from the people with whom they have formed attachments so they will need fair warning for any forthcoming changes in learning locations.

Jupiter transits through signs at a pace of about one sign per year. It is important to note that as children are taught by year group, they will learn alongside other children with Jupiter in Leo. Depending on the time of year they were born, they will also have classmates with either Jupiter in Cancer or Jupiter in Virgo. This topic has been explored in depth in *Growing Pains: Astrology in Adolescence.*

Children who have Jupiter in Leo usually take pride in their work and they want their parents and teachers to notice. Praise goes a long way with these learners—but they can spot sympathy applause from a mile away. Leo is ruled by the Sun and, whilst everyone loves to bask in the warmth of the sun, this rulership can have its drawbacks: everyone needs a little rain sometimes just to cool off. Jupiter in Leo learners can be very sensitive to criticism (watch out for this if there are Jupiter in Virgo learners in the same classroom) so it's important to catch them being good as often as you can.

Let's look at Jupiter as it transits through the other signs of the zodiac for Jupiter in Leo.

The First Jupiter Square

All babies need the basics of adequate nutrition, a safe place to sleep, cleanliness and a comfortable environment. They also need the human touch in order to build trust and to feel the caregiver is responding to their signals for these necessities. Eye contact, talking/singing to the baby and providing a daily rhythm of sleep, cleaning, feeding and playing with age appropriate toys are essential for all babies, irrespective of the Jupiter sign. As the baby grows into a toddler, it is important caregivers have adequately "baby proofed" the child's environment. These essential needs are important all the way into old age. Once these needs are met consistently, a bit of astrology can help the caregivers find the learner's internal "beat" for development.

Here are just a few suggestions for Jupiter in Leo learners:

At some point during the first year of their life, the Jupiter in Leo learner will experience Jupiter transiting through the sign of Virgo. As the learner is a baby, the world is simply full of learning opportunities. Natally, the Jupiter in Leo learners may lean towards pungent foods such as garlic, onion and ginger but, as with all young babies, sweet foods may be a preference.

As Jupiter transits through Libra during the second year, the Jupiter in Leo child is usually learning how to move around more efficiently. Although success in walking and crawling varies according to factors such as genetics, Jupiter in Leo learners quite instinctively have a sense of self preservation that may mean they are afraid to let others see them make mistakes. Applause and encouragement are the keys to helping them to learn that everyone makes mistakes. Of course they can't express this concept but what harm can it do to let them know they are pleasing you? This is also a fantastic time to instil the good manners that will last them for a lifetime. Even shortened versions of "please", "thank you" and "excuse me" can help them get the idea that good decorum can assist them in charming even the harshest critic when they get older. Getting children to verbalise can also help professionals diagnose any potential speech/language difficulties so these can be dealt with as soon possible.

During the third year, Jupiter will transit through the sign of Scorpio and will complete its first opening square for Jupiter in Leo learners. Usually by the time any child is three years old, they are able to walk and talk with limitations that are appropriate for their age group. However, it could be that the Jupiter in Leo learner has come to understand that the only way to get attention is through getting into trouble or by causing unnecessary concern. During this year, it becomes important for carers and parents to be able to discern if their child is doing or saying (or not doing or saying) something in order to cause a crisis. Clearly, early intervention is important if a parent suspects something is not quite right. However, it is equally a good idea to see if praise for the right kind of behaviour encourages the child to reach expected milestones under an appropriate doctor's guidance.

The First Jupiter Opposition

Between the ages of about three to six years old, most young children are preparing for formal education and socialisation. These are just some ideas to help Jupiter in Leo learners prepare for their first adventures away from their immediate care givers.

As Jupiter transits through Sagittarius, another fire sign, any doubt about a Jupiter in Leo's progress in reaching milestones should probably be resolved. Sagittarius is daredevil energy and parents and carers should see their child coming right out of any shell they thought the Jupiter in Leo learner was in. And of course, this is just in time for preparing for school. Many children are ready for day care at this age and Jupiter in Leo learners generally thrive amongst their peers. Whilst this group of learners may wear their teachers out, astrology can be enormously helpful in tempering some of this fire energy down by pairing these learners with their less physically energetic classmates such as Jupiter in Cancer (slightly older children) and Jupiter in Virgo (slightly younger children). Either of these signs intuitively understands the importance of pacing, observing and fixing on a goal to work on.

Activities for enjoyment and learning outside of school: taking part in charity work, visiting places of worship, learning to discuss politics and identifying political leaders, learning about different countries (their map, geographical features, language, etc.).

Jupiter will begin transiting through the sign of Capricorn during the Jupiter in Leo's fifth year. Having experienced a classroom/day care centre full of fellow Jupiter in Leo learners, they may start to get the idea that it's not all about tearing around the place getting into trouble. Suddenly, they may crave being productive and making progress. For teachers and parents, this is fertile training grounds for getting these young Jupiter in Leo children to enjoy the satisfaction that comes from achievement. Even play time can be seen by these learners as the opportunity to learn new skills and build on the knowledge they have already acquired.

Activities for enjoyment and learning outside of school: hobbies that encourage one step at a time, like wool crafts, learning to do simple carpentry skills, learning to do "handyman/woman" jobs around the house, activities that encourage business skills.

As Jupiter begins its transit through the sign of Aquarius in their sixth year, Jupiter in Leo learners may begin to realise that there are people and experiences outside of their own expectations. They may be surprised to learn there are different religions to the one they are familiar with or the idea of cultures different to their own begins to capture their imaginations. Whilst these children are young, having a variety of friends will teach them the most basic of human concepts: no matter how different we are on the outside, we are all equal on the inside. We all deserve respect and we all deserve to be treated nicely.

Activities for enjoyment and learning outside of school: leading/forming a new club and setting rules and expectations, simple science experiments (YouTube is full of ideas of home science experiments—ensure they have permission and understand they have to clean up), learning how to do simple tasks like changing light bulbs, fuses and understanding electrical circuits, recording and monitoring data accurately as part of an experiment.

Through the opportunity of change, these fixed sign children develop the confidence to step outside of what they think they know and step into a world of wonder and diversity.

The Closing Jupiter Square

By this stage, children will have settled into a home/school routine and it is likely schools will begin to prepare students for the Scholastic Achievement Tests (or their equivalents). Debate rages as to whether these tests cause stress for the children but, drawing from personal experience, students tend not to get too upset if the adults around them don't behave as if the world is coming to an end. The purpose of these tests is to help identify strengths and weaknesses in the child's development. The results establish a baseline, not a final outcome.

Here are some ways to help support the learners during these formative times:

During their seventh year, Jupiter in Leo pupils will experience Jupiter's transit through the sign of Pisces. They may become more thoughtful and reflective and may express a desire to exercise their ample creativity through poetry, music or other art forms. Their teachers may press them to begin preparation for their SATs but these learners are developing their intuition—and they instinctively know that in order to secure prior learning, they need the time to digest everything. They will understand that they have come a long way and they may just need a bit of time out to get used to that. How can they show their appreciation? How do they demonstrate what they have learned? Just by watching them one can see that through their playacting (when they think adults aren't watching them) the children take on adult roles and show exactly what they need in order to continue to grow. Watch the productions and plays that they so carefully plan, organise and perform—designed only for the eyes of a hand-picked audience.

Activities for enjoyment and learning outside of school: Music lessons, art projects not found in school like pottery courses that allow the learner to complete a project in step-by-step stages, studying a particular artist and their work medium (painting, sculpture, carving, etc.).

As Jupiter transits into Aries during their eighth year, usually another burst of energy hits the year group like a proverbial explosion. Now the competition begins. These previously thoughtful students can declare war on each other unless that energy is directed through activities like sports, speed rounds in learning or frequent play breaks. If they don't have a way of burning off this excess energy, they could resort to attention-seeking tactics that are not only wearing to observe but could be outright dangerous. Harness this energy, aim it into productive directions (school plays, dance classes, singing lessons and/or extra sports at the weekends) and a ton of money could be saved in broken furniture, chipped teeth and visits to Accidents and Emergency.

Activities for enjoyment and learning outside of school: any activities that involve racing, focusing on perfecting a singular skill, physical exercise, activities that help them understand their own strengths and limits

Children do tend to wear themselves down eventually and as they enter their ninth year, Jupiter will be about to enter into the sign of Taurus, another fixed sign. By the time Jupiter in Leo children hit this stage of development, they will need a bit of extra time to complete the tasks they used to speed through without a second thought. And this is the key: "without a second thought". Once they show signs of being ready to pace and steady themselves through their lessons, it may be time to spend some learning sessions going back and doing some basics such as handwriting and other means of presentation. They may need time just to spend on making their workbooks tidier, getting more organised and generally enjoying the process of learning without pressure. It's very much like a re-set button and they want to get off to a good start. Activities for enjoyment and learning outside of school: outdoor walks, animal watching, tasting different foods, sensory activities and toys, simple physical strength exercises, collecting interesting things (and keeping them organised).

The Jupiter Return

As the learner heads towards their final years of primary school, they should be able to work more independently, understand the general rules of the classroom/playground and see home and school as two separate environments.

As they enter their tenth year, the Jupiter in Leo learners begin to experience a broadening of their interests as Jupiter transits through the sign of Gemini. If they've been given an opportunity to re-boot, they will take more time in preserving the good habits they have learned whilst Jupiter was transiting through Taurus. If they've been pushed, they may never quite feel they are ready to learn new material. Learning resources get messier, disorganisation could become a bigger problem and their sense of time keeping could become nonexistent. Jupiter in Leo learners at this stage of their development need to have extremely clear expectations. Given the right encouragement, they may very well exceed expectations but not letting them know what to do is like a speedboat without a rudder. Another possible challenge with this year is that the class could polarise into super-speedy learners and those who are terrified they will get caught out for not knowing what to do. Parents and teachers should aim to understand the strengths and weaknesses of the individual learners and avoid letting Jupiter in Leo learners charm their way into taking on tasks that are too difficult (or too easy) for them.

Activities for enjoyment and learning outside of school: singing, synonyms for common words, giving names to unfamiliar items, becoming familiar with numbers and letters through learning the skills of simple calligraphy (far different from their previous handwriting lessons), learning marketing or networking skills, learning to touch type.

As they prepare for secondary school, Jupiter in Leo students may begin exhibiting signs that they are nervous about their new journey into the bigger school as Jupiter transits into the sign of Cancer. Of course this is to be expected: there is no doubt that this is a big step. However, there could be something far more hidden than just starting all over again at a new school. Consider how hard Jupiter in Leo learners have worked to establish themselves as school royalty: the younger children looked up to them, the teachers found them a lot of fun to teach, parents admired their talents. And now they have to start all over again. It's terribly daunting for Jupiter in Leo learners and they will need a lot of reassurance that they will have a lot to offer their new school. Of course there will be new friends, of course they will have to get to know their new teachers but almost certainly all the lessons they learned in previous years will help them settle in. It's likely to be nothing more than stage fright.

Activities for enjoyment and learning outside of school: taking care of animals, singing (as a way to cope with negative emotions), helping with the cooking, taking responsibility for the management of one area of their living space, learning how to take care of their clothes and beds, visiting museums or investigating certain times in history.

During their Jupiter return, as transiting Jupiter returns to its position in Leo at their birth, the confidence of Jupiter in Leo children will return if they are given the chance to shine. Fortunately, secondary school teachers are trained to help new students at secondary school to settle in (it's a shame not more of them use astrology but one has to work with the available tools). As the year progresses and more and more of the pupils of the academic year reach their Jupiter returns, the better these learners get the measure of themselves and find their places.

When we return to a place have visited before, it is our nature to make comparisons to what has changed since the first time we were there. We may want to seek out the things we did before or perhaps try something completely different.

As almost all students will have had their first Jupiter returns by the end of their first year of secondary school, schools could hold an end of year festival that would allow pupils to demonstrate their individual skills. Schools tend to hold sporting events during this time but how about a talent competition? Students could perform a Variety Show for the public and donate proceeds to an agreed charity.

The Jupiter and Uranus Sextiles: In the Thick of Puberty

As noted in the Introduction, the thirteenth year of a child's life is usually when rebellion and defiance begin to become noticeable. Astrologically, transiting Jupiter forms a sextile aspect to its natal position at the same time Uranus, the planet of rebellion, will also make its first Ptolemaic aspect to its own natal position (also by sextile aspect). This combination quite literally means "big rebellion" and marks the time when adolescents (and their parents) begin the struggle to make that separation into adulthood.

Identifying when and how a young adolescent may struggle with the changing social rules they must face could be helpful for parents. For example, if an adolescent experiences the Uranus sextile before the Jupiter sextile, parents may view their child as needing more guidance for following the expectations of the home environment (which would include expectations in school). In the Case Studies section, subjects with this tendency are noted as "rebels". If an adolescent experiences the Jupiter sextile before the Uranus sextile, parents may view their child as needing more encouragement for academic work and possibly with social skills. In the Case Studies section, subjects with this tendency are noted as "truth seekers". There is no "good" or "bad" with these notations and they are only presented as starting points for understanding the life-long impact this stage of development has on learners as they continue their journey all the way into old age. To demonstrate how this particular stage of development can vary from person to person, there is a summary of the time frame for the subjects of the case studies on page 208.

Furthermore, an adolescent's developing body means they may be interested in forming intimate relationships but their brain needs time to catch up with all the new situations it finds itself in. For children born with Jupiter in Leo, Jupiter will be transiting through the sign of Libra as it had been during their second year. It can be helpful for parents to recall the lessons of this year as difficulties with relationships and learning can typically come down to simple manners. At this stage of development, young people of this age are exploring relationships of all types. Boundaries and levels of trust need to be set both at school and at home in order for healthy interactions to flourish.

The Saturn Opposition

The Saturn opposition begins some time during the fourteenth or fifteenth year (possibly earlier or later depending on individual cases) and marks the end of astrological adolescence. Parents and teachers usually notice that the adolescent begins to calm down and take a more mature approach to their academic progress. In the UK, this coincides with choosing academic subjects (as opposed to trying a little bit of everything), formal exam preparation and a marked change in mood. Depression, anxiety and their symptoms must be monitored and taken seriously. Schools will have access to support mechanisms for parents and carers, teachers will have been trained in how to identify potential difficulties and for parents who are home schooling, social services can be a sound source for help.

As they head towards their transiting Saturn opposition, Jupiter in Leo students will also re-visit what they had learned as transiting Jupiter usually (it can vary from person to person) passes through the signs of Scorpio and Sagittarius. They will develop a sense of personal power as well as a need to explore new places and situations. Re-visiting the appropriate stage of astrological development can be helpful to provide the right sort of help and support.

The Second Jupiter Opposition

By the time a young adult finishes mandatory education, they will have a good idea of what they want to do with their lives and yet they still have time to re-take exams or re-train if they discover they want to do something else. The second Jupiter opposition is a time of making serious decisions: the young adult is no longer a child. The learner now knows there are consequences for undesirable behaviour and can no longer blame "the system" for their poor choices. Sadly, our prison services are filled with young people who have slipped through the net. As a collective whole, society could do with using a little astrology to help these young people get back on track. A more comprehensive mentoring service could be helpful.

Here are some ideas to help young adults focus on the rest of their adult lives:

Transiting Jupiter will be in Aquarius as the young adult finishes their formal education at around the age of eighteen. Jupiter in Aquarius is tends to be concerned with platonic friendships but, as they are Jupiter in Leo learners, their primary concern is preserving their ego. A heartbroken Jupiter in Leo could take a long time before they feel ready to be vulnerable to another person again. As always, there is the possibility of the other extreme of rushing into another relationship just to avoid looking wounded to their friends. Either extreme needs tender loving care, a good support system from the family and if they are away from home for the first time, they also need a strong network of friends.

The Second and Subsequent Jupiter Returns

As a person continues to develop emotionally, physically and spiritually they will build on the lessons they learned in the formative years. Jupiter returns occur at (roughly) the ages of 24, 36, 48 and 60 (and beyond). The suggestions for activities can be modified to suit the developmental cycle for each Jupiter cycle. For example, a Jupiter in Leo learner experiencing a Jupiter in Libra transit during their third year of life can be encouraged to study the fine arts; during their fifteenth year, they may wish to extend these skills to bigger projects; during their twenty-seventh year, they may want to take on a professional development course to help them hone their artistic skills. The key for all Jupiter returns is to choose a skill (or even one per year) and exercise the brain, all the way to the final years of life. As always, with Jupiter, the sky is the limit.

Jupiter returns at all ages should be celebrated and an experienced astrologer can help locate the exact moment of the return. New clothes to reflect a changing style, a good meal (with a magnificent dessert) with influential friends and maybe even a holiday to some exotic place are just a few ideas. To celebrate the ingress (entry) of Jupiter in a new sign, consult the table in the appendix. The Chinese culture does a wonderful job with celebrating, "The Year of the…". While theirs may be a different culture and system, the similarity of intention is still there.

Fine Tuning Jupiter in Leo

Like everything else with Leo, finding the ruler of Jupiter is not difficult: it is their Sun sign and is obvious from just the date of their birth.

Sun in Aries: These pupils creatively find ways to express themselves when learning. Their work stands out as their own and often there is some sort of hallmark making their product easy to identify.

Sun in Taurus: These pupils are adept at creating beauty and comfort wherever they are. They can turn even the most austere surroundings into an art gallery. There may be some fuss over material goods that may need to be addressed once the child starts to understand the power of money.

Sun in Gemini: These pupils are adept at creatively communicating with anyone. They can adjust their manner, tone of voice and choice of words to suit any occasion. Seldom lost for words, teachers usually can't keep them quiet for long.

Sun in Cancer: These pupils learn best when they feel secure. Disliking unfamiliar people or places, these pupils need to feel protected and looked after. Or they need to feel they are the ones offering the comfort and security.

Sun in Leo: These pupils learn best when they are at the centre of attention—whether for good behaviour or bad. It is important they understand from an early age that only good behaviour is awarded with attention.

Sun in Virgo: These pupils learn best when they are allowed to express their creativity through precision. They require learning tools to help them do this: clear lesson objectives, equipment in good working order and a clean working environment.

Sun in Libra: These pupils learn best by being given opportunities to engage with others. Unfortunately, the current examination system does not make allowances for this and these learners would greatly benefit by being taught independent skills.

Sun in Scorpio: These pupils learn best by exercising their power over their learning. Track their progress and show them how their efforts pay off. In the right circumstances, these pupils can obsess over seemingly innocuous points.

Sun in Sagittarius: These pupils learn best when allowed to explore their creativity. They will find inspiration in adventures, faraway lands and people who hold unusual philosophical views. Carers usually discover, after several sessions in A and E, that safety precautions are necessary to keep these children safely corralled.

Sun in Capricorn: These pupils learn best when allowed to exercise their creativity in a step-by-step process. Give them a blank canvas and they will leave it blank and go back to their Lego constructions.

Sun in Aquarius: These pupils learn best when allowed to experiment. Yes, they will make a lot of noise and create a lot of mess but they almost always see mistakes as a chance to improve.

Sun in Pisces: These pupils learn best by being allowed to explore alternative outcomes to known situations. They like "What if?" questions and the further removed from reality, the better they will like it.

Case Studies

Gordon Ramsay

Born: 8 November 1966, 18:05, Johnstone, Scotland (RR: AA; Collector: Wright) with Jupiter in Leo and Sun in Scorpio.

Gordon Ramsay is a multi-talented celebrity who has become one of the most influential and best-known chefs in the world. Beyond his culinary mastery, Ramsay is also a successful restaurateur, television personality, and author. As of 2025, he has six children and divides his time between London and Los Angeles with his wife, Tana.

In adolescence, like many boys his age, Ramsay dreamed of becoming a footballer. He was selected to play for an under-14 team during the year of his first Jupiter return, which included three conjunctions by transit. However, a serious knee injury forced him to give up this dream. During adolescence, transiting Uranus in Scorpio was sextile to its natal position about thirteen months before the first transiting Jupiter in Libra was sextile his natal Jupiter in Leo—an astrological indicator of a rebellious streak. Notably, Ramsay experienced his Saturn oppositions before these Jupiter sextiles.

At age sixteen, he left his family home and an abusive, alcoholic father to live in Oxfordshire. When transiting Jupiter in Aquarius opposed its natal position, Ramsay made the pivotal decision to pursue a career in culinary arts. Just before his second Jupiter return in 1989, he moved to France to train under Michelin-starred chefs for three years. He also

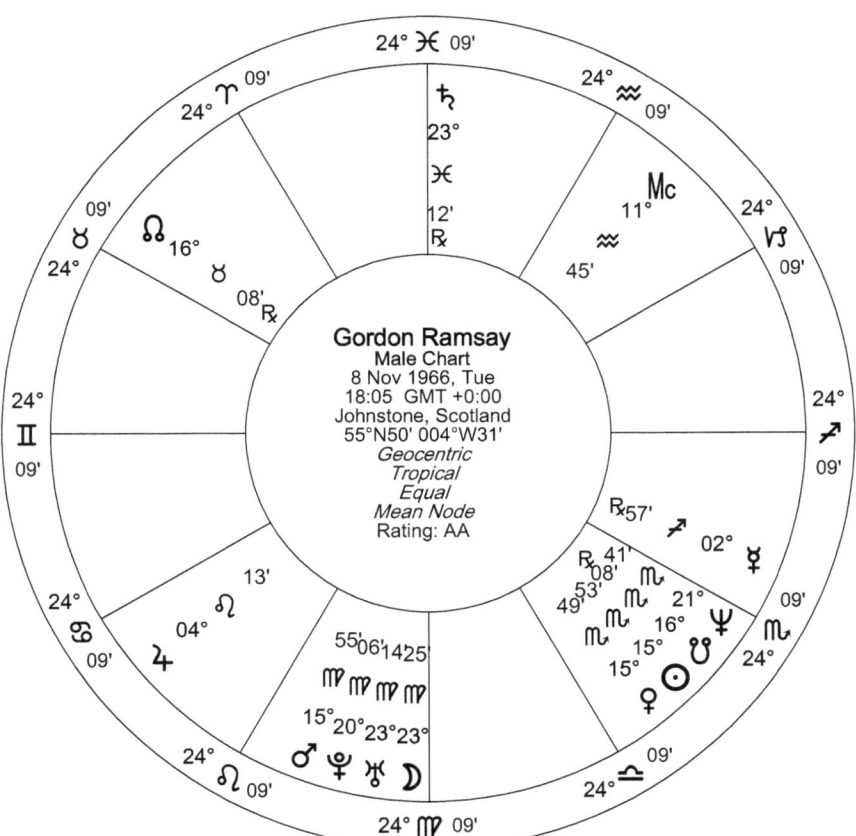

worked aboard a yacht as a personal chef and later travelled to Italy to refine his skills in Italian cuisine.

By 1993, during the opening square of his Jupiter cycle, Ramsay opened a restaurant in Chelsea with Marco Pierre White. He left this partnership in 1998, the year transiting Jupiter opposed his natal Pluto three times—an experience Ramsay later described as the most important turning point in his life. That same year, with the help of his father-in-law, he opened his own restaurant.

In 1999, during his closing Jupiter square, Ramsay made his television debut in *Boiling Point*. In 2001, his restaurant earned a third Michelin star, making him the first Scottish chef to achieve this. At the time, transiting Jupiter was opposing his natal Mercury in Sagittarius. As his success mounted, he continued opening restaurants globally. In 2006, when transiting Jupiter was conjunct his natal Mercury, Ramsay was awarded an OBE for services to the hospitality industry.

He became a household name through the show *Kitchen Nightmares*, launched in 2004, as transiting Jupiter was conjunct his natal Pluto. Since then, Ramsay has been a consistent presence on television and has participated in numerous charitable efforts, including running ten marathons in ten years for the Spina Bifida Association and working with UNICEF and Women's Aid.

Despite his talent, Ramsay is equally known for his fiery temper, perfectionism, and frequent use of expletives—traits that may reflect a fiercely guarded ego and a reaction to childhood trauma. Jupiter in Leo learners often thrive when given recognition, but if their emotional needs are not met, they may develop an exaggerated response to authority and criticism.

Gary Busey

Born: 29 June 1944, 11:50, Baytown, TX (RR: A; Collector: Rodden) with Jupiter in Leo and Sun in Cancer.

Gary Busey is an American actor whose career spans several decades, with roles in prominent films from 1974 to 2015. He was nominated for an Academy Award for Best Actor in 1978 for his portrayal of Buddy Holly in *The Buddy Holly Story*. Despite his talent, Busey's career was marked by serious injuries, substance abuse, and controversy.

During adolescence, transiting Uranus in Leo was sextile to its natal position about three months before transiting Jupiter in Libra formed a sextile to his natal Jupiter in Leo, marking him as a classic rebel.

In 1974, as transiting Jupiter in Aquarius opposed its natal position, Busey starred in the TV comedy *The Texas Wheelers* and appeared in *Thunderbolt and Lightfoot* alongside Clint Eastwood and Jeff Bridges. Two years later, during a Jupiter square, he featured in *A Star Is Born* with Barbra Streisand. But his breakout came in 1978 with *The Buddy Holly Story*, released as transiting Jupiter in Cancer was conjunct his natal Sun.

He continued to find success throughout the 1980s, most notably with *Lethal Weapon* in 1987, as Jupiter in Aries opposed his natal Sun and squared his nodal axis. However, in 1988, Busey suffered a near-fatal motorcycle accident—he wasn't wearing a helmet—and sustained

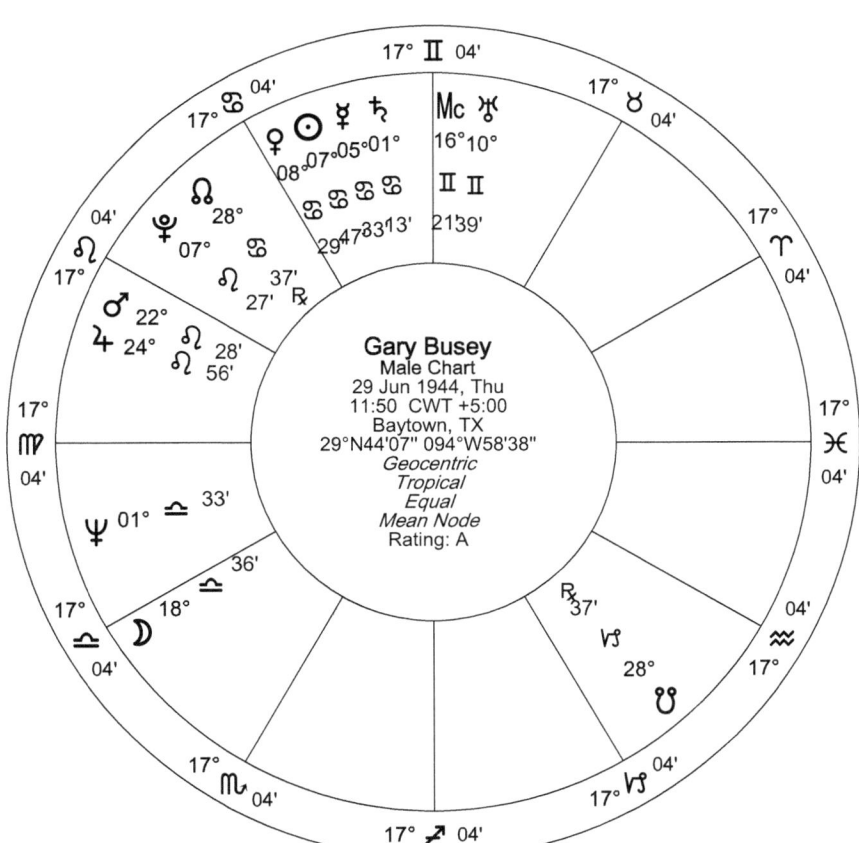

permanent brain damage. During this period, transiting Jupiter squared both his natal Mars and Sun.

Despite the injury, Busey remained active in film through the 1990s. His resurgence came in 2008 when he won *Celebrity Big Brother 14*, under a Jupiter opposition to its natal position in Capricorn.

In 1996, he declared himself a born-again Christian, citing his motorcycle accident and near-fatal cocaine overdose in 1995 as pivotal moments in his spiritual journey. Transiting Jupiter opposed its natal position three times during this period, a classic indicator of reassessing one's personal beliefs.

Busey's Jupiter in Leo shows the full arc of the sign's potential: meteoric rise, dramatic personal crises, and eventual redemption through spiritual growth. His later years reflect the softened ego and wisdom that can come when Jupiter in Leo matures and learns to direct its brilliance with humility.

Jupiter in Virgo

Virgo is an earth sign by element and a mutable sign by modality. Transiting squares and oppositions to its natal position will take place roughly every three years in the other mutable signs, Sagittarius, Pisces and Gemini. This pattern will repeat for the rest of the native's life, defining how a person learns, grows and develops a personal philosophy. Mutable signs are flexible, co-operative and interested in what goes on around them. They are usually very curious and collect and distribute information that passes their way. Jupiter in Virgo generally likes to keep their belongings and tools for learning in an organised space for easy reference.

Jupiter transits through signs at a pace of about one sign per year. It is important to note that as children are taught by year group, they will learn alongside other children with Jupiter in Virgo. Depending on the time of year they were born, they will also have classmates with either Jupiter in Leo or Jupiter in Libra. This topic has been explored in depth in *Growing Pains: Astrology in Adolescence.*

Children who have Jupiter in Virgo tend to thrive by being given the opportunity to analyse, discern and improve. They tend to be natural critics and are usually able to turn chaos into order simply by being able to identify the problems and then taking steps to solve them. As Jupiter in Virgo is ruled by Mercury, they tend to have a talent for transcribing or translating texts as well. In peer assessment situations, they can come across as harsh so it is important to lay down firm guidelines or they could cause upset amongst their peers (particularly if they have Jupiter in Leo classmates, who tend not to appreciate criticism).

The First Jupiter Square

All babies need the basics of adequate nutrition, a safe place to sleep, cleanliness and a comfortable environment. They also need the human touch in order to build trust and to feel the caregiver is responding to their signals for these necessities. Eye contact, talking/singing to the baby

and providing a daily rhythm of sleep, cleaning, feeding and playing with age appropriate toys are essential for all babies, irrespective of the Jupiter signs. As the baby grows into a toddler, it is important caregivers have adequately "baby proofed" the child's environment. These essential needs are important all the way into old age. Once these needs are met consistently, a bit of astrology can help the caregivers find the learner's internal "beat" for development.

Here are just a few suggestions for Jupiter in Virgo learners:

At some point during the first year of their life, the Jupiter in Virgo child will experience Jupiter transiting through the sign of Libra. As the learner is a baby, the world is simply full of learning opportunities. Natally, the Jupiter in Virgo learner could develop a fussy palette so it is important to maintain a wide variety of tastes for them to enjoy.

As their attention span increases, the Jupiter in Virgo baby may show signs of interest in music and dance. If their interest in the fine arts continues to grow into their second year, it is likely Jupiter in Virgo learners may fixate on certain performers, even though they are still quite young. Transiting Jupiter in Scorpio can bring edginess to the learning process. They may be observed doing the same movement or making the same sounds over and over again. As their verbal abilities may only be rudimentary at this stage, they are already practising the precision in their language that is likely to become the hallmark of a Jupiter in Virgo learner.

By the time of their third year, Jupiter in Virgo children will experience transiting Jupiter in Sagittarius. Sagittarius tends to be a fun, energetic and occasionally careless sign that is not worried about being bogged down by rules and regulations. However, this tends to not be the nature of Jupiter in Virgo which usually prefers to have things tamed, predictable and manageable. They like routines and knowing what comes next. They tend to micromanage if not encouraged to do otherwise. For these reasons, Jupiter in Virgo learners may find this a challenging time as they have to watch their careful plans go up in smoke. Fortunately, Jupiter in Virgo learners tend to be even-tempered. However, what they do very well is express their displeasure without saying all that much: they may huff and sigh, tut just loud enough for you to hear… and then give everyone a taste of their own medicine by being reckless while making it look like an accident. That wonderful Lego tower? Oops. Sorry it fell down by itself. Your favourite shirt? Oh sorry the lid fell off the permanent marker. Got somewhere to go? Sorry I can't find my shoes. For all these "little accidents" it is important that Jupiter in Virgo learners take responsibility, apologise and learn how to be a little more forthcoming with what is really bothering them.

It doesn't take much to upset Jupiter in Virgo learners but they must learn patience and tolerance for those who find it challenging to keep up with their high standards. They are beginning to learn that not everyone does things the way they like to do them.

The First Jupiter Opposition

Between the ages of about three and six years old, most young children are preparing for formal education and socialisation. These are just some ideas to help Jupiter in Virgo learners prepare for their first adventures away from their immediate care givers.

As transiting Jupiter moves into Capricorn during their fourth year, Jupiter in Virgo learners begin to understand that things get done a lot faster if they stop fussing over the smallest details. Hard work can get the job done faster and these learners begin to get very good at assessing the talents of other people and putting them to good use—even though they are still very young. They may also begin to understand the power of words: they learn how to motivate other people and direct them to finding the most efficient way to accomplish the task at hand. Even if it's only a simple task in the local park, the Jupiter in Virgo learner has a way of examining a situation, pulling the right people together and resolving the problem. Adults may stare at them in wonder, playmates may retreat for fear of being put to work but the Jupiter in Virgo will get the job done.

During their fifth year, Jupiter in Virgo children are usually preparing to start school as Jupiter transits through the sign of Aquarius. Having firsthand experience in seeing that different people operate in different ways, they may want to experiment with new ways of getting things done. They tend to put a lot of thought into inventing new routines or even using every day gadgets in ways no one has thought of before. It usually won't matter to them if their latest "time saving device" takes far longer than it would if it was done the way it has always been done. Trying new things is their way of gathering information. It is highly likely they will want to share their inventions with you, get feedback and then return to the drawing board to try something else. They tend to search relentlessly for perfection but at the same time, they also seem to make things more complicated than they need to be. Their learning process is all about trial and error.

Jupiter will transit through Pisces during their sixth year. By now, the Jupiter in Virgo child has started school and they may be feeling a bit overwhelmed. Their routines are not the same as they were when they were at home so they are confused about what they should do. School lunches may be a particular challenge as mass-produced food is not what they are used to. Suddenly, they may feel as if they have lost control. Teachers may keep telling them there is nothing to be worried about but that is a bit like asking the wind not to blow. As their classmates seem to be getting on with school life, they may feel completely overwhelmed by all the information they have to process so may begin to shut down. They can't concentrate on phonics because they may be wondering about who else has sat in the carpet space and why something smells funny. Jupiter in Virgo pupils need firm routines and reminders about what is coming up next. It might help to spend a bit longer going over what to expect during the day (including what is for lunch) and ensuring they have everything they need (a spare change of clothing could go a long way to offering some comfort amidst the chaos). Having a bit of quiet space with some soft music and lowered lights may also help regulate them after a busy morning.

Learning to take time out to calm an active mind is usually a fantastic lesson for Jupiter in Virgo learners.

The Closing Jupiter Square

By this stage, children will have settled into a home/school routine and it is likely schools will begin to prepare students for the Scholastic Achievement Tests (or their equivalents). Debate rages as to whether these tests cause stress for the children but, drawing from personal experience, students tend not to get too upset if the adults around them don't behave as if the world is coming to an end. The purpose of these tests is to help identify strengths and weaknesses in the child's development. The results establish a baseline, not a final outcome. Here are some ways to help support the learners during these formative times:

During their seventh year, Jupiter will be transiting through the sign of Aries. This is the year Jupiter in Virgo children tend to learn that doing things a little faster clears up some thinking space so they can have the freedom to do one of their favourite activities: planning and organising. They tend to lose their fear of making mistakes (but it doesn't stop them from fussing over someone else's) and they seem to invent shortcuts for everything. However, they can, at times, get stuck in doing the same things over and over. To adults, it can look like they are messing around but to the Jupiter in Virgo learner, they are practising making things move as smoothly as they can. They may, for example, repeatedly empty out their toy boxes and time themselves to see how quickly they can put everything away. They'll practise this repeatedly until they are satisfied they are getting better and faster.

Activities for enjoyment and learning outside of school: any activities that involve racing, focusing on perfecting a singular skill, physical exercise, activities that help them understand their own strengths and limits.

As Jupiter transits through Taurus during their eighth year, they may get the urge to not only get better at getting things done faster but they want things to look good too. A lot of Jupiter in Virgo learners have a wonderful artistic eye and they have a good instinct for other people's taste too. They could probably spend many happy hours planning the ideal kitchen or bedroom and, with a little support, they could help measure the amount of material needed. And this could literally mean they become good at putting menus together and, for the most part, they are also very good at shopping. If ever there were A* shoppers, it would be Jupiter in Virgo at this stage of development. They can spot a good deal from a mile away, calculate how much you could save and then produce the perfect coupon at checkout. At this age, their food choices should be starting to broaden too (even if they still like to read the labels on everything).

Activities for enjoyment and learning outside of school: outdoor walks, animal watching, tasting different foods, sensory activities and toys, simple physical strength exercises, collecting interesting things (and keeping them organised).

By the time they reach their ninth year, Jupiter in Virgo learners will be experiencing Jupiter transiting through the sign of Gemini. As very young children, they appreciated being read to but by this stage of development, they will be able to read for themselves and have a huge appetite for reading everything. However, as a mutable sign, these learners could polarise. Weak readers will pretend they understand much more than they really do and teachers/parents could be lulled into a false sense of security. Stronger readers may get too hung up on details and lose the overall message of the book so teacher/parents fret that the child isn't "getting it". Either side of the divide causes unnecessary worry: the really good thing about Jupiter in Virgo children is that they tend to like to learn and, perhaps even better, they know they can always do better so they tend to be ambitious as well.

Activities for enjoyment and learning outside of school: singing, synonyms for common words, giving names to unfamiliar items, becoming familiar with numbers and letters through learning calligraphy (such as Shodo), a skill different to their basic handwriting skills.

During the closing square, Jupiter in Virgo learners start to hone the basic skills it takes to manage a household. As they continue to grow, they will practise these skills. To observers, it may feel as if Jupiter in Virgo learners are making slow progress. However, like the fable of the tortoise and the hare, their carefully laid foundations tend to stand the test of time.

The Jupiter Return

As the learner heads towards their final years of primary school, they should be able to work more independently, understand the general rules of the classroom/playground and see home and school as two separate environments.

During their tenth year, Jupiter in Virgo learners will be experiencing Jupiter transiting through the sign of Cancer. As Virgo is ruled by Mercury, these learners can be quite nervous by nature and adding the fretfulness of Cancer can only heighten their anxiety. They will worry—even if they still have a couple of years left—that they won't get into the secondary school of their choice. They will fret over the notion that they won't be able to provide for the family and children they have yet to have and, if you let them, they can drive themselves up the wall over getting a mortgage for a house they have yet to even plan. Perhaps even worse, they can have the kind of attitude that gives up because of some mistake that happened a few years prior. These guys can fuss over anything until their teachers and parents help to rein it all in: they need to be helped with focusing on the here and now.

Activities for enjoyment and learning outside of school: taking care of animals, singing (as a way to cope with negative emotions), helping with the cooking, taking responsibility for the management of one area of their living space, learning how to take care of their clothes and beds, visiting museums or investigating certain times in history.

As their eleventh year rolls around, Jupiter in Virgo pupils may begin to feel more confident as they prepare to leave their primary schools. As a matter of fact, they may agree that they have grown out of being educated with all the other "little kids" and begin to look forward to the academic challenges they will find in secondary school. The final year of primary school usually finishes with some sort of musical production. This really is their chance to shine and to feel good about all their achievements. Be sure to take plenty of photos (to share within the family and to save for posterity). Celebrate their achievements, their progress and their hopes for the future.

Activities for enjoyment and learning outside of school: stage play, making and wearing costumes and masks, dressing up to go to an event.

By the time they reach their Jupiter return, they should be more than ready to step up to the plate if they have been encouraged to shake off the small stuff that just does not matter. Help them purge their bedrooms of childhood games, decor and furniture. Allow them to re-decorate to their tastes and be sure to leave plenty of room for bookshelves (or if they prefer electronic versions of books, help them back up their data).

When we return to a place have visited before, it is our nature to make comparisons to what has changed since the first time we were there. We may want to seek out the things we did before or perhaps try something completely different.

As almost all students will have had their first Jupiter return by the end of their first year of secondary school, schools could hold an end of year festival that would allow pupils to demonstrate their individual skills. Schools tend to hold sporting events during this time but how about a Health Awareness Fair? Students could do research on the environmental factors that have a direct impact on their general well being. They could do follow up research at future Jupiter returns to see if their recommendations have made a difference.

The stages of development during their first twelve years will repeat in the same sequence, for roughly the same amount of time, for the rest of their lives.

The Jupiter and Uranus Sextiles: In the Thick of Puberty

As noted in the Introduction, the thirteenth year of a child's life is usually when rebellion and defiance begin to become noticeable. Astrologically, transiting Jupiter forms a sextile aspect to its natal position at the same time Uranus, the planet of rebellion, will also make its first Ptolemaic aspect to its own natal position (also by sextile aspect). This combination quite literally means "big rebellion" and marks the time when adolescents (and their parents) begin the struggle to make that separation into adulthood.

Identifying when and how a young adolescent may struggle with the changing social rules they must face could be helpful for parents. For example, if an adolescent experiences the Uranus sextile before the Jupiter sextile, parents may view their child as needing more guidance for following the expectations of the home environment (which would include expectations in school). In the Case Studies section, subjects with this tendency are noted as "rebels". If an adolescent experiences the Jupiter sextile before the Uranus sextile, parents may view their child as needing more encouragement for academic work and possibly with social skills. In the Case Studies section, subjects with this tendency are noted as "truth seekers". There is no "good" or "bad" with these notations and they are only presented as starting points for understanding the life-long impact this stage of development has on learners as they continue their journey all the way into old age. To demonstrate how this particular stage of development can vary from person to person, there is a summary of the time frame for the subjects of the case studies on page 208.

Furthermore, an adolescent's developing body means they may be interested in forming intimate relationships but their brain needs time to catch up with all the new situations it finds itself in. For children born with Jupiter in Virgo, Jupiter will be transiting through the sign of Scorpio as it had been during their second year. It can be helpful for parents to recall the lessons of this year as difficulties with relationships and learning often stem from early habits. Young adolescents can become too focused on a certain style or type of music so it might be a good idea to help them broaden their interests. They may not like the same music as their parents and teachers but they can learn how to imitate and analyse the sounds and cultures.

The Saturn Opposition

The Saturn opposition begins some time during the fourteenth or fifteenth year (possibly earlier or later depending on individual cases) and marks the end of astrological adolescence. Parents and teachers usually notice that the adolescent begins to calm down and take a more mature approach to their academic progress. In the UK, this coincides with choosing academic subjects (as opposed to trying a little bit of everything), formal exam preparation and a marked change in mood. Depression, anxiety and their symptoms must be monitored and taken seriously. Schools will have access to support mechanisms for parents and carers, teachers will have been trained in how to identify potential difficulties and for parents who are home schooling, social services can be a sound source for help.

As they head towards their transiting Saturn opposition, in Virgo children will also re-visit what they had learned as transiting Jupiter once again passes through the signs of Sagittarius and Capricorn. They may take on new interests very quickly only to lose interest just as fast because they see themselves as being more mature than others in their peer group (even if they are all the same age).

The Second Jupiter Opposition

By the time a young adult finishes mandatory education, they will have a good idea of what they want to do with their lives and yet they still have time to re-take exams or re-train if they discover they want to do something else. The second Jupiter opposition is a time of making serious decisions: the young adult is no longer a child. The learner now knows there are consequences for undesirable behaviour and can no longer blame "the system" for their poor choices. Sadly, our prison services are filled with young people who have slipped through the net. As a collective whole, society could do with using a little astrology to help these young people get back on track. A more comprehensive mentoring service could be helpful.

Here are some ideas to help young adults focus on the rest of their adult lives:

For the Jupiter in Virgo learner, transiting Jupiter will be in Pisces as the young adult finishes their formal education at around the age of eighteen. Because Pisces is associated with the imagination, Jupiter in Virgo learners may feel overwhelmed by information and the pressure to make decisions. Helping these learners focus on the desired outcomes of their goals can help them prioritise what is important for them.

The Second and Subsequent Jupiter Returns

As a person continues to develop emotionally, physically and spiritually they will build on the lessons they learned in the formative years. Jupiter returns (roughly) at the ages of 24, 36, 48 and 60 (and beyond). The suggestions for activities can be modified to suit the developmental cycle for each Jupiter cycle. For example, a Jupiter in Virgo learner experiencing a Jupiter in Scorpio transit during their third year of life can be encouraged to sort and categorise colours and shapes; during their fifteenth year, they may wish to extend these skills to bigger research projects involving data collection; during their twenty-seventh year, they may want to take on a professional development course based on action research. The key for all Jupiter returns is to choose a skill (or even one per year) and exercise the brain, all the way to the final years of life. As always, with Jupiter, the sky is the limit.

Jupiter returns at all ages should be celebrated and an experienced astrologer can help locate the exact moment of the return. New clothes to reflect a changing style, a good meal (with a magnificent dessert) with influential friends and maybe even a holiday to some exotic place are just a few ideas. To celebrate the ingress (entry) of Jupiter in a new sign, consult the table in the appendix. The Chinese culture does a wonderful job with celebrating "The Year of the…". While theirs may be a different culture and system, the similarity of intention is still there.

Fine Tuning Jupiter in Virgo

Mercury in Aries: These pupils quite literally learn by using their heads. Like Vulcans, they are orderly, methodical and quite adept at removing human emotion from any situation.

Mercury in Taurus: These pupils learn by touching things and talking things through. Typically these pupils resist new ideas and prefer to chew over previous lessons.

Mercury in Gemini: These pupils learn by using precise language. They typically have extensive vocabularies with lots of big words such as those found in medical dictionaries.

Mercury in Cancer: These pupils learn by using their gut instincts. If something doesn't feel right, they won't go with it. Teachers usually find these pupils have a nose for reliable resources and can spot anachronisms with ease.

Mercury in Leo: These pupils learn by using their natural abilities to gain attention. If the spotlight isn't on them, giving them the incentive to show what they can do, they lose interest.

Mercury in Virgo: These pupils learn by using their methodical thought processes to analyse information. Natural pupils, these pupils usually favour mathematics and sciences or any activity which allows them to employ precision.

Mercury in Libra: These pupils learn by measuring differences. They are usually able to get people to work together by pairing strengths and weaknesses. Teachers often appreciate their manners but despair at their inability to make firm decisions for themselves.

Mercury in Scorpio: These pupils learn by using their personal power to get people to do things they would not ordinarily do. Some people might call this a hypnotic hold over others, some might attribute it to considerable psychic powers.

Mercury in Sagittarius: These pupils learn by using the fearless sense of adventure to explore strange new worlds and philosophies. Teachers appreciate the enthusiasm for learning but secretly wish they would stop breaking things.

Mercury in Capricorn: These pupils learn by using their talents for building firm and lasting foundations. They understand step one thoroughly before they progress onto step two.

Mercury in Aquarius: These pupils learn best by using their ability to embrace experimentation. There's really nothing these pupils won't try—except the tried and trusted method of doing things.

Mercury in Pisces: These pupils learn best by using their ability to tune into the mood of others. They have the uncanny talent of understanding artists' or writers' intentions. They even understand that mathematicians intend to bore the socks off them.

Case Studies

Julia Roberts

Julia Roberts was born on 28 October 1967 at 00:16 in Atlanta, Georgia (RR: AA; Collector: Rodden), with Jupiter in Virgo and Mercury in Scorpio. Roberts has had leading roles in numerous well-known films and has received many accolades over nearly forty years of professional acting. She is widely recognised as one of Hollywood's most bankable stars, and *People* magazine has named her the most beautiful woman a record-breaking five times.

Both of Roberts' parents were actors and playwrights who met while performing in theatrical productions for the armed services. As a child, Roberts originally wanted to be a veterinarian but later moved to New York to pursue acting after finishing high school. During adolescence, transiting Jupiter in Scorpio was sextile to its natal position in Virgo about a year before transiting Uranus in Scorpio was sextile her natal Jupiter, indicating she is a truth seeker.

She began her screen career with small roles in *Crime Story*, but got her first significant film role in *Satisfaction* (1988), starring alongside Liam Neeson and Justine Bateman. That year, Jupiter was in the middle of three closing squares to her natal Jupiter. She also starred in *Mystic Pizza* the same year—a film that critic Roger Ebert suggested might later be remembered for its rising stars. As transiting Jupiter in Gemini continued to square her Virgo placements in 1989, she filmed *Steel Magnolias* with an ensemble cast. For that performance, Roberts received her first Academy Award nomination (Best Supporting Actress) and her first Golden Globe win.

Later that year, she began filming the movie she's most known for - *Pretty Woman* - playing "a hooker with a heart of gold" opposite Richard Gere. Fittingly, transiting Jupiter in Cancer opposed her natal Mars in Capricorn three times, with the final pass occurring just days after the film's release in March 1990. The role earned Roberts significant critical acclaim and solidified her Hollywood status. That same year, Jupiter in Cancer crossed her Ascendant as she starred in *Flatliners* and later squared her natal Sun during the filming of *Sleeping with the Enemy*. After filming *Dying Young* and *Hook,* Roberts took a two-year break following her second Jupiter return.

She returned in 1993, just after a series of three Jupiter oppositions to her natal Saturn, to star in *The Pelican Brief.* After a string of less successful films, she bounced back with the romantic comedy *My Best Friend's Wedding* (1997). During filming, transiting Jupiter crossed her

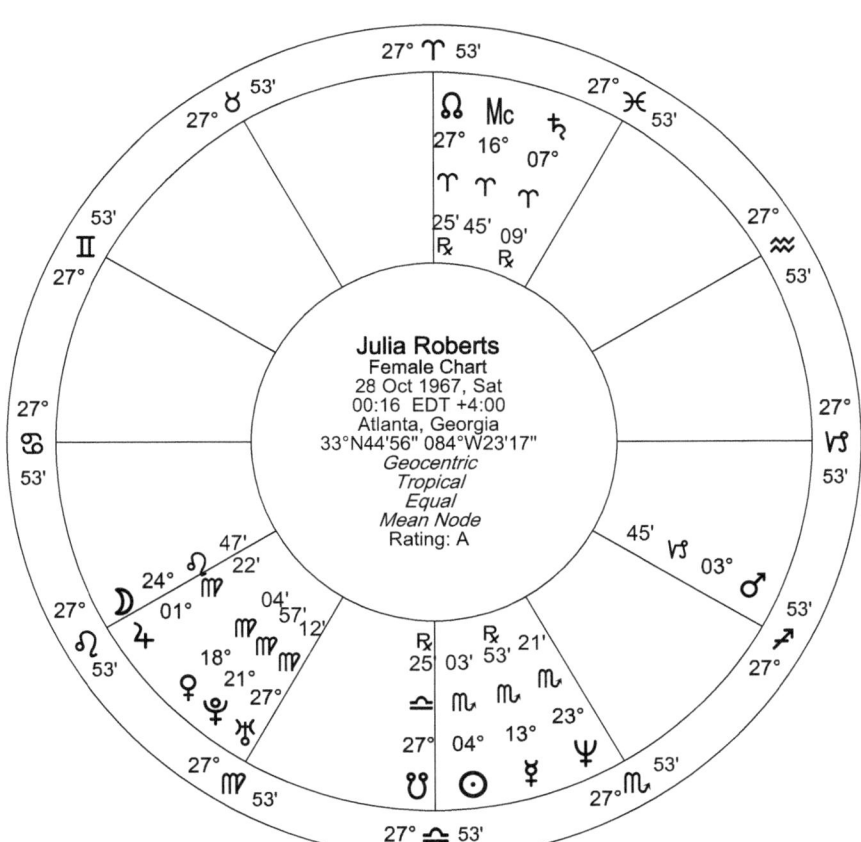

Descendant. In 1999, she reunited with Gere in *Runaway Bride*, as Jupiter opposed her Sun.

In 2000, Roberts became the first actress to earn $20 million for a role, portraying environmental activist *Erin Brockovich*. The performance won her the Academy Award for Best Actress. Just months after the film's release, transiting Jupiter in Taurus opposed her natal Neptune, an apt transit for a role centred on exposing environmental toxins.

Roberts' personal life has also attracted attention. She famously called off her wedding to actor Kiefer Sutherland and later married country singer Lyle Lovett—though the marriage ended in divorce. Shortly after the success of *Erin Brockovich*, she began a relationship with married cameraman Daniel Moder, who divorced his wife and married Roberts in 2002—as transiting Jupiter again crossed her Ascendant.

Although she has starred in many films since, some less iconic than *Pretty Woman* or *Erin Brockovich*, Roberts has used the discernment and craftsmanship of Jupiter in Virgo to establish herself as one of the most successful - and highest-paid - actresses in Hollywood.

Will Smith

Will Smith was born on 25 September 1968 at 21:47 in Philadelphia, Pennsylvania (RR: A; Collector: Rodden) with Jupiter in Virgo ruled by Mercury in Libra. He is a rapper, actor, and film producer with numerous accolades. However, his talents were recently overshadowed by a moment of impulsive behaviour when he slapped comedian Chris Rock at the 2022 Academy Awards—the same ceremony in which he won the Best Actor award.

Smith was raised in a Baptist household and attended a private Catholic school. At his first Jupiter return, he began rapping—a skill demanding the kind of precision, rhythm, and verbal dexterity we expect from a Jupiter in Virgo learner.

During adolescence, transiting Uranus in Scorpio was sextile his natal Uranus in Virgo about a year before transiting Jupiter in Scorpio made its sextile—confirming his status as a rebel. Notably, he committed early in his career to avoiding profanity in his music. During this time, however, his parents also separated.

Smith's first breakout hit came with DJ Jazzy Jeff in 1988 with *Parents Just Don't Understand*, as Jupiter in Aries was conjunct his natal Saturn—a perfect example of Jupiter expressing itself within Saturnian boundaries. In 1990, he was forced to learn a hard Saturnian lesson when the IRS seized assets due to unpaid taxes.

Smith bounced back quickly, using his Virgoan analytical skills to study box office trends and setting a clear goal: to become the biggest movie star in the world. He starred in *The Fresh Prince of Bel-Air* starting in 1990. Jupiter in Cancer made several squares to his natal planets in cardinal signs, and he earned a Golden Globe nomination shortly after his second Jupiter return in 1993. That same year, he starred in *Six Degrees of Separation*.

Bad Boys was released in 1995, during three transits of Jupiter over his Descendant, and *Independence Day* followed in 1996, with Jupiter in

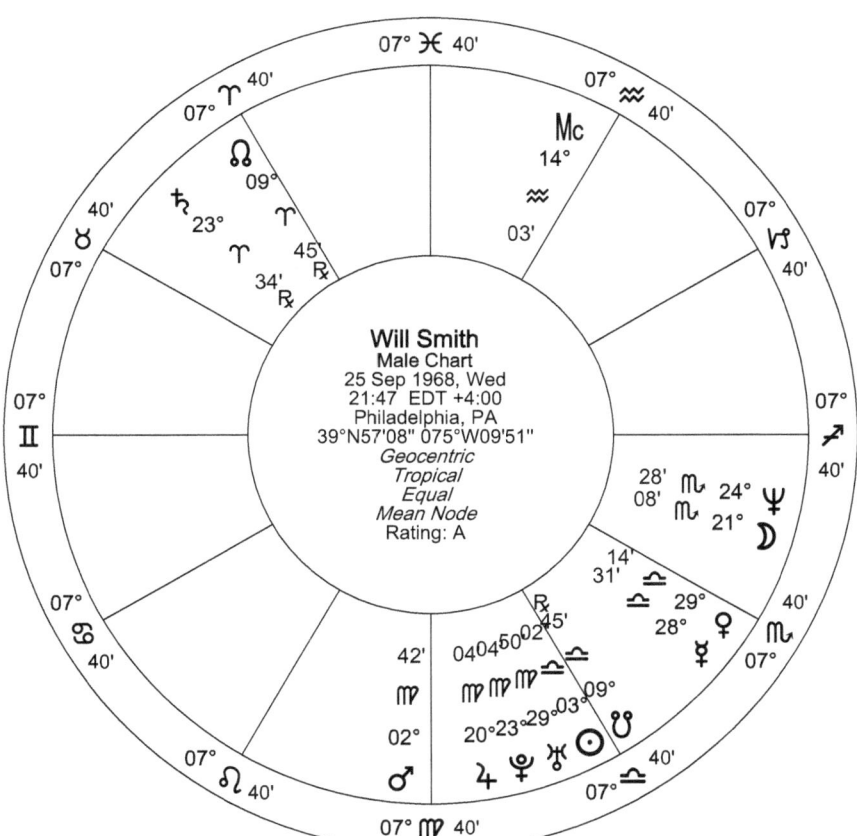

Capricorn squaring his nodes. In 1997, *Men in Black* premiered just as Jupiter in Aquarius squared his Moon in Scorpio—excellent transits for chasing aliens while wearing black.

Enemy of the State (1998) was released during a series of oppositions from Jupiter to his natal Jupiter. In 2001, he earned an Oscar nomination for Ali as Jupiter in Cancer again squared his cardinal nodes. He filmed *I, Robot* during his third Jupiter return in 2004.

In 2005, Smith set a Guinness World Record for attending the most film premieres in 24 hours, with Jupiter crossing his South Node three times. The following year, he starred in *The Pursuit of Happyness*, earning another Oscar nomination, with transiting Jupiter conjunct his Descendant in Sagittarius. In 2007, he cemented his Hollywood legacy with a ceremony at Grauman's Chinese Theatre, while Jupiter in Scorpio was conjunct his Moon.

Smith's career has been remarkably successful, with blockbuster hits like the *Men in Black* sequels, *I Am Legend*, *Hancock*, and many more. However, on 27 March 2022, he stunned viewers at the Oscars by slapping Chris Rock. To the day, Jupiter in Pisces was in exact opposition to his natal Jupiter in Virgo. He resigned from the Academy and was banned from its events for ten years. The incident led to film delays and project cancellations, a stark reminder of the consequences a single impulsive moment can have—even for someone with a track record as strong as a Jupiter in Virgo native.

Jupiter in Libra

Libra is an air sign by element and cardinal sign by modality. Transiting squares and oppositions to its natal position will take place roughly every three years in the other cardinal signs, Capricorn, Aries and Cancer. This pattern will repeat for the rest of the native's life, defining how a person learns, grows and develops a personal philosophy. Cardinal signs are independent, self-sufficient and enterprising and they need to be led towards learning how to work with others. While Jupiter in Libra is fixated on relationships, they can often lose their sense of self as they measure themselves against the opinions of others. It is important for Jupiter in Libra to learn how to work independently and also with others without losing their own identity in the mix.

Jupiter transits through signs at a pace of about one sign per year. It is important to note that as children are taught by year group, they will learn alongside other children with Jupiter in Libra. Depending on the time of year they were born, they will also have classmates with either Jupiter in Virgo or Jupiter in Scorpio. This topic has been explored in depth in *Growing Pains: Astrology in Adolescence.* Children who have Jupiter in Libra tend to be diplomats when it comes to learning: they don't want to upset people with their opinion and try to counterbalance emotional situations rather than risk riling others into anger. Whilst this can make a very pleasant learning environment with everyone patiently waiting for someone else to finish speaking, a teacher may just wish there was a little *passion* in their opinions. More than any other sign, Jupiter in Libra needs provocation. Just about the only way to get through to these learners is by encouraging them to debate. At first, they may not be so good at it, but if they are given the right tools, they will want to please their parents and teachers by showing them that yes, they do have important opinions and yes, they are willing to support them with facts. And manners. Always with the manners.

The First Jupiter Square

All babies need the basics of adequate nutrition, a safe place to sleep, cleanliness and a comfortable environment. They also need the human touch in order to build trust and to feel the caregiver is responding to their signals for these necessities. Eye contact, talking/singing to the baby and providing a daily rhythm of sleep, cleaning, feeding and playing with age appropriate toys are essential for all babies, irrespective of the Jupiter sign. As the baby grows into a toddler, it is important caregivers have adequately "baby proofed" the child's environment. These essential needs are important all the way into old age. Once these needs are met consistently, a bit of astrology can help the caregivers find the learner's internal "beat" for development.

At some point during the first year of their life, the Jupiter in Libra child will experience Jupiter transiting through the sign of Scorpio. As the learner is a baby, the world is simply full of learning opportunities. Natally, the Jupiter in Libra learner, ruled by Venus, may lean towards sour foods such as yoghurt, apples, and pomegranates may be a preference during this stage though, like all children, they could develop a sweet tooth if this preference is not monitored.

During the second year, Jupiter in Libra learners begin to experience transiting Jupiter in Sagittarius, a much easier going sign that can be full of playful mischief. As they usually have a good sense of balance, Jupiter in Libra learners of this age may become daredevils and risk takers. Physically, it may be a good time to introduce some sort of sport (they may veer towards gymnastics or trampolining) to soak up some of their excess energy. If the family has a religious faith, it might be a good time to get more involved with the local place of worship so the child can begin to develop a personal philosophy that can be supported by other family members. Another activity the child might find useful is travelling. By this stage of development, the child is likely learning independent skills such as walking. However, once they do start getting around, they might wear their parents out as they struggle to keep their toddler safe.

The third year, as Jupiter transits through the sign of Capricorn, is when Jupiter in Libra learners begin to apply and commit more to their interests. Toys such as Lego can help them increase their confidence and give them a sense of achievement. Building toys not only help develop eye-hand coordination but they help Jupiter in Libra learners understand the importance of independent play (sharing Lego and building blocks with other children who may knock down their structures is no fun at all) and taking responsibility for their creations. However Jupiter in Libra learners like to socialise. The trick is to get the balance right at this stage: a good mix of independent learning so they can get the measure of themselves and a good dose of play dates so they can meet children who are different to them.

By the time of their first transiting square, Jupiter in Libra children will typically become the peacemakers of the playgroup. They will have learned that teamwork is the most efficient way to work and they will usually have a strong sense of democracy and an innate need to keep conversations (and even disagreements) gentle and open to further discussion.

The First Jupiter Opposition

Between the ages of about three years and six years old, most young children are preparing for formal education and socialisation. These are just some ideas to help Jupiter in Libra learners prepare for their first adventures away from their immediate care givers.

Heading into their fourth year, Jupiter will transit into the sign of Aquarius. By this time, language acquisition is usually in full swing and Jupiter in Libra learners have a lot to say even if they can't quite express their opinions as clearly as they would like. However, the gist is clear: in their world, everyone is an equal. They probably won't have any difficulties sharing their toys or standing up for the underdog. In fact, they'll be so busy making sure everyone else has a voice that they forget they have their own. Under these kinds of conditions, they could just step back and play referee to the conflicts around them. Of course, there is nothing wrong with this—except that sooner or later, they will find themselves with their backs against the proverbial wall and have to learn how to fight their own corner. This can be a difficult lesson for any child but for the peacemakers, it can feel like they have lost some sort of competition. Parents and carers may have to show these learners how to balance not being a pushover with overusing their authority.

Activities for enjoyment and learning outside of school: leading/ forming a new club and setting rules and expectations, simple science experiments (YouTube is full of ideas for home science experiments—ensure they have permission and understand they have to clean up), learning how to do simple tasks like changing light bulbs, fuses and understanding electrical circuits, recording and monitoring data accurately as part of an experiment (simplified data gathering).

As the fifth year rolls around, transiting Jupiter will move into the sign of Pisces. Having learned how to deal more assertively with conflict, they may need to step back into a gentler mode of easy conversations and yielding to the needs of others. At this stage of development, Jupiter in Libra children tend to dislike the suffering of others. They may develop genuine sympathy for the less fortunate and may actually lose sleep over feeling powerless to do anything about. One possible way to counterbalance this is by encouraging the whole family to take part in some sort of charity work. There are many aid organisations that would positively welcome the support of young people and their parents. By teaching the Jupiter in Libra learners that there are ways to help that doesn't involve just throwing money at a problem can assist them in seeing they are not as weak or as powerless as they thought they were.

Activities for enjoyment and learning outside of school: Music lessons, art projects not found in school like pottery courses that allow the learner to complete a project all the way to a good level of proficiency, studying a particular artist and their work medium (painting, sculpture, carving, etc.).

During their sixth year, transiting Jupiter will be in Aries for Jupiter in Libra learners. For most children of this age, they will be starting school and if parents had any concerns that their child was in danger of letting life pass by without a fight, they are likely to be assured this won't be the case during this stage of development. The first half of the Jupiter cycle was all about considering other people but now Jupiter in Libra learners may be getting the idea that if they want something, they just might have to put up a bit of a fight. Whilst no one advocates violence, there is something very satisfying when a sweet, gentle pupil lets others know they don't exist to let others push them around.

Activities for enjoyment and learning outside of school: any activities that involve racing, focusing on perfecting a singular skill, physical exercise, activities that help them understand their own strengths and limits.

Developing an awareness of self is just one of the many challenges Jupiter in Libra children face during their first Jupiter opposition. This is a vital and necessary step for them. As they continue to grow, they will become more confident with who they are and bolder when expressing their needs.

The Closing Jupiter Square

By this stage, children will have settled into a home/school routine and it is likely schools will begin to prepare students for the Scholastic Achievement Tests (or their equivalents). Debate rages as to whether these tests cause stress for the children but, drawing from personal experience, students tend not to get too upset if the adults around them don't behave as if the world is coming to an end. The purpose of these tests is to help identify strengths and weaknesses in the child's development. The results establish a baseline, not a final outcome. Here are some ways to help support the learners during these formative times:

In their seventh year, Jupiter in Libra learners will experience Jupiter transiting through the sign of Taurus. Like Libra, Taurus is a Venus-ruled sign. However, whereas Libra is concerned with relationships, Taurus is concerned with acquiring people or things of value. This is a wonderful opportunity for both parents and teachers to help these pupils understand basic economics and how money works in the real world. How do people earn money? What do they do with it once they get it? And who decides what is of value and what isn't? Although peaceful by nature, Jupiter in Libra learners are likely to have witnessed disputes over money or they may have heard something on the news about the economy. Because they tend to be sensitive to the feelings of other people, they understand finances are a taboo topic. However, opening up these types of conversations can help them manage real world challenges and discover how to resolve them.

Activities for enjoyment and learning outside of school: outdoor walks, animal watching, tasting different foods, sensory activities and toys, simple physical strength exercises, collecting interesting things (and keeping them organised), money games.

During their eighth year, Jupiter in Libra children will experience Jupiter transiting through the sign of Gemini. As Libra and Gemini are both air signs, the Jupiter in Libra learner may feel as if they are on familiar ground. They love to meet people and make a good impression and Jupiter's transit through Gemini often creates opportunities for this. However, Jupiter in Gemini provides much more than this: Jupiter in Gemini creates a sense of curiosity about the world and a deep, burning passion to learn more. Often what can happen when Jupiter transits through Gemini is that the class polarises into super speedy learners and reluctant learners who are worried that they will be caught out on their lack of knowledge. To counterbalance this, teachers can identify learning gaps through the data that has been gathered during SATs. Parents can also use these test results to practise reading with their children to strengthen their weaknesses and also practise other skills such as handwriting and times tables at home (being careful not to overdo it). This tandem approach supports the child and allows them the opportunity to discover that with effort, they can overcome any difficulties they are faced with.

Activities for enjoyment and learning outside of school: singing, synonyms for common words, giving names to unfamiliar items, becoming familiar with numbers and letters through simple calligraphy, touch typing.

Jupiter will be transiting through the sign of Cancer during Jupiter in Libra learners' ninth year. With the intellectual stimulation of the previous year, Jupiter in Libra pupils may have the desire to pay a little more attention to their creature comforts. They may need to be encouraged to get out of the house a bit more and parents may need to support them in regulating their sleeping schedules. They may also become quite territorial and need their own space. One possible solution is to help them re-decorate their bedrooms in the home or personal space at school (or other individual areas) with the understanding that said space is to be kept clean and organised with clear rules and boundaries about what is allowed (whether parents allow the child to take food into their bedroom, for example). Another problem that may arise is the issue of privacy. Children at this stage of development are adept at keeping secrets and it is in a parent's best interest to ensure they know what their children are getting up to on the internet. Schools have a duty of care to prevent pupils in their care from breeching security when using computer devices on the premises but it is completely up to the parents whether the child is allowed to do so at home. For parents or carers who are uncertain about the consequences of not carefully monitoring their child's online activity, they need only to check out guidance available from their local police stations.

Activities for enjoyment and learning outside of school: taking care of animals, singing (as a way to cope with negative emotions), helping with the cooking, taking responsibility for the management of one area of their living space, learning how to take care of their clothes and beds, visiting museums or investigating certain times in history.

The Jupiter Return

As the learner heads towards their final years of primary school, they should be able to work more independently, understand the general rules of the classroom/playground and see home and school as two separate environments.

During the Jupiter in Libra's tenth year, Jupiter will be transiting through the sign of Leo. This tends to be a time when a child's confidence in him/herself grows as they overcome their shyness and learn to embrace the limelight. Many schools allow each year group to take turns hosting an assembly and this is an ideal opportunity to allow Jupiter in Libra learners to strut their stuff. There is room for all manner of talents in a school assembly: from the technical side to the musical side, to dancing or showing off the recorder skills they learned in Music classes, assemblies often show parents and teachers things they never knew about their children. As children of this age are approaching the end of their time in primary school, leading assemblies also makes for a wonderful chance to see the potential for their final performance in primary school which will take place during their eleventh year.

Activities for enjoyment and learning outside of school: stage play, making and wearing costumes and masks, dressing up to go to an event, developing their speaking skills.

Jupiter in Virgo will transit Jupiter in Libra's eleventh year usually and this time typically corresponds to their final year in primary school. They may feel the pressure to find closure as they hurtle (as it may seem to them) towards secondary school. Naturally, they will be nervous and will want to be as prepared as possible. For Jupiter in Libra learners, a new school is all about meeting the right people. And this could be a problem because, as important as their social life is (or will be), these children need to get a handle on their education too. Another potential problem is not getting into the school of their choice. Unfortunately, in the bigger cities, it is just not possible to continue their education with the same children they have grown up with. This could be devastating to the Jupiter in Libra learners because it more or less ruins all their perfect plans. Parents and teachers, once they help dry the eyes of the disappointed, can help support these learners by helping them to arrange get-togethers for children going to the same secondary school or parties for children who will continue to live in the same neighbourhood. No matter the outcome, moving on is a necessary part of life and, once the Jupiter in Libra learner understands this, the sooner they can see the changes as an opportunity for new adventures.

Activities for enjoyment and learning outside of school: learning about the physical body of people or animals, learning about sickness and how to take care of someone (or a pet) who is not feeling well, understanding the basics of medicine. Learning to identify plants and different species of animals, and applying complex measuring skills to practical projects such as those found in design and technology.

As the Jupiter return in Libra begins to affect children in their twelfth year, school can be seen not as a place of learning but as one great big social gathering. Of course, schools do strive to ensure their pupils are settled in and happy but Jupiter in Libra take things just that extra step from learning about the world to throwing one great big party (usually there's dancing involved too). They are easily distracted by potential romances or being overly concerned about someone else's love life. They may spend a lot of time ensuring they look good and then get swallowed up by that rabbit hole that is social media. Again, parents must be pro-active and monitor their child's online activities. Teachers too would do well to remember that Algebra and/or the Table of Elements may not necessarily be on the minds of Jupiter in Libra. However, school isn't just about facts and figures. It is about understanding human relationships and all its intricacies. And there's no group quite like Jupiter in Libra to teach all of us what it means to be a part of a world filled with partnerships and associations.

When we return to a place have visited before, it is our nature to make comparisons to what has changed since the first time we were there. We may want to seek out the things we did before or perhaps try something completely different.

As almost all students will have had their first Jupiter return by the end of their first year of secondary school, schools could hold an end of year festival that would allow pupils to demonstrate their individual skills. Schools tend to hold sporting events during this time but how about a school wide Human Rights Convention? Students could display their concerns through debate, political campaigns with local politicians or even by spearheading a particular headline to draw attention to problems and potential solutions. At their next Jupiter return, they could do follow up work on their efforts.

The stages of development during their first twelve years will repeat in the same sequence, for roughly the same amount of time, for the rest of their lives.

The Jupiter and Uranus Sextiles: In the Thick of Puberty

As noted in the Introduction, the thirteenth year of a child's life is usually when rebellion and defiance begin to become noticeable. Astrologically, transiting Jupiter forms a sextile aspect to its natal position at the same time Uranus, the planet of rebellion, will also make its first Ptolemaic aspect to its own natal position (also by sextile aspect). This combination quite literally means "big rebellion" and marks the time when adolescents (and their parents) begin the struggle to make that separation into adulthood.

Identifying when and how a young adolescent may struggle with the changing social rules they must face could be helpful for parents. For example, if an adolescent experiences the Uranus sextile before the Jupiter sextile, parents may view their child as needing more guidance for following the expectations of the home environment (which would include expectations in school). In the Case Studies section, subjects with this tendency are noted as "rebels". If an adolescent experiences the Jupiter sextile before the Uranus sextile, parents may view their child as needing more encouragement for academic work and possibly with social skills. In the Case Studies section, subjects with this tendency are noted as "truth seekers". There is no "good" or "bad" with these notations and they are only presented as starting points for understanding the life-long impact this stage of development has on learners as they continue their journey all the way into old age. To demonstrate how this particular stage of development can vary from person to person, there is a summary of the time frame for the subjects of the case studies on page 208.

Furthermore, an adolescent's developing body means they may be interested in forming intimate relationships but their brain needs time to catch up with all the new situations it finds itself in.

For children born with Jupiter in Libra, Jupiter will be transiting through the sign of Sagittarius as it had been during their second year. It can be helpful for parents to recall the lessons of this year as difficulties with risk-taking and recklessness can lead these learners into making poor relationship choices. At this stage of development, firm boundaries need to be in place and respect and trust must be carefully monitored. Whilst generally speaking strict rules can lead to rebellion, a lack of limitations can open the door to peer pressure and poor decision making.

The Saturn Opposition

The Saturn opposition begins some time during the fourteenth or fifteenth year (possibly earlier or later depending on individual cases) and marks the end of astrological adolescence. Parents and teachers usually notice that the adolescent begins to calm down and take a more mature approach to their academic progress. In the UK, this coincides with choosing academic subjects (as opposed to trying a little bit of everything), formal exam preparation and a marked change in mood. Depression, anxiety and their symptoms must be monitored and taken seriously. Schools will have access to support mechanisms for parents and carers, teachers will have been trained in how to identify potential difficulties and for parents who are home schooling, social services can be a sound source for help.

As they head towards their transiting Saturn opposition, Jupiter in Libra learners will also re-visit what they had learned as transiting Jupiter usually (it can vary from person to person) passes through the signs of Capricorn and Aquarius. They will develop a sold work ethic as well as a strong desire for societal equality. Re-visiting the appropriate stage of astrological development can be helpful to provide the right sort of help and support.

The Second Jupiter Opposition

By the time a young adult finishes mandatory education, they will have a good idea of what they want to do with their lives and yet they still have time to re-take exams or re-train if they discover they want to do something else. The second Jupiter opposition is a time of making serious decisions: the young adult is no longer a child. The learner now knows there are consequences for undesirable behaviour and can no longer blame "the system" for their poor choices. Sadly, our prison services are filled with young people who have slipped through the net. As a collective whole, society could do with using a little astrology to help these young people get back on track. A more comprehensive mentoring service could be helpful.

Here are some ideas to help young adults focus on the rest of their adult lives:

For the Jupiter in Libra learner, transiting Jupiter will be in Aries as the young adult finishes their formal education at around the age of eighteen. Because Aries is associated with self-development, the Jupiter in Libra learner may feel they need time to polish up on certain skills they may have missed out on during secondary school. Helping these learners weigh the pros and cons of their decisions can help them maintain their independence and encourage self-reliance.

The Second and Subsequent Jupiter Returns

As a person continues to develop emotionally, physically and spiritually they will build on the lessons they learned in their formative years. Jupiter returns (roughly) at the ages of 24, 36, 48 and 60 (and beyond). The suggestions for activities can be modified to suit the developmental cycle for each Jupiter cycle. For example, a Jupiter in Libra learner experiencing a Jupiter in Sagittarius transit during their third year of life can be encouraged to take an interest in a sport for the social benefits such an interest can provide; during their fifteenth year, they may wish to play for a team; during their twenty-seventh year, they may wish to coach a sport and so on. The key for all Jupiter returns is to choose a skill (or even one per year) and exercise the brain, all the way to the final years of life. As always, with Jupiter, the sky is the limit.

Jupiter returns at all ages should be celebrated and an experienced astrologer can help locate the exact moment of the return. New clothes to reflect a changing style, a good meal (with a magnificent dessert) with influential friends and maybe even a holiday to some exotic place are just a few ideas. To celebrate the ingress (entry) of Jupiter in a new sign, consult the table in the appendix. The Chinese culture does a wonderful job with celebrating "The Year of the…". While theirs may be a different culture and system, the similarity of intention is still there.

Fine Tuning Jupiter in Libra

Venus in Aries: These pupils like to work independently if there is an opportunity to share progress afterwards. There is often a strong need for social approval in these pupils.

Venus in Taurus: These pupils take pride in their classroom so artistic displays usually grab their attention. They will show others around the classroom - often using a guiding hand - as if they are personally responsible for the beautiful surroundings.

Venus in Gemini: These pupils simply love to socialise and most of the conversation is about the next party. They are bright and keen learners but are not quiet for long. These are the kind of learners that plan the school prom when they should be studying for exams.

Venus in Cancer: These pupils love to prepare for their family's future. Even from a young age, these pupils have a good understanding of relationships on all different levels.

Venus in Leo: These pupils like to learn by being the centre of attention. Usually there is something striking about their hair or its bold style.

Venus in Virgo: These pupils like to learn by making clear choices about the people they work with. It can be very difficult to persuade them to work with someone they have taken a dislike to.

Venus in Libra: These pupils like to learn by socialising with their polar opposites. Girls are fascinated with boys and vice versa. Although there is usually no problem with getting these pupils to mix, teachers are typically challenged to keep them quiet.

Venus in Scorpio: These pupils like to learn by de-coding the mysteries of a lesson—which can often mean why they are learning in the first place. They are often fascinated by danger or situations which may seem unsafe. These pupils understand power games on all sorts of different levels.

Venus in Sagittarius: These pupils love anything that enhances the speed at which they can grow but they need to compare progress with others. They often have more than one full-on project on the go and may fantasise about some adventure or another.

Venus in Capricorn: These pupils like to learn by exploring traditional roles in society. Their lips curl in distaste when discussing major advances in civilisation.

Venus in Aquarius: These pupils like to learn by exploring the unusual or the downright strange. They are naturally rebellious and like to experiment.

Venus in Pisces: these pupils like to learn by submerging themselves in information. To anyone else, they look lost. To themselves, they are tuning in to their environment.

Case Studies

Beyoncé Knowles

Beyoncé was born on 4 September 1981, at 9.47pm (RR:AA, Source: Nakti), in Houston, Texas with Jupiter in Libra, ruled by Venus—also in Libra. Although primarily known as a highly skilled singer with an impressive four-octave vocal range, she is also an actress and businesswoman.

She won a school talent show at the age of seven (circa 1988), the year transiting Jupiter opposed her natal Pluto in Libra and shortly after her first Jupiter opposition.

As an adolescent, Beyoncé was a rebel. She experienced her transiting Uranus in Capricorn sextile its natal position just weeks before her transiting Jupiter in Sagittarius made a series of three sextiles to her natal Jupiter in 1995. During this time, the Knowles family endured financial hardship so that Beyoncé could perform with her girl group on national television. Her parents separated under the strain but reconciled the following year when Beyoncé and her group were signed to Sony, as transiting Jupiter in Aquarius squared her fixed planets. When Jupiter changed signs to Pisces, it opposed her Sun in Virgo. During this period, the group changed its name to Destiny's Child and featured on the *Men in Black* soundtrack.

The group's album The *Writing's on the Wall*, containing the breakout hit 'Say My Name', was recorded and released during the winter of 1998–99, with transiting Jupiter in Aries opposite her natal Mercury in Libra. It's so astrologically fitting, it's pure poetry.

In 2000, *Charlie's Angels* featured the hit *Independent Women Part I*, just after transiting Jupiter in Taurus opposed her natal Uranus in Scorpio. Shortly after, Beyoncé landed a major role in the TV film *Carmen: A Hip Hopera*, with transiting Jupiter in Gemini opposing her natal Neptune in Sagittarius.

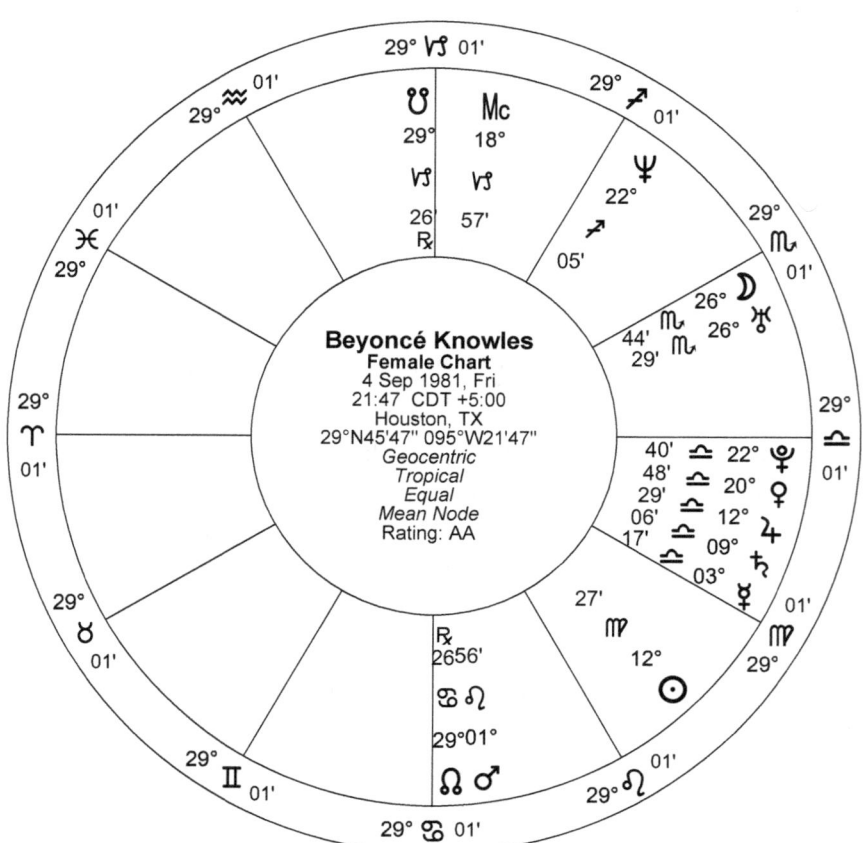

In autumn 2002, she recorded her first solo album just after transiting Jupiter in Cancer was conjunct her natal North Node. The following year, 'Crazy in Love' was released just before transiting Jupiter in Virgo conjoined her natal Sun. She performed the U.S. National Anthem in the middle of three Jupiter in Libra conjunctions to her natal Sun.

Destiny's Child released their final studio album in November 2004, almost to the day that transiting Jupiter conjoined her natal Saturn in Libra—a fitting ending to a collaboration that made way for her solo path. The group accepted a star on the Hollywood Walk of Fame a few months after Beyoncé's second Jupiter return in March 2006. Around the same time, as transiting Jupiter in Sagittarius squared her natal Sun, she starred in the hit film *Dreamgirls*.

On 8 October 2008, Beyoncé released 'Single Ladies' as a double A-side with 'If I Were a Boy', highlighting the contrast between her real self and her aggressive alter ego, Sasha Fierce. Transiting Jupiter in Capricorn was in the middle of a series of three squares to her natal Venus in Libra—a powerful moment for unleashing the repressed woman within.

Beyoncé's many accomplishments are too numerous to list individually. With thirty-five Grammys (and many other honours), she is the most awarded female artist of all time and one of the best-selling music artists in history. She has her own fashion line and has been a creative partner with Adidas, Pepsi, and Levi Strauss. She is also known for her philanthropic work and has coined popular phrases such as "put a ring on it" and "I woke up like this".

And she has done it all while rarely falling out with anyone - and never seeming to have a bad hair day. All hail Queen B and the power of Jupiter in Libra ruled by Venus in Libra.

Judy Garland

Judy Garland was born on 10 June 1922 at 6:00 a.m. in Grand Rapids, Minnesota (RR: AA, Collector: Steinbrecher). She starred in one of the most beloved films of all time, *The Wizard of Oz*, and her career spanned nearly across the entirety of her life.

Garland was a child performer alongside her sisters in the Gumm Sisters trio. At age six, she enrolled in dance school with her sisters as Jupiter in Aries opposed her natal Jupiter in Libra. In 1935, at just 13, she was signed by Metro-Goldwyn-Mayer (MGM). She experienced her first transiting Jupiter sextile in Sagittarius to her natal Jupiter in Libra significantly earlier than her Uranus sextile, marking her as a truth seeker. Sadly, the pressures of early stardom led to lasting mental health struggles, exacerbated by constant criticism from film executives who deemed her "not attractive enough". Louis B. Mayer cruelly referred to her as his "little hunchback". On 16 November 1935, her father died of meningitis—almost to the day transiting Jupiter in Sagittarius sextiled her natal Saturn in Libra.

She was cast with Mickey Rooney in *Thoroughbreds Don't Cry* in 1937 during her second opening Jupiter square in Capricorn. Rooney and Garland starred in several Andy Hardy films in the late 1930s. She began filming her most famous role as Dorothy in *The Wizard of Oz* just before her transiting Saturn opposition. Two weeks before filming ended, transiting Jupiter in Pisces conjoined her natal Uranus.

Garland's image was carefully managed: she was kept on amphetamines and had her breasts bound to appear younger than her sixteen years. After *The Wizard of Oz*, she was sent on a promotional tour with Rooney for *Babes in Arms*. During this time, transiting Jupiter was conjunct her South Node three times.

From 1940, she began adult romances and married David Rose in 1941, when transiting Jupiter in Gemini squared her natal Uranus. That same year, she had an abortion under her mother's insistence, fearing damage to her daughter's career. A second abortion followed her separation from Rose in 1943, as transiting Jupiter in Cancer squared her natal Venus. These events surely left deep wounds.

She gave birth to Liza Minnelli in March 1946, as transiting Jupiter made a series of conjunctions to her natal Venus in Cancer. Though her image matured, Garland attempted suicide in 1947 and had a breakdown in 1948. She was hospitalised as transiting Jupiter in Sagittarius conjoined her natal Neptune.

Despite being suspended by MGM for drug use, she continued to work. After another suicide attempt, Garland left MGM in 1950 as Jupiter in Aquarius squared her fixed-sign planets. She rebounded with a successful tour alongside Bing Crosby. Jupiter in Pisces opposed her Sun in late 1950 and her natal Jupiter in Libra in 1951. She married Sidney Luft in 1952 and gave birth to a daughter as Jupiter made three oppositions to her Descendant.

In 1955, she was nominated for an Academy Award for *A Star is Born*, though she couldn't attend the ceremony due to giving birth to her son weeks earlier—at the same time that Jupiter in Cancer squared her natal Venus.

In late 1959, Garland was diagnosed with acute hepatitis and told she had less than five years to live and would never sing again. She later said this gave her a sense of relief, as it lifted the pressure to perform. Transiting Jupiter in Sagittarius was square to her natal Sun almost to the day of the diagnosis.

In 1962, she began her own television series to stabilise her finances. Jupiter in Aries opposed her natal Mercury and Saturn. In 1964, she

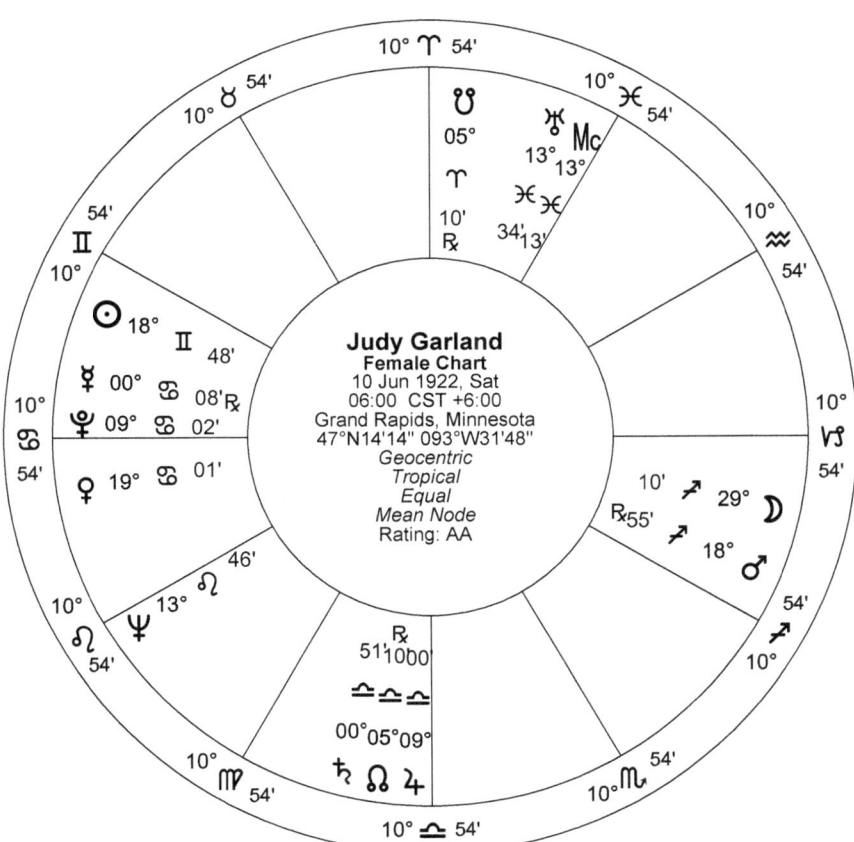

appeared at The London Palladium with her 18-year-old daughter, Liza, as Jupiter opposed her natal Moon in Scorpio.

On 22 June 1969, Judy Garland died of a barbiturate overdose. From late 1968 to shortly after her death, transiting Jupiter in Libra had been conjunct her natal Mercury. Despite personal tragedy and addiction, she is forever remembered for her transcendent voice and enduring legacy.

Jupiter in Scorpio

Scorpio is a water sign by element and a fixed sign by modality. Transiting squares and oppositions to its natal position will take place about every three years in the other fixed signs, Aquarius, Taurus and Leo. This pattern will repeat for the rest of the native's life, defining how a person learns, grows and develops a personal philosophy. Generally speaking, the fixed signs tend to hold strong opinions and for Scorpio, this usually manifests in quite literal matters of life and death. Like the other fixed signs, Jupiter in Scorpio is a creature of habit and they need fair warning of any upcoming changes.

Jupiter transits through signs at a pace of about one sign per year. It is important to note that as children are taught by year group, they will learn alongside other children with Jupiter in Scorpio. Depending on the time of year they were born, they will also have classmates with either Jupiter in Libra or Jupiter in Sagittarius. This topic has been explored in depth in *Growing Pains: Astrology in Adolescence.*

Children who have Jupiter in Scorpio tend to enjoy cloak and dagger type lessons where they can put their ability to delve deeply into the problem itself in order to solve it. If sold well by teachers and parents, they should enjoy using formulas in Maths and Chemistry and, at a stretch, could also use these skills to crack the mysteries of language syntax. It could be said, Jupiter in Scorpio learners are the silent watchers of the classroom: they don't say much but they notice everything. Traditionally, Scorpio is ruled by Mars so to add more detail, one can look to this planet. Modern astrologers also look at Pluto (although this has a large orbit and changes signs from about 12 years to just over 30 years) to understand how this sign uses its potential powers.

Let's look at Jupiter as it transits through the other signs of the zodiac for Jupiter in Scorpio.

The First Jupiter Square

All babies need the basics of adequate nutrition, a safe place to sleep, cleanliness and a comfortable environment. They also need the human touch in order to build trust and to feel the caregiver is responding to their signals for these necessities. Eye contact, talking/singing to the baby and providing a daily rhythm of sleep, cleaning, feeding and playing with age appropriate toys are essential for all babies, irrespective of the Jupiter sign. As the baby grows into a toddler, it is important caregivers have adequately "baby proofed" the child's environment. These essential needs are important all the way into old age. Once these needs are met consistently, a bit of astrology can help the caregivers find the learner's internal "beat" for their development.

Here are just a few suggestions for Jupiter in Scorpio learners:

At some point during the first year of their life, the Jupiter in Scorpio learner will experience Jupiter transiting through the sign of Sagittarius. As the learner is a baby, the world is simply full of learning opportunities. Natally, the Jupiter in Scorpio learner may lean towards spicy or garlicky foods but bitter foods like green leafy vegetables or broccoli (in a texture they can manage) might be something they like. As they get older, they may like the taste of coffee.

As Jupiter moves into the sign of Capricorn in their second year, Jupiter in Scorpio learners tend to understand the step-by-step process it takes to get what they want. It may seem to parents that they almost have things planned out. Even though babies of this age may not be able to verbally express themselves, they have a way of letting their carers know exactly what it is they want. And they will persist until they get it. For carers, the easiest thing to do would be to go for the quiet life and just give in. What needs to be remembered is that babies grow up into adolescents who will come to understand that if they persist, they will wear their parents down until they give in. Parents and carers would be well advised to begin forming boundaries: what does the child need versus what do they want? No one would advocate causing a child to suffer by withholding love and affection but the line has to be drawn somewhere. It will become more and more important for carers of Jupiter in Scorpio learners to have a united front because these children can find the chink in the armour well before others.

During their third year, these learners will begin to walk and their vocabulary will begin to develop as Jupiter transits through the sign of Aquarius. It may seem to the carers that they do things a little differently to other children—and they may seem to dislike any sort of restraint even if it is for their own safety. They may delight in keeping you on your toes and may find highly creative uses for their toys that the manufacturers have probably never thought of. One very good aspect of this stage of development is their sociability: they tend to like to be with others but are perfectly capable of entertaining themselves in equal measure. These days, most young children are fascinated with technology but Jupiter in Scorpio learners may take to these devices like proverbial ducks to water. They may also be gifted in communicating in ways that seem unconventional: Morse code, sign language, soundboards and more cryptic methods of speaking may uncover truly unexpected—and probably highly complicated—thought processes and ideas.

Through the early stages of play, Jupiter in Scorpio learners are creating the basis for discovering the answers to questions that may have out-foxed the older minds of previous generations.

The First Jupiter Opposition

Between the ages of about three and six years old, most young children are preparing for formal education and socialisation. These are just some ideas to help Jupiter in Scorpio learners prepare for their first adventures away from their immediate care givers.

As their fourth year rolls around, Jupiter in Scorpio learners will have transiting Jupiter in Pisces. As has been noted, these children do not miss anything. They see and hear all, even if they are not reacting. However, there are some things they cannot control and those include their dreams. As the water signs tend to be worriers, sometimes suppressed feelings, unprocessed by the conscious mind, can be turned into nightmares by the unconscious mind. The young Scorpio learner may not have the vocabulary to express their fears (or their bad dreams) but they can find other ways of showing their stress. Not eating or becoming very fussy, refusing to go to sleep by themselves or actively showing signs of terror are all possible manifestations. Telling these children they shouldn't worry is not going to help. They may have been accidentally exposed to genuine horrors such as a death in the family or they may have heard something online or on TV. Whilst not advocating further exposure to frightening events, it is important to be honest if these children ask difficult questions. Jupiter in Pisces is transitionally ruled by Jupiter itself and therefore helps us to form our personal belief systems. Jupiter in Scorpio children at this stage of development may have some very big questions. As they grow older, they may not continue to share the faith of their carers but understanding what they believe can be a soothing balm to an unsettled dreamer.

Activities for enjoyment and learning outside of school: music lessons, art projects not found in school like pottery courses that allow the learner to complete a project step-by-step, studying a particular artist and their work medium (painting, sculpture, carving, etc.).

During their fifth year, transiting Jupiter will enter Aries for the Jupiter in Scorpio child. Aries is also a Mars-ruled sign and so the Jupiter in Scorpio learner, having confronted their worst fears, may be motivated to take part in activities that have a sense of danger to them. Fire may be particularly fascinating. Obviously allowing children of this age carte blanche access to matches and accelerants is not a great idea but there are ways of satisfying their curiosity without danger. If they show an interest, starting a contained fire, such as a campfire, is one possible way of teaching them fire safety. They may also be interested in vehicles that move fast. Go-carting or taking them to see a car race might take the edge off their inquisitiveness. In terms of learning in a classroom and getting ready to start school, they may be very eager indeed. These learners tend to love a good thrill so it may be a good idea for teachers to be extra vigilant in the playground and to be sure the equipment is used as it is intended.

Activities for enjoyment and learning outside of school: any activities that involve racing, focusing on perfecting a singular skill, physical exercise, activities that help them understand their own strengths and limits

By the time Jupiter transits into Taurus during their sixth year, most Jupiter in Scorpio learners will be in school. They may become interested in the platonic interactions amongst peers or even be fascinated by relations between adults. A little word of warning: Jupiter in Scorpio learners do not miss anything and that will include seemingly innocuous flirting amongst staff. A teacher's pregnancy could open up a whole can of worms as could a crisis such as a serious accident or illness. It is always best to tell children the truth but particularly for Jupiter in Scorpio learners who have probably figured out the answers anyway. Their questions are their secret way of quizzing you to see if you are smart enough or honest enough to be trusted.

Activities for enjoyment and learning outside of school: outdoor walks, animal watching, tasting different foods, sensory activities and toys, simple physical strength exercises, collecting interesting things (and keeping them organised), managing money.

The Jupiter opposition for Jupiter in Scorpio children is an opportunity to analyse the information they have been provided with. They will always have an in-depth understanding of life's deepest mysteries and are far more mature than they are often given credit for.

The Closing Jupiter Square

By this stage, children will have settled into a home/school routine and it is likely schools will begin to prepare students for the Scholastic Achievement Tests (or their equivalents). Debate rages as to whether these tests cause stress for the children but, drawing from personal experience, students tend not to get too upset if the adults around them don't behave as if the world is coming to an end. The purpose of these tests is to help identify strengths and weaknesses in the child's development. The results establish a baseline, not a final outcome. Here are some ways to help support the learners during these formative times:

By the time Jupiter in Scorpio learners are in their seventh year, transiting Jupiter will be in the sign of Gemini. If their questions made you squirm in previous years then you had better get the defibrillator ready. Now the name of the game is: "Make everyone blush". Toilet humour for these learners tends to be the strong favourite. Lord help the pregnant teachers for this academic year too. There can be so many giggles and wink-winks behind the backs of authority figures that there might be a fear these learners will never be ready for SATs. The thing to remember is that these children are sensitive: if the teachers and parents take exams seriously, Jupiter in Scorpio learners will as well. Even if they pretend they don't care (they are just trying to scare you into an early grave).

Activities for enjoyment and learning outside of school: singing, synonyms for common words, giving names to unfamiliar items, becoming familiar with numbers and letters through simple calligraphy, learning to touch type.

With SATs over and done with during their eighth year, these learners may develop concerns that they didn't take things seriously enough as Jupiter transits into Cancer. They may be haunted by the memories of poor answers or regret not working hard enough. Whilst it might be tempting to tell them they deserve every bit of worry, it should be remembered these are young children who have been put under too much pressure. Allowing them a bit of time to re-group is the sensitive thing to do for them. Encourage family time so they can feel loved and supported by those closest to them. A good in-school buddy system can also be enormously helpful as they will all be at the same Jupiter stage of learning. Above all, be as reassuring as possible: they really do care about pleasing the people they like the most.

Activities for enjoyment and learning outside of school: taking care of animals, singing (as a way to cope with negative emotions), helping with the cooking, taking responsibility for the management of one area of their living space, learning how to take care of their clothes and beds, visiting museums or investigating certain times in history.

Transiting Jupiter will be in Leo as Jupiter in Scorpio pupils are in their ninth year. During this stage of development these children seem to have the desire to show their creativity through music, writing, poetry or their sense of fashion. Do not expect butterflies and unicorns. These guys tend to have a worryingly dark sense of expression. They may even say their favourite colour is black. Or blood red. And all the while they are watching you for your reaction (act shocked and they will love you forever). Playing with the more macabre topics of human life is their way of understanding the human condition. And playing with death is just one possible manifestation of understanding God and exploring their faith (they may express a desire to stray away from the family faith at this time too just to see how everyone is going to react). These learners like to be "safely scared". Let them play in the dark and test the mirrors for Bloody Mary. They like to see who can act the most scared by screaming the loudest.

Activities for enjoyment and learning outside of school: stage play, making and wearing costumes and masks, dressing up to go to an event, taking part in a musical.

The Jupiter Return

As the learner heads towards their final years of primary school, they should be able to work more independently, understand the general rules of the classroom/playground and see home and school as two separate environments.

Jupiter in Scorpio learners will have Jupiter transiting through the sign of Virgo during their tenth year. As they prepare to leave their primary schools behind, they can be given the opportunity to put their ample analytical skills to good use. They may become interested in the microscopic or telescopic world but they may show discontent in taking theories at their basic interpretation. Very often, with a little guidance, they can show precision when recording their findings. For teachers, these abilities can give them a jump start with future research projects. In fact, what is the harm in allowing them to extend their scientific interests by conducting a full-on investigation into a topic they are interested in? Of course they will need guidance but it's far better than wasting that X-ray vision on songs, games and TikTok videos.

Activities for enjoyment and learning outside of school: learning about the physical body of people or animals, learning about sickness and how to take care of someone (or a pet) who is not feeling well, understanding the basics of medicine. Learning to identify plants and different species of animals, and applying complex measuring skills to practical projects such as those found in design and technology.

Transiting Jupiter in Libra, as the Jupiter in Scorpio students prepare for secondary school in their eleventh year, can be a time of intensity in friendships and other kinds of relationships. To the Jupiter in Scorpio learner, it's all change in how people interact with each other. As they enter puberty, they tend to be hyper-aware of sexuality and it tends to become important to keep communication about intimacy as open as possible in this tricky time. Sometimes Jupiter in Scorpio demands too much of others and, conversely, they may be terrified of making commitments because they sense the end even before anything has really begun. Of course behind all this tension is the inevitability of change—something which fixed signs fear. It can help if parents, teachers and carers can openly take steps to plan get-togethers, reunions and ways of keeping in contact as far in advance as possible to help Jupiter in Scorpio understand "the end" doesn't always mean "the end".

Activities for enjoyment and learning outside of school: planning a themed party with a few friends (try themes based around *Horrible Histories* or their favourite kids' movies) and have "preparation parties" where all the invitees have to make their own party favours and costumes, plan their food and activities, etc.

At some point during their twelfth year, Jupiter in Scorpio students will experience their first Jupiter return. Parents, carers and teachers may find these learners are reflective and contemplative. However, this doesn't mean there is nothing much going on. They are back to the stage of observing and gathering information for future use. They will instinctively know who they can trust and who has it in for them (according to their perceptions). At this stage in development, starting secondary school introduces a lot of new adults—and children—to their social skills. This can feel overwhelming with too much information to sift through all at once. Jupiter in Scorpio learners may need to spend more time in their rooms (don't be alarmed if they prefer the lights off), lost in their all thoughts as they mull over the day's events. Their energy and confidence will return and they will let you know when they are ready to join in with social activities again.

Activities for enjoyment and learning outside of school: mysteries and puzzles, being *gently* frightened (Halloween or cold, dark autumn nights are a good time to share simple ghost stories), nature walks so they can observe the cycle of life in plants and animals (NB: learners at this stage may take an interest in death and pregnancies so be prepared to explain).

When we return to a place have visited before, it is our nature to make comparisons to what has changed since the first time we were there. We may want to seek out the things we did before or perhaps try something completely different.

As almost all students will have had their first Jupiter return by the end of their first year of secondary school, schools could hold an end of year festival that would allow pupils to demonstrate their individual skills. Schools tend to hold sporting events during this time but how about organising a Business Fair? Students could arrange community events to see who (or which team) can raise the most money for their charity of choice.

The Jupiter and Uranus Sextiles: In the Thick of Puberty

As noted in the Introduction, the thirteenth year of a child's life is usually when rebellion and defiance begin to become noticeable. Astrologically, transiting Jupiter forms a sextile aspect to its natal position at the same time Uranus, the planet of rebellion, will also make its first Ptolemaic aspect to its own natal position (also by sextile aspect). This combination quite literally means "big rebellion" and marks the time when adolescents (and their parents) begin the struggle to make that separation into adulthood.

Identifying when and how a young adolescent may struggle with the changing social rules they must face could be helpful for parents. For example, if an adolescent experiences the Uranus sextile before the Jupiter sextile, parents may view their child as needing more guidance for following the expectations of the home environment (which would include expectations in school). In the Case Studies section, subjects with this tendency are noted as "rebels". If an adolescent experiences the Jupiter sextile before the Uranus sextile, parents may view their child as needing more encouragement for academic work and possibly with social skills. In the Case Studies section, subjects with this tendency are noted as "truth seekers". There is no "good" or "bad" with these notations and they are only presented as starting points for understanding the life-long impact this stage of development has on learners as they continue their journey all the way into old age. To demonstrate how this particular stage of development can vary from person to person, there is a summary of the time frame for the subjects of the case studies on page 208.

Furthermore, an adolescent's developing body means they may be interested in forming intimate relationships but their brain needs time to catch up with all the new situations it finds itself in.

For children born with Jupiter in Scorpio, Jupiter will be transiting through the sign of Capricorn as it had been during their second year. It can be helpful for parents to recall the lessons of this year as the young Jupiter in Scorpio learner began to understand step-by-step processes. It is a similar manner of handling challenges during the thick of puberty: taking things at a steady pace and keeping an eye on the desired outcome (which will most likely be career-focused).

The Saturn Opposition

The Saturn opposition begins some time during the fourteenth or fifteenth year (possibly earlier or later depending on individual cases) and marks the end of astrological adolescence. Parents and teachers usually notice that the adolescent begins to calm down and take a more mature approach to their academic progress. In the UK, this coincides with choosing academic subjects (as opposed to trying a little bit of everything), formal exam preparation and a marked change in mood. Depression, anxiety and their symptoms must be monitored and taken seriously. Schools will have access to support mechanisms for parents and carers, teachers will have been trained in how to identify potential difficulties and for parents who are home schooling, social services can be a sound source for help.

As they head towards their transiting Saturn opposition, in Scorpio children will also re-visit what they had learned as transiting Jupiter once again passes through the signs of Aquarius and Pisces. Adolescents, especially since the invention of social media, tend to have a broader range of friends now with the added complexity of never feeling they can deepen relationships without trivial distractions and a multitude of methods of peer pressure. Although "circle time" may seem childish, it may help if teachers could somehow hold a more profound, live social space to encourage real friendships and connections.

The Second Jupiter Opposition

By the time a young adult finishes mandatory education, they will have a good idea of what they want to do with their lives and yet they still have time to re-take exams or re-train if they discover they want to do something else. The second Jupiter opposition is a time of making serious decisions: the young adult is no longer a child. The learner now knows there are consequences for undesirable behaviour and can no longer blame "the system" for their poor choices. Sadly, our prison services are filled with young people who have slipped through the net. As a collective whole, society could do with using a little astrology to help these young people get back on track. A more comprehensive mentoring service could be helpful.

Here are some ideas to help young adults focus on the rest of their adult lives:

Transiting Jupiter will be in Taurus as the young adult finishes their formal education at around the age of eighteen. There may be a need to establish themselves financially rather than academically and they need the adults in their lives to help them make the choices that are right for them. Not everyone who grew up in a working class family will want to learn a trade and not everyone whose family hold advance degrees wish to follow in those footsteps. Career counselling (which is woefully underfunded in schools) needs support from the home environment. Good communication between home and school is essential.

The Second and Subsequent Jupiter Returns

As a person continues to develop emotionally, physically and spiritually they will build on the lessons they learned in the formative years. Jupiter returns (roughly) at the ages of 24, 36, 48 and 60 (and beyond). The suggestions for activities can be modified to suit the developmental cycle for each Jupiter cycle. For example, a Jupiter in Scorpio learner experiencing a Jupiter in Capricorn transit during their third year of life might enjoy dressing up as a workperson they admire; during their fifteenth year, they may wish to try the more advanced skills of a given vocation (one that is different from their work experience tasks); during their twenty-seventh year, they may want to extend these skills into something more lucrative and so on. The key for all Jupiter returns is to choose a skill (or even one per year) and exercise the brain, all the way to the final years of life. As always, with Jupiter, the sky is the limit.

Jupiter returns at all ages should be celebrated and an experienced astrologer can help locate the exact moment of the return. New clothes to reflect a changing style, a good meal (with a magnificent dessert) with influential friends and maybe even a holiday to some exotic place are just a few ideas. To celebrate the ingress (entry) of Jupiter in a new sign, consult the table in the appendix. The Chinese culture does a wonderful job with celebrating "The Year of the…". While theirs may be a different culture and system, the similarity of intention is still there.

Fine tuning the role of Jupiter:

Jupiter in Scorpio is traditionally ruled by the planet Mars and co-ruled by Pluto (either or both planets can be used). For the interpretation, the element of power and control is added to the traditional Mars drive. As Scorpios are co-ruled by the god of the underworld, there can be an element of sneakiness in these pupils.

Mars/Pluto in Aries: These pupils learn by exercising self-control. They get what they want by understanding themselves and their limitations.

Mars/Pluto in Taurus: These pupils learn by controlling their working environment. They sneakily adjust the heating or air conditioning and take an abnormal interest in school acquisitions.

Mars/Pluto in Gemini: These pupils learn by keeping everyone on their toes. They are nervous and fidgety and want everyone else to be too. They need short, sharp learning objectives and plenty of breaks.

Mars/Pluto in Cancer: These pupils like to learn by manipulating emotional context of lessons. They cry out in over exaggerated pain or laugh hysterically at inappropriate times. These learners should be encouraged to convey facts rather than resorting to emotional outbursts.

Mars/Pluto in Leo: These pupils learn by creating drama, sometimes of a sexual nature, to draw attention to themselves. Precocious, they are adept at turning the most innocent gesture into something much more sinister.

Mars/Pluto in Virgo: These pupils learn by exploring the dark side of life without getting themselves dirty in the process. Keen observers and brilliant interviewers, these pupils have the knack of teasing information out of whatever they are studying.

Mars/Pluto in Libra: these pupils learn by controlling the people they work and play with. They understand human psychology and are adept at making themselves appear faultless. Carers can help these children learn by encouraging them to get what they want by asking politely rather than resorting to psychological warfare.

Mars/Pluto in Scorpio: These pupils learn by tuning into the undercurrents of social situations. They seem to understand that humans are motivated by three things: power, money and sex. Carers can help them learn by teaching them "survival" and/or coping skills in the classroom.

Mars/Pluto in Sagittarius: These pupils learn by taking risks and putting themselves in dangerous situations. They like life or death situations because it allows them to form their own philosophies about the bigger questions.

Mars/Pluto in Capricorn: These pupils learn by using their social status to garner special attention from the teacher. Although usually quite hard working, these pupils seem to be under the impression such displays of power actually endear themselves to others.

Mars/Pluto in Aquarius: These pupils learn by using their skills in experimentation. These children resist rules and the more that are put into place, the more they will see to it they are broken.

Mars/Pluto in Pisces: These pupils learn by pretending to be more lost than they really are. Typically, they have too much self control to become completely lost but this doesn't prevent them from trying to get you to do their work for them.

Case Studies

Stephen King

Stephen King was born on 21 September 1947 at 1:30 am (RR: A; Collector: Rodden) in Portland, Maine, with Jupiter in Scorpio and Mars in Cancer. He is a prolific and internationally renowned author known primarily for his work in the horror genre. Many of his books have been adapted into critically acclaimed films, and King himself has made cameo appearances in several of them.

Interestingly, King recalls using panels from comic books to create his own stories at the age of six or seven—around the time of his first Jupiter opposition. His transiting Jupiter in Capricorn made a sextile to its natal position about six months before his transiting Uranus in Leo formed a sextile to his natal Uranus in Gemini, indicating that he is a truth seeker. His incredibly prolific output attests to this.

In 1965, he published his first short story, *I Was a Teenage Grave Robber*, printed by his brother on a mimeograph and sold to friends. At the time, transiting Jupiter in Taurus was opposing his natal Jupiter in Scorpio—aptly mirroring the content. While attending the University of Maine in 1967, he sold his first professional short story as transiting Jupiter in Leo was conjunct his natal Saturn.

His first novel, *Carrie*, was published shortly after transiting Jupiter in Aquarius opposed his natal Saturn. *Salem's Lot* followed in 1975, published the same autumn his mother passed away from uterine cancer. At the time, transiting Jupiter in Aries was squaring his natal Mars in Cancer and opposing his natal Mercury in Libra three times. That same year, King moved with his family to Boulder, Colorado, where he wrote *The Shining*, inspired by an eerie hotel during a winter stay. All three early novels were later adapted into iconic films.

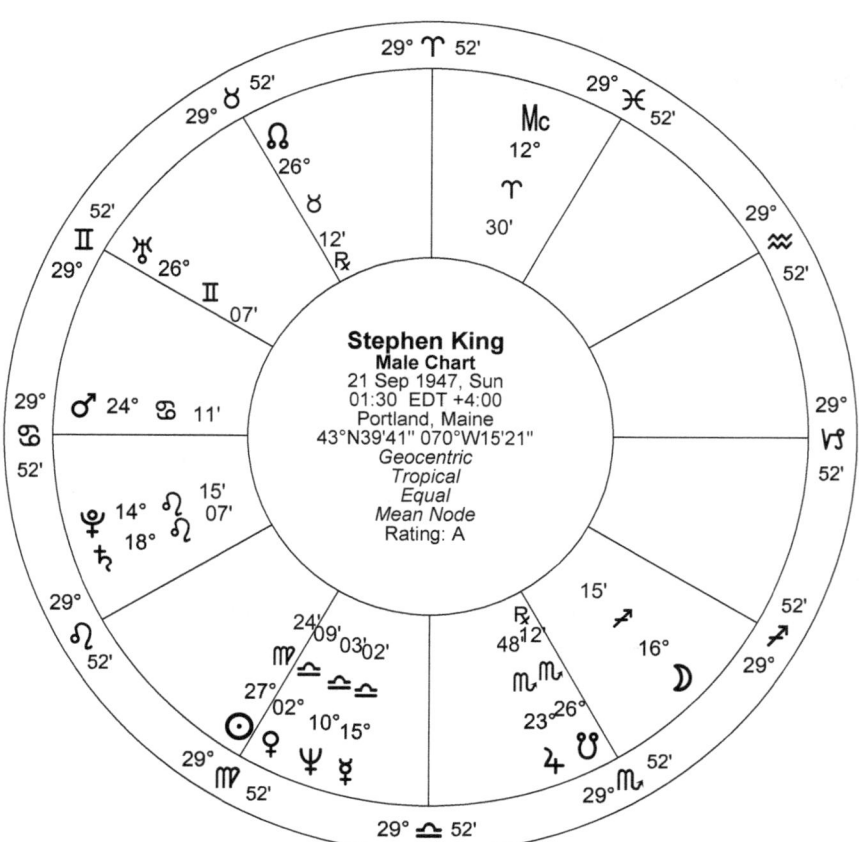

Upon returning to Maine, he completed *The Stand*, which was published just weeks before transiting Jupiter in Aries squared his Cancer Ascendant. Remarkably, transiting Jupiter again opposed his natal Mars in Cancer in early 2020 during the onset of the COVID-19 pandemic, prompting many to draw eerie parallels between the novel and real life.

In 1982, King published *Different Seasons*, a collection of four novellas—three of which were adapted into major films. In August 1983, as transiting Jupiter formed a series of squares to his natal Chiron in Scorpio, *The Body* was in negotiations for film rights. The resulting film, *Stand By Me*, was released in 1986 during a series of transiting Jupiter squares to his natal Moon in Sagittarius.

Another novella from the collection, *Rita Hayworth and the Shawshank Redemption*, became the award-nominated *The Shawshank Redemption* in 1994. The film was released during a series of three Uranus oppositions to King's Mars in Cancer and is now frequently cited as one of the greatest films of all time.

In April 1983, just before *The Body* negotiations began, King published *Christine*, later adapted into a film. Both the novel and the film were released while he was experiencing his Jupiter return in Sagittarius. At the same time, he published *Pet Sematary*, which was made into a film released in April 1989, just before transiting Jupiter in Gemini opposed his natal Moon in Sagittarius. A remake of the film was released in April 2019 during a series of Jupiter conjunctions to that same Moon.

Another notable success was *The Green Mile*, released as six serialised paperback volumes. The first was published in March 1986 shortly after transiting Jupiter in Aquarius squared his natal Jupiter in Scorpio. The 1999 film adaptation, starring Tom Hanks, was released as transiting Jupiter in Capricorn squared King's natal Mercury in Libra.

Stephen King's literary output is too vast to summarise fully in one case study. But it's clear: with Jupiter in Scorpio, he found his purpose in exploring the darker corners of the human psyche and sharing those stories with the world.

Kevin Spacey

Kevin Spacey was born on 26 July 1959 (no time) in South Orange, New Jersey (source: Wikipedia). He has Jupiter in Scorpio with Mars in Virgo. Over the course of his career, he won two Academy Awards and was made an honorary Knight Commander of the Order of the British Empire in 2015.

During adolescence, Spacey experienced a sextile from transiting Uranus in Libra to his natal Uranus in Gemini about a year before transiting Jupiter in Capricorn formed a sextile to his natal Jupiter in Scorpio, indicating he is a rebel. He has publicly spoken out against his father's racist and homophobic views and has noted that his father didn't believe acting was a viable career—so Spacey defied that authority figure.

Spacey's early career began on the stage. His first professional appearance came at age 22, just as transiting Jupiter in Libra formed three

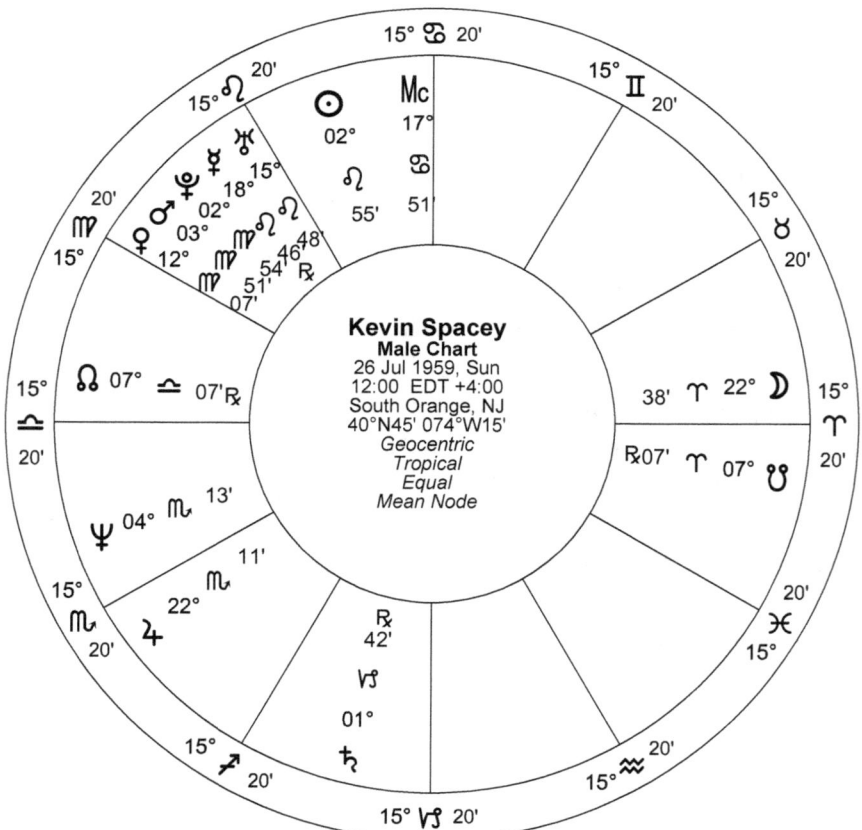

conjunctions to his North Node. While he would later find major success in film, he remained closely tied to theatre. In 2003, during a series of three conjunctions from transiting Jupiter in Leo to his natal Uranus, he became the artistic director of the Old Vic, one of London's most prestigious theatres.

Spacey began appearing in films in the late 1980s, during the opening stages of his Jupiter cycle. At his third Jupiter return in 1995, he rose to international prominence, winning an Oscar for *The Usual Suspects* and appearing in the thriller *Seven*. His Oscar-winning performance in *American Beauty* followed in 1999, released during a series of oppositions from transiting Jupiter in Scorpio to his natal Neptune—an astrologically fitting backdrop for a film about blurred boundaries and disillusionment.

In 2004, Spacey co-wrote, directed, produced, and starred as Bobby Darin in *Beyond the Sea*, a deeply personal project. Transiting Jupiter crossed his Ascendant just prior to the film's release. Notably, the real Bobby Darin's natal Sun in Taurus was exactly opposite Spacey's Jupiter, with Mars transiting this opposition at the time of the film's release.

In 2011, transiting Jupiter crossed Spacey's South Node as he was cast in the Netflix series *House of Cards*, earning widespread acclaim. However, in 2017, multiple allegations of sexual misconduct came to light. Transiting Jupiter in Scorpio was conjunct his natal Neptune almost to the day, highlighting a potent period of public scandal. He was later found not liable in a civil lawsuit (2022) and acquitted of charges in London (2023), but his professional reputation remains significantly damaged.

Kevin Spacey's chart reflects a powerful manifestation of Jupiter in Scorpio's themes: talent, charisma, secrecy, and the potential for downfall when the quest for power and control goes too far.

Jupiter in Sagittarius

Sagittarius is a fire sign by element and a mutable sign by modality. Transiting squares and oppositions to its natal position will take place about every three years in the other mutable signs, Pisces, Gemini and Virgo. This pattern will repeat for the rest of the native's life, defining how a person learns, grows and develops a personal philosophy. Mutable signs are flexible, co-operative and interested in what goes on around them. They are usually very curious and collect and distribute information that passes their way. Jupiter in Sagittarius is a highly spiritual combination and the native may learn through extensive travels and adventures or through experiencing religious rituals outside of their family's influence. However, they can also be overly confident in assuming others want to hear their strong opinions.

Jupiter transits through signs at a pace of about one sign per year. It is important to note that as children are taught by year group, they will learn alongside other children with Jupiter in Sagittarius. Depending on the time of year they were born, they will also have classmates with either Jupiter in Scorpio or Jupiter in Capricorn. This topic has been explored in depth in *Growing Pains: Astrology in Adolescence.*

Children who have Jupiter in Sagittarius are the embodiment of Zeus himself—in all his glory and in all his hubris. They are confident learners, they are inquisitive and tend to be well read. However, as cocky as they may seem academically, they lack experience in real life situations. It's as if they have read the instruction booklet, but they haven't put anything together yet. They need adults to guide them and help to keep them within safe limits.

The First Jupiter Square

All babies need the basics of adequate nutrition, a safe place to sleep, cleanliness and a comfortable environment. They also need the human touch in order to build trust and to feel the caregiver is responding to their signals for these necessities. Eye contact, talking/singing to the baby and providing a daily rhythm of sleep, cleaning, feeding and playing with age appropriate toys are essential for all babies, irrespective of their Jupiter sign. As the baby grows into a toddler, it is important caregivers have adequately "baby proofed" the child's environment. These essential needs are important all the way into old age. Once these needs are met consistently, a bit of astrology can help the caregivers find the learner's internal "beat" for development.

At some point during the first year of their life, the Jupiter in Sagittarius learner will experience Jupiter transiting through the sign of Capricorn. As the learner is a baby, the world is simply full of learning opportunities. Natally, Jupiter in Sagittarius learners may develop quite a sweet tooth if indulged too much. As they get older, they tend to prefer rich foods.

During their second year, the Jupiter in Sagittarius learner will have Jupiter transiting through the sign of Aquarius. Most children of this age experience the "terrible twos" but for children with this combination, accepting the word "no" may not be high on their learning agendas. They may take great satisfaction in defying authority figures or inventing new ways of navigating their environments: "bottom scooching" or other unusual methods of crawling are all a part of their way of expressing their individuality and need for autonomy. As they learn to talk, they may experiment with all sorts of sounds not found in their native language.

Jupiter will transit through the sign of Pisces during a Jupiter in Sagittarius' third year. Faith and/or religious beliefs may become prominent themes as the toddler begins to work out how the world outside of his own experience operates. Family religious routines and celebrations may become a source of fascination as well as inspiration. Getting the Jupiter in Sagittarius learner involved with these rituals, through craft, decorating, praying, meditating and visiting sacred sites is likely to make a big impression on children at this stage of development. Exploring religious artefacts (and perhaps attempting to replicate them if appropriate) and listening to spiritually uplifting music can give the learner the opportunity to find a belief system s/he is comfortable with.

Developing a personal philosophy may be a topic that is too advanced for young children. However, providing a wide range of experiences for these curious Jupiter in Sagittarius learners stimulates their very active minds and helps prepare the groundwork for further investigation as they seek a version of the truth (which will be in a constant state of flux) that suits them.

The First Jupiter Opposition

Between the ages of about three and six years old, most young children are preparing for formal education and socialisation. These are just some ideas to help Jupiter in Sagittarius learners prepare for their first adventures away from their immediate care givers.

During the fourth year, Jupiter in Sagittarius learners will experience Jupiter transiting through the sign of Aries. For the already active Sagittarius learner, this is the metaphorical equivalent of a triple espresso. Even the most robust toys may not be able to withstand the forces of nature that these children are. As difficult as it may be to impose, these children need very firm boundaries and rules around keeping their hands to themselves, tidying up their messes and listening to their bodies so they can develop habits that will allow them to nurture self care routines. Their modus operandi tends to be running around until they no longer have the strength to carry on. This is fun for the child but exhausting for parents and carers—and children who have Jupiter in the adjacent signs (Scorpio and Capricorn) who are likely to be simultaneously shocked and annoyed by the aftermath of sharing a playing space with these learners. Jupiter in Sagittarius learners at this stage of development tend to need to be taught how to pace themselves.

Activities for enjoyment and learning outside of school: any activities that involve racing, focusing on perfecting a singular skill, physical exercise, activities that help them understand their own strengths and limits.

As Jupiter in Sagittarius learners prepare to begin their formal education, transiting Jupiter will be in the sign of Taurus during their fifth year. Their fascination may turn from doing everything at breakneck speed to slowing down (at least comparatively) and enjoying what is around them. Long hikes through nature will help them manage their excess energy and encourage them to cultivate a genuine interest in the Great Outdoors can help open up new opportunities for learning. They may also enjoy learning how to manage their ever-increasing collections. Through taking care of their belongings, Jupiter in Sagittarius learners practise responsibility and organisation which they will need to continue to develop as their learning journey continues.

Activities for enjoyment and learning outside of school: outdoor walks, animal watching, tasting different foods, sensory activities and toys, simple physical strength exercises, collecting interesting things (and keeping them organised).

Jupiter will transit the sign of Gemini sometime during the Jupiter in Sagittarius learner's sixth year. As their written and spoken vocabulary expands, so will their social circles. Whilst this sounds encouraging, it should be noted that Jupiter in Gemini repeats everything it hears. As these learners approach their first Jupiter opposition, it is like a talking review of everything they have ever heard. Parents and teachers who think they don't use personal key phrases may not recognise when a Jupiter in Sagittarius imitates them at this particular stage of development, but everyone else will. There are many advantages of this phase. One is simply they love to write, read and talk. Use these skills by setting clear ground rules about appropriate topics, the amount of time needed for the set tasks and the intended outcomes. Possible concerns about this stage may include the tendency for mutable signs to polarise into super speedy learners who can't get enough information and the more reluctant type of learners who seem to live in terror that they are not as clever as anyone else. For these reasons, it is important for teachers (and parents if there is more than one child at home) to be wary of comparing progress amongst these learners.

Activities for enjoyment and learning outside of school: singing, synonyms for common words, giving names to unfamiliar items, becoming familiar with numbers and letters through simple calligraphy.

As these learners approach their first Jupiter opposition, check for comprehension before getting more complex texts out of the cupboard and use this opportunity to keep expanding their vocabulary.

The Closing Jupiter Square

By this stage, children will have settled into a home/school routine and it is likely schools will begin to prepare students for the Scholastic Achievement Tests (or their equivalents). Debate rages as to whether these tests cause stress for the children but, drawing from personal experience, students tend not to get too upset if the adults around them don't behave as if the world is coming to an end. The purpose of these tests is to help identify strengths and weaknesses in the child's development. The results establish a baseline, not a final outcome. Here are some ways to help support the learners during these formative times:

During their seventh year, Jupiter will transit into the sign of Cancer. Like Pisces, Cancer is a water sign but its cardinal modality indicates learners at this stage of development may struggle to utilise the lessons of this very sensitive sign. Jupiter in Sagittarius learners tend to be quite provocative as they search for their truth. Initially, as they begin their learning journey during this transit, they are likely to come across as extremely insensitive and, in the worst possible scenario, as downright offensive. Sagittarius learners may experience the ire of their fellow pupils (and possibly their teachers too) over their self-perceived sense of "honesty". Nothing thrills Jupiter in Sagittarius more than a good debate, even if it means they are proven wrong. These learners thrive on stirring the passions of others and seeing otherwise sedate fellow learners becoming enraged by being forced to see things from a different point of view. Teachers can support Jupiter in Sagittarius learners by reminding them that it's not always a good thing to upset other people: they need to be taught moderation and how to recognise the signs when someone is getting a bit overheated.

Activities for enjoyment and learning outside of school: taking care of animals, singing (as a way to cope with negative emotions), helping with the cooking, taking responsibility for the management of one area of their living space, learning how to take care of their clothes and beds, visiting museums or investigating certain times in history.

As Jupiter transits through the sign of Leo in their eighth year, Jupiter in Sagittarius learners begin to take pride in their strong opinions IF they were not taught how to gauge other people's feelings whilst Jupiter was transiting through Cancer the previous year. A double dose of fire (as both Leo and Sagittarius are fire signs) can lead to physical altercations unless careful ground rules are laid out. If Jupiter in Sagittarius learners have been carefully trained, they tend to make fine orators with strong political leanings who are respectful to others as well as entertaining. Managed well, Jupiter in Sagittarius learners will always remember the year they got their start in politics.

Activities for enjoyment and learning outside of school: stage play, making and wearing costumes and masks, dressing up to go to an event.

Jupiter moves on to transit through the sign of Virgo during the ninth year for Jupiter in Sagittarius learners. This will tend to be a year of refining their knowledge rather than taking in more information. Keeping on top of daily news and topical events will help these learners use discernment rather than debate to find their answers. Learning how to cite sources could be a valuable lesson as will teaching them how to spot reliable resources. Already well-read, they can take analysing literature to levels far more advanced than their chronological years. However, the trick to managing these learners is to prevent them from becoming so cocky over what they already know that they will not acknowledge that they lack the experience of application. Indeed it can be easy to forget this because they can sound so erudite. As they are still quite young, they may still respond to incentives such as merits but what can truly motivate them are opportunities to explore new fields of knowledge.

Activities for enjoyment and learning outside of school: learning about the physical body of people or animals, learning about sickness and how to take care of someone (or a pet) who is not feeling well, understanding the basics of medicine. Learning to identify plants and different species of animals, and applying complex measuring skills to practical projects such as those found in design and technology.

As the closing transiting Jupiter square comes to a close, Jupiter in Sagittarius learners will have discovered a sensitivity to the feelings of others which helps them to become the leaders they are meant to be. They will also have learned how to balance what they know, with what they need to know.

The Jupiter Return

As the learner heads towards their final years of primary school, they should be able to work more independently, understand the general rules of the classroom/playground and see home and school as two separate environments.

Jupiter in Sagittarius learners will experience Jupiter transiting through the sign of Libra in their tenth year. Already adventurous academically, these learners may become curious about the nature of relationships.

Being Jupiter in Sagittarius learners, their questions can be quite invasive and are asked without consideration for the feelings of others. There tends not to be a concern about privacy or a sense of embarrassment, therefore their questions need to be met in the same manner. These learners respect honesty, so when they ask their parents or teachers about their first kiss or ask at what age they fell in love, if they are married, engaged, divorced, widowed or on the lookout, it helps to be as frank as possible (including reminding them that everyone has the right to privacy). Friendship circles will probably be important as these learners try to work out the social rules of relationships of all levels. Teachers should be aware of learners who attempt to hold the fort as they are masters at pretending they know the answers about intimacy. And on the topic of intimacy, this is a year for emphasising the importance of love and companionship in favour of physical closeness. Teachers should ensure these learners understand the steps needed to create solid relationships and not try to get too far ahead of themselves.

Activities for enjoyment and learning outside of school: planning a themed party with a few friends (try themes based around *Horrible Histories* or their favourite kids' movies) and have "preparation parties" where all the invitees have to make their own party favours and costumes, plan their food and activities, etc.

Transiting Jupiter in Scorpio during the eleventh year is generally the age when some pupils begin puberty. They may be curious about sex and may have no problem asking about the mechanics of intimate acts. A good home-school relationship is essential during this year because not all parents want their child to learn about intimacy outside of the family circle. However, in this age of social media and unlimited access to the internet, it can be pretty much impossible to isolate sex education to the home. Sadly, many children are exposed to subject material they are not ready for and if it seems taboo to discuss these things at home, Jupiter in Sagittarius learners will just take their questions to the playground where their burning questions will be answered by inexperienced peers who may like to pretend they know what they are talking about. It may be best to provide an environment that allows these learners to feel comfortable talking to their favourite adult without shame or fear of ridicule or judgment.

Activities for enjoyment and learning outside of school: mysteries and puzzles, being *gently* frightened (Halloween or cold, dark autumn nights are a good time to share simple ghost stories), nature walks so they can observe the cycle of life in plants and animals (NB: learners at this stage may take an interest in death and pregnancies so be prepared to explain).

By the time of their first Jupiter return, Jupiter in Sagittarius learners will be starting secondary school (or at least preparing for it). The bigger school can seem like freedom to these young, curious learners. They may thrive with so many teachers, a bigger library, older friends and more room to move around. As is usually the case with these learners, it is important to remember they are still young and no matter how big they talk, they still lack the experience to do what they like without supervision.

Activities for enjoyment and learning outside of school: taking part in charity work, visiting places of worship, learning to discuss politics and identifying political leaders, learning about different countries (their map, geographical features, language, etc.).

When we return to a place have visited before, it is our nature to make comparisons to what has changed since the first time we were there. We may want to seek out the things we did before or perhaps try something completely different.

As almost all students will have had their first Jupiter return by the end of their first year of secondary school, schools could hold an end of year festival that would allow pupils to demonstrate their individual skills. Schools tend to hold sporting events during this time but how about a Cultural Exhibition? Students work together to bring a wide variety of experiences to the armchair travellers in their community.

The Jupiter and Uranus Sextiles: In the Thick of Puberty

As noted in the Introduction, the thirteenth year of a child's life is usually when rebellion and defiance begin to become noticeable. Astrologically, transiting Jupiter forms a sextile aspect to its natal position at the same time Uranus, the planet of rebellion, will also make its first Ptolemaic aspect to its own natal position (also by sextile aspect). This combination quite literally means "big rebellion" and marks the time when adolescents (and their parents) begin the struggle to make that separation into adulthood.

Identifying when and how a young adolescent may struggle with the changing social rules they must face could be helpful for parents. For example, if an adolescent experiences the Uranus sextile before the Jupiter sextile, parents may view their child as needing more guidance for following the expectations of the home environment (which would include expectations in school). In the Case Studies section, subjects with this tendency are noted as "rebels". If an adolescent experiences the Jupiter sextile before the Uranus sextile, parents may view their child as needing more encouragement for academic work and possibly with social skills. In the Case Studies section, subjects with this tendency are noted as "truth seekers". There is no "good" or "bad" with these notations and they are only presented as starting points for understanding the life-long impact this stage of development has on learners as they continue their journey all the way into old age. To demonstrate how this particular stage of development can vary from person to person, there is a summary of the time frame for the subjects of the case studies on page 208.

Furthermore, an adolescent's developing body means they may be interested in forming intimate relationships but their brain needs time to catch up with all the new situations it finds itself in.

For children born with Jupiter in Sagittarius, Jupiter will be transiting through the sign of Aquarius as it had during their second year. What Jupiter in Sagittarius learners may crave more than anything is freedom. They may resist boundaries so much that it may feel easier to just give in and let them get on with it. Don't. One of the methods these learners might try is to get the parents and teachers to disagree so they are so busy arguing with each other that no one notices the learner has wandered off to do whatever it was they were trying to get to do in the first place. It's worth trying to keep a united front and to be sure all involved understand the rules of engagement during this very tricky time.

The Saturn Opposition

The Saturn opposition begins some time during the fourteenth or fifteenth year (possibly earlier or later depending on individual cases) and marks the end of astrological adolescence. Parents and teachers usually notice that the adolescent begins to calm down and take a more mature approach to their academic progress. In the UK, this coincides with choosing academic subjects (as opposed to trying a little bit of everything), formal exam preparation and a marked change in mood. Depression, anxiety and their symptoms must be monitored and taken seriously. Schools will have access to support mechanisms for parents and carers, teachers will have been trained in how to identify potential difficulties and for parents who are home schooling, social services can be a sound source for help.

As they head towards their transiting Saturn opposition, Jupiter in Sagittarius children will also re-visit what they had learned as transiting Jupiter once again passes through the signs of Pisces and Aries. During these years, there may be a sort of awakening that inspires the Jupiter in Sagittarius learner to put some action behind their dreams. These adolescents tend to be ambitious and, if given the chance during their Jupiter return, are deeply curious about the world outside of their homes and classrooms.

Re-visiting the appropriate stage of astrological development can be helpful in providing the right sort of help and support.

The Second Jupiter Opposition

By the time a young adult finishes mandatory education, they will have a good idea of what they want to do with their lives and yet they still have time to re-take exams or re-train if they discover they want to do something else. The second Jupiter opposition is a time of making serious decisions: the young adult is no longer a child. The learner now knows there are consequences for undesirable behaviour and can no longer blame "the system" for their poor choices. Sadly, our prison services are filled with young people who have slipped through the net. As a collective whole, society could do with using a little astrology to help these young people get back on track. A more comprehensive mentoring service could be helpful.

Here are some ideas to help young adults focus on the rest of their adult lives:

Transiting Jupiter will be in Gemini as the young adult finishes their formal education at around the age of eighteen. Because Gemini is associated with gathering information, Jupiter in Sagittarius learners may be drawn to media studies, teaching, journalism or marketing. Obviously this tendency varies wildly between individuals but usually there is a strong need for disseminating knowledge.

The Second and Subsequent Jupiter Returns

As a person continues to develop emotionally, physically and spiritually they will build on the lessons they learned in their formative years. Jupiter returns (roughly) at the ages of 24, 36, 48 and 60 (and beyond). The suggestions for activities can be modified to suit the developmental cycle for each Jupiter cycle. For example, a Jupiter in Sagittarius learner experiencing a Jupiter in Aquarius transit during their third year of life can be encouraged to take an interest into make believe lands; during their fifteenth year, they may wish to plan a trip for their gap year; during their twenty-seventh year, they may wish to learn a different language or take a unique course that no one else in the social group has taken. The key for all Jupiter returns is to choose a skill (or even one per year) and exercise the brain, all the way to the final years of life. As always, with Jupiter, the sky is the limit.

Jupiter returns at all ages should be celebrated and an experienced astrologer can help locate the exact moment of the return. New clothes to reflect a changing style, a good meal (with a magnificent dessert) with influential friends and maybe even a holiday to some exotic place are just a few ideas. To celebrate the ingress (entry) of Jupiter in a new sign, consult the table in the appendix. The Chinese culture does a wonderful job with celebrating "The Year of the…". While theirs may be a different culture and system, the similarity of intention is still there.

Fine Tuning Jupiter in Sagittarius

Jupiter in Sagittarius is ruled by Jupiter. Jupiter in this sign is at its most potent.

Case Studies

Timothée Chalamet

Timothée Chalamet was born on 27 December 1995 at 21:16 (RR:AA; Collector: de Jabrun) in Manhattan, NY, with Jupiter in Sagittarius. Although he has only just reached his first Saturn return, he has already received several accolades for his performances.

Transiting Jupiter in Capricorn was conjunct his natal Mars when he was inspired to pursue a career in acting after watching *The Dark Knight*, released in the summer of 2008. He experienced his transiting Jupiter in Aquarius sextile his natal Jupiter about five months before transiting Uranus in Pisces formed a sextile to his natal Uranus in Capricorn—marking him as a truth seeker. Unusually, he experienced his Saturn opposition before these Jupiter and Uranus sextiles.

Chalamet is bilingual in French and English and eventually learned Italian for a film role. He is Jewish on his mother's side and has a Protestant background on his father's—an enriching mix of languages and philosophies for a truth-seeking Jupiter in Sagittarius native. He was accepted into a performing arts school in 2009.

In 2011, he played a sexually curious twelve-year-old in *The Talls*, as transiting Jupiter in Aries opposed both his natal Chiron and Venus

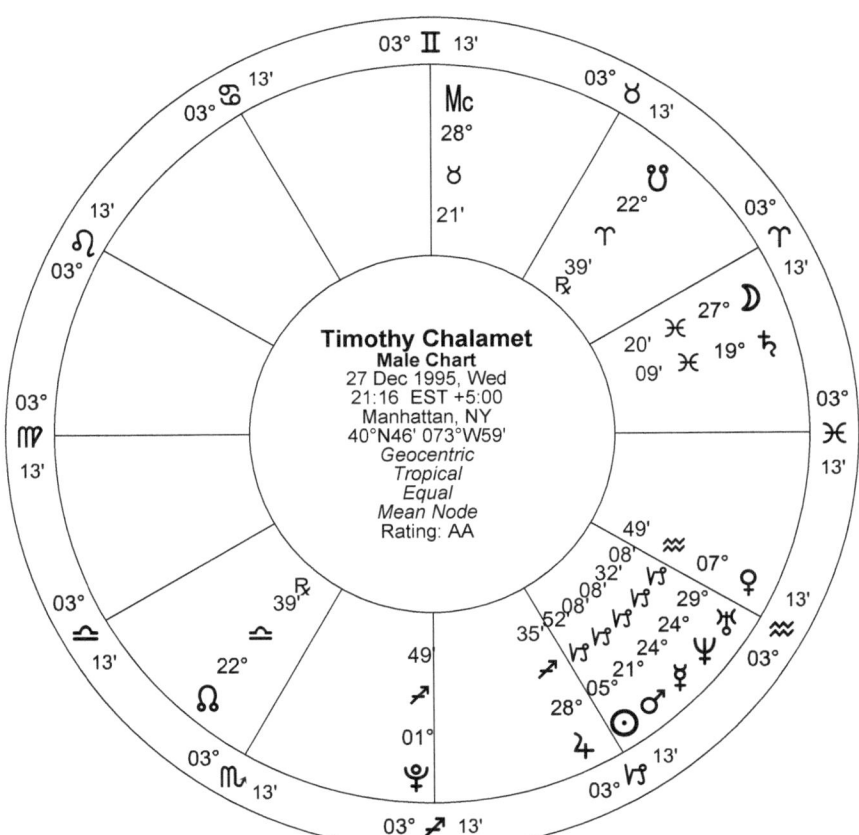

in Aries. After high school, he attended Columbia University but found it difficult to return to his studies following the release of *Interstellar* in November 2014, as transiting Jupiter in Cancer opposed his natal Uranus. He eventually transferred but later dropped out to focus on acting and avoid student debt.

Chalamet continued to play minor roles for several years until transiting Jupiter approached its second opposition. He came to international attention in *Call Me by Your Name*, released in January 2017, as transiting Jupiter in Libra was conjunct his natal Chiron three times. The film, a coming-of-age story, earned him an Oscar nomination for Best Actor—making him the third-youngest nominee in that category. For the role, Chalamet learned to play both guitar and piano.

In 2018, he starred in *Beautiful Boy*, based on a true story of a son's descent into addiction. Transiting Jupiter in Sagittarius was conjunct his natal Pluto.

In 2019, as the film *A Rainy Day in New York* was released, Chalamet came under fire due to renewed allegations against director Woody Allen. This occurred just prior to his second Jupiter return. Chalamet publicly distanced himself from the controversy by donating his salary to charity.

Chalamet's next major film, *Wonka* (2023), was filmed as transiting Jupiter in Aries again opposed his natal Chiron. This was followed by *Dune: Part Two*, which *Variety* noted as solidifying Chalamet's status as a major star—just as Jupiter in Gemini opposed his natal Pluto in Sagittarius.

However, it is likely that *A Complete Unknown*—a Bob Dylan biopic—will become one of his most iconic roles. Filming began during his second Jupiter return (2019) and the film was released in 2024, as transiting Jupiter in Gemini made a series of squares to his natal Saturn in Pisces. In the film, Chalamet sings 40 Dylan songs, plays guitar and harmonica, and also served as producer. It may be worth noting that his Moon in Pisces is conjunct Dylan's natal North Node.

With encouragement and innate confidence, it would seem Jupiter in Sagittarius can do just about anything—except be put in a box.

Dua Lipa

Dua Lipa was born on 22 August 1995 at 00:18 in London, UK (RR: A; Collector: Astrodienst). She has Jupiter in Sagittarius and her Albanian name "Dua" translates to "Love" in English—a fitting name for someone with a Sun-Venus conjunction in Leo in the third house.

Her father was the lead singer and guitarist of an Albanian rock band, an early musical influence on Lipa. When Kosovo declared independence in 2008, the family moved to Pristina. At this time, she was around thirteen years old and experienced transiting Jupiter in Pisces sextile her natal Jupiter in Sagittarius about eight weeks before transiting Uranus in Pisces sextile her natal Uranus in Capricorn - indicating a truth seeker.

While in Pristina, she reconnected with her Albanian roots and began considering a career in music. Transiting Jupiter in Aquarius opposed her Sun–Venus conjunction in Leo when she returned to the UK alone in 2010

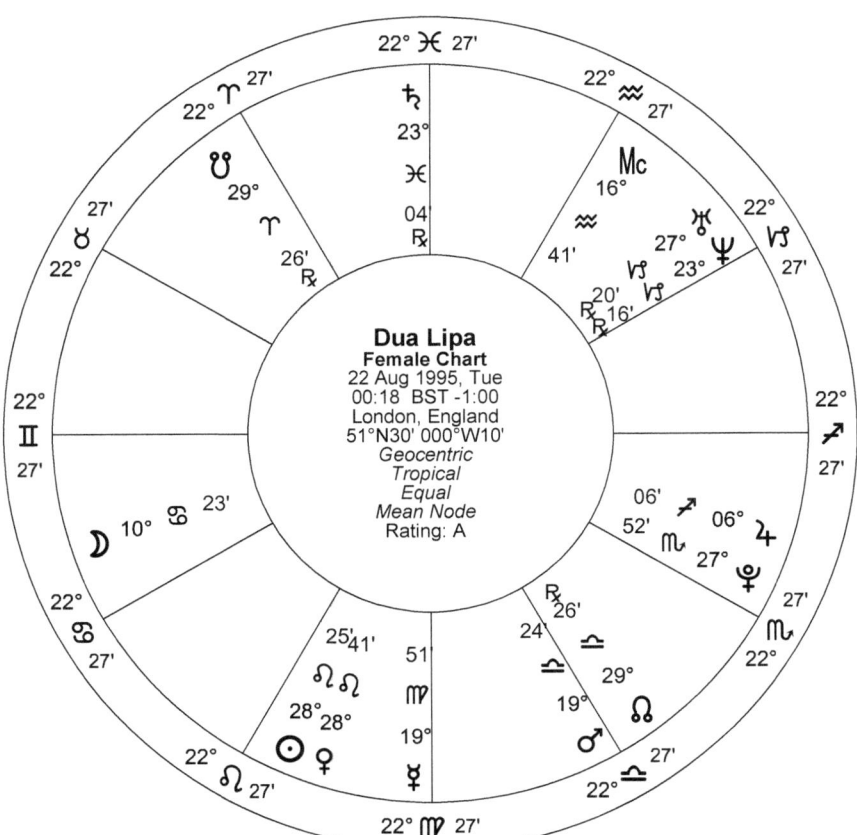

to attend the Sylvia Young Theatre School part-time. She began uploading song covers to YouTube and worked as a model for Topshop. In 2013, her agency helped her land a spot in an *X Factor* commercial, coinciding with Jupiter in Cancer crossing over her Moon. She also worked at a cocktail bar and hired a lawyer to help her secure a record deal that same year. Only a Jupiter in Sagittarius native would have a lawyer at eighteen.

In 2015, she signed with Warner Bros. Records as transiting Jupiter crossed over her natal Leo placements. Appropriately, her first single was titled 'New Love'. In late 2016, she featured on Sean Paul's single 'No Lie', just before transiting Jupiter in Libra made three conjunctions to her natal Mars. Six years later, the single became a top-ten hit in ten countries as transiting Jupiter in Aries began to square her natal planets in Leo.

Her debut album was released in June 2017, just before the final hit of Jupiter conjunct her Mars. As of 2024, *New Rules* had streamed over three billion views on YouTube, and Lipa performed at Glastonbury that summer, as transiting Jupiter in Libra opposed her Mars and North Node.

Lipa has earned seven Brit Awards, three Grammy Awards, an MTV Music Award, and numerous other honours. She has received nine Spotify 1-billion-stream plaques, holds two Guinness World Records (including most tickets sold for a livestreamed concert), and in 2024, was named one of *Time* magazine's 100 most influential people in the world.

Sagittarius rules the hips and thighs—symbols of freedom and movement. It's safe to say that Dua Lipa, with her Jupiter in Sagittarius, was born to run—and dance—all the way to global superstardom.

Jupiter in Capricorn

Capricorn is an earth sign by element and a cardinal sign by modality. Transiting squares and oppositions to its natal position will take place about every three years in the other cardinal signs, Aries, Cancer and Libra. This pattern will repeat for the rest of the native's life, defining how a person learns, grows and develops a personal philosophy. Cardinal signs are independent, self-sufficient and enterprising and they need to be led towards learning how to work with others. Jupiter in Capricorn is very dutiful and responsible. They will complete their work to a high standard but often need to be encouraged to push themselves out of their safety zones.

Jupiter transits through signs at a pace of about one sign per year. It is important to note that as children are taught by year group, they will learn alongside other children with Jupiter in Capricorn. Depending on the time of year they were born, they will also have classmates with either Jupiter in Sagittarius or Jupiter in Aquarius. This topic has been explored in depth in *Growing Pains: Astrology in Adolescence*. Jupiter in Capricorn children tend to be quite cautious and conservative when it comes to their education. They tend to play it safe career-wise, opting for occupations that are traditionally meant to last a lifetime and make as much money as possible. Although associated with ambition and achievement, Jupiter in Capricorn pupils may need to be pushed to achieve beyond expectations. Saturn, Jupiter in Capricorn's ruling planet, holds such tight boundaries that these learners will keep to the required syllabus and avoid independent study if they are allowed to.

The First Jupiter Square

All babies need the basics of adequate nutrition, a safe place to sleep, cleanliness and a comfortable environment. They also need the human touch in order to build trust and to feel their caregiver is responding to their signals for these necessities. Eye contact, talking/singing to the baby

and providing a daily rhythm of sleep, cleaning, feeding and playing with age appropriate toys are essential for all babies, irrespective of the Jupiter signs. As the baby grows into a toddler, it is important caregivers have adequately "baby proofed" the child's environment. These essential needs are important all the way into old age. Once these needs are met consistently, a bit of astrology can help the caregivers find the learner's internal "beat" for development.

At some point during the first year of their life, the Jupiter in Capricorn learner will experience Jupiter transiting through the sign of Aquarius. As the learner is a baby, the world is simply full of learning opportunities. Natally, the Jupiter in Capricorn learner may lean towards astringent, legume-based foods, pears, apples and sprouts.

Jupiter will transit through the sign of Pisces during the Jupiter in Capricorn's second year. It can be easy to imagine babies of this age attending festivals with their parents where they are both inspired and inspiring to those around them. If the parents (or grandparents) are not the New Age type, there may be something about these toddlers that seems ethereal or even other worldly. They may prefer unusual music (and no matter how young they are, they will let you know their preferences as well as remember their early choices later in life). Children of this age tend to be extremely impressionable and sensitive to harsh sounds, colours or tastes and textures.

As they enter their third year, Jupiter in Capricorn learners will experience transiting Jupiter in Aries. A calm, placid Jupiter in Capricorn learner may suddenly wake up as a toddler who has no fear in letting anyone know what they want. As their speech is still developing, they may resort to tactics such as physically lashing out when they don't get their own way. As with all aggressive behaviour, the parents must be clear on what is acceptable and have a united front: these learners tend to have both the energy and endurance to persist until they get what they want.

Young Jupiter in Capricorn children tend to play the game of life in a step-by-step fashion: they'll put up with the parents being a little different, then they'll watch and wait as the right time approaches and they'll explode with their own ideas of how they want to do things. For parents and carers, this can be tiring. As it is often said in childhood, if this stage seems difficult, it won't last forever.

The First Jupiter Opposition

Between the ages of about three and six years old, most young children are preparing for formal education and socialisation. These are just some ideas to help Jupiter in Capricorn learners prepare for their first adventures away from their immediate care givers.

During the fourth year, Jupiter will transit through the sign of Taurus for Jupiter in Capricorn learners. Both Capricorn and Taurus are "down to earth" signs and are concerned with the practical sides of life. For children at this stage of development, there may be a marked period of growth, matched by a voracious appetite—and it's usually the sweet stuff they will go for. As persistent as these learners can be, it is worth noting that Saturn (Capricorn's ruler) governs the bones and teeth. And we all know sugar can be bad for both the teeth and for bone growth as well as for weight gain. Whilst it may be true most people like the sugary stuff, for Jupiter in Capricorn learners, it is usually important to promote healthy eating from a young age. These children should be able to understand that junk for is for "now and again" and not for every day consumption. They will appreciate rules to help them manage their growing bodies and steady routines so they know what is expected of them.

Activities for enjoyment and learning outside of school: outdoor walks, animal watching, tasting different foods, sensory activities and toys, simple physical strength exercises, collecting interesting things (and keeping them organised).

As Jupiter transits the sign of Gemini in their fifth year, Jupiter in Capricorn children may become frustrated with what they perceive as a lack of structure in their education. These are learners who like to know what it is they are supposed to be getting out of the tasks that are set for them and they tend not to like a frivolous approach to learning. For these reasons, learning intentions (even at this young age) should be clear with no ambiguity and a rewards structure should be in place to keep them motivated. They tend to work at their best if they understand that once their work is finished, they can go outside and play. However, there should also be incentives to encourage them to go above and beyond the basics. Here is where teachers need a delicate balance: if you dangle achievement in front of them like a carrot on a stick, they will keep going for the reward - but they won't learn to enjoy learning for the intrinsic value of it. Praise them for when they do a bit extra and ensure they can see how they compare to others in a way that doesn't intimidate them into silence (it is generally necessary to understand their targets at all times). Ensure parents understand this as well so they can reinforce hard work at home without adding undue pressure at such a young age. Activities for enjoyment and learning outside of school: singing, synonyms for common words, giving names to unfamiliar items, becoming familiar with numbers and letters through simple calligraphy.

Jupiter moves on to transit through the sign of Cancer during a Jupiter in Capricorn learner's sixth year. This is a time of plumbing emotional depths, and issues regarding the family or the family lineage will likely hit a raw nerve. A family secret may come to light or there may be crises that distract the otherwise hardworking learner into allowing education to take a backseat. Schools have resources that can help families find the support they need and it is important that Jupiter in Capricorn children understand that they never have to shoulder burdens on their own: they need to see parents and carers (and even teachers) be vulnerable and unafraid to ask for help if they need it.

Activities for enjoyment and learning outside of school: taking care of animals, singing (as a way to cope with negative emotions), helping with the cooking, taking responsibility for the management of one area of their living space, learning how to take care of their clothes and beds, visiting museums or investigating certain times in history.

This Jupiter opposition is about learning to harness their resources, taking stock of their capabilities and dealing effectively with their emotions. If they see adults managing then they will be able to develop into capable adults when it's their turn to successfully run a household. Children really do learn from what they observe.

The Closing Jupiter Square

By this stage, children will have settled into a home/school routine and it is likely schools will begin to prepare students for the Scholastic Achievement Tests (or their equivalents). Debate rages as to whether these tests cause stress for the children but, drawing from personal experience, students tend not to get too upset if the adults around them don't behave as if the world is coming to an end. The purpose of these tests is to help identify strengths and weaknesses in the child's development. The results establish a baseline, not a final outcome. Here are some ways to help support the learners during these formative times:

During their seventh year, Jupiter in Capricorn learners will experience Jupiter as it transits through the sign of Leo. This is the learners' chance to show what they can do and just in time for SATs too. Many parents and carers may not agree about the importance of SATs to children of this age but the results help educators find gaps in learning and then support the students as they fill in where their weaknesses lie. The learners themselves tend to take pride in their work and they may be keen to show off exactly what they have been learning. However, one aspect Jupiter in Capricorn pupils may struggle with at this stage of development is the lack of opportunity to show off their creative skills. Unfortunately SATs are not about measuring their progress in physical education or how well they manage the watercolours or their beautiful vocabulary in short stories. SATs are about the basic structures in education: reading, writing (spelling, punctuation and grammar) and Maths. Jupiter in Capricorn is about stripping everything down to the essentials so if these learners understand the purpose of being tested, they will be motivated to do well.

Activities for enjoyment and learning outside of school: stage play, making and wearing costumes and masks, dressing up to go to an event.

As their eighth year approaches, Jupiter in Capricorn learners will have Jupiter transiting through the sign of Virgo. By this time, the results of the SATs are in and schools will be carefully analysing the results to ensure their precious resources are put into the right places to do the most good. Pupils can feel they have no control over their learning which can be frustrating for Jupiter in Capricorn learners who will most likely be aware of where their weaknesses lie. Instead of simply allocating extra assistance where the data indicates it is needed, it may help to consult the children about what kind of help they think they need. Student conferencing need not take up lots of time: simple surveys or even brief discussions with them can help identify where the child lacks confidence. Listening to concerns not only builds relationships, it also builds confidence.

Activities for enjoyment and learning outside of school: learning about the physical body of people or animals, learning about sickness and how to take care of someone (or a pet) who is not feeling well, understanding the basics of medicine. Learning to identify plants and different species of animals, learning to measure accurately with simple tools such as rulers.

Jupiter will transit Libra during the ninth year of a Jupiter in Capricorn's academic journey. These pupils are likely to be very sensitive to any difficulties in the relationships of the adults they care about. They may dislike the messiness of conflict and may try to use methods of resolution that can seem like far more mature skills than they are ready for—and as young children, they lack the experience to do this type of reconciliation with consistent success. Rather than allowing them to leave it up to the adults, it could be a great learning opportunity to help them understand why people argue and why they can't resolve their own difficulties with relationships. Children (and adults too) often fall back on their instincts when faced with a dispute: people either fight, fly away or freeze with indecision. Getting to the bottom of a problem and bringing it into the light teaches these children a skill they will never forget: that everyone has disputes at some point and that agreeing to find solutions together can preserve a relationship. And sadly, they will also learn not everyone is willing to find a middle ground.

Activities for enjoyment and learning outside of school: planning a themed party with a few friends (try themes based around *Horrible Histories* or their favourite kids' movies) and have "preparation parties" where all the invitees have to make their own party favours and costumes, plan their food and activities, etc.

It is a tough lesson but as they face their closing Jupiter square, Jupiter in Capricorn children can develop the confidence to face challenges with a cool, analytical head.

The Jupiter Return

As the child heads towards their final years of primary school, they should be able to work more independently, understand the general rules of the classroom/playground and see home and school as two separate environments.

During their tenth year, Jupiter in Capricorn learners will experience Jupiter transiting through the sign of Scorpio. As with their lessons when Jupiter transited through Cancer, learning may tend to be around emotional issues, particularly with letting go of people and/or situations that are no longer serving their purpose. As these learners get ready to leave their childhoods behind and start secondary school, they may come across as if they really can't wait to start their new life. More sensitive fellow pupils may be slightly offended but really, most of them at this stage of development have outgrown the family-style learning environment and look forward to taking a bigger bite of the academic pie. However, beneath the eagerness to move forward is a sort of grieving process for leaving the past behind. Changes can be difficult for anyone, but Jupiter in Capricorn can wish they could go back in time to make things better. They may worry about their SATs papers (both the past one and the one that will come up the following year). Something about moving forward can haunt them. Allowing them to express their concerns gives parents, teachers and carers the chance to reassure them that change is inevitable and that we can only look ahead to the future.

Activities for enjoyment and learning outside of school: mysteries and puzzles, being *gently* frightened (Halloween or cold, dark autumn nights are a good time to share simple ghost stories), nature walks so they can observe the cycle of life in plants and animals (NB: learners at this stage may take an interest in death and pregnancies so be prepared to explain).

As their eleventh year approaches, Jupiter in Capricorn learners will experience Jupiter transiting through the sign of Sagittarius. These learners will leave the melancholy of the previous year behind, their physical energy tends to begin to perk up and they seem to look forward to the challenges of secondary school. One thing they really know how to do at this stage of their development is throw a party. Let them (within careful boundaries). School carnivals/festivals are just a couple of ways of ensuring everyone can take part in the celebrations without costing the parents/carers (or school) an arm and a leg. These students have learned to be incredibly savvy and, despite their over-the-top enthusiasm, they have enough common sense to keep safety measures in mind as well as keep to a budget (no one can bargain like an earth sign). This is the last hurrah of childhood. Let them let their hair down.

Activities for enjoyment and learning outside of school: taking part in charity work, visiting places of worship, learning to discuss politics and identifying political leaders, learning about different countries (their map, geographical features, language, etc.).

Jupiter in Capricorn will return to its natal position at some time during the twelfth year. The raw exuberance of the previous year may morph into a mature approach to learning but the enthusiasm to gain knowledge is there. Young adolescents of this age (just starting secondary school) often feel engulfed by the new experiences of the bigger school. They tend to be overwhelmed by all the things they have to do and may often need to be reminded that everything is just a step-by-step process. They have five years to prepare for the GCSE exams and at least two more years beyond that before they have to worry about college in earnest. What they will need is parents and carers to help keep them focused on prioritising tasks—at least at first. Jupiter in Capricorn learners will soon get to grips with all the challenges of their first term and will soon become experts in this thing called secondary school.

Activities for enjoyment and learning outside of school: hobbies that encourage one step at a time, like wool craft, learning to do simple carpentry skills, learning to do "handyman/woman" jobs around the house, activities that encourage business skills.

When we return to a place have visited before, it is our nature to make comparisons to what has changed since the first time we were there. We may want to seek out the things we did before or perhaps try something completely different.

As almost all students will have had their first Jupiter return by the end of their first year of secondary school, schools could hold an end of year festival that would allow pupils to demonstrate their individual skills. Schools tend to hold sporting events during this time but how about a Careers Fair? Students could interview successful people from a variety of careers and put together a show piece of the best projects.

The Jupiter and Uranus Sextiles: In the Thick of Puberty

As noted in the Introduction, the thirteenth year of a child's life is usually when rebellion and defiance begin to become noticeable. Astrologically, transiting Jupiter forms a sextile aspect to its natal position at the same time Uranus, the planet of rebellion, will also make its first Ptolemaic aspect to its own natal position (also by sextile aspect). This combination quite literally means "big rebellion" and marks the time when adolescents (and their parents) begin the struggle to make that separation into adulthood.

Identifying when and how a young adolescent may struggle with the changing social rules they must face could be helpful for parents. For example, if an adolescent experiences the Uranus sextile before the Jupiter sextile, parents may view their child as needing more guidance for following the expectations of the home environment (which would include expectations in school). In the Case Studies section, subjects with this tendency are noted as "rebels". If an adolescent experiences the Jupiter sextile before the Uranus sextile, parents may view their child as needing more encouragement for academic work and possibly with social skills. In the Case Studies section, subjects with this tendency are noted as "truth seekers". There is no "good" or "bad" with these notations and they are only presented as starting points for understanding the life-long impact this stage of development has on learners as they continue their journey all the way into old age. To demonstrate how this particular stage of development can vary from person to person, there is a summary of the time frame for the subjects of the case studies on page 208.

Furthermore, an adolescent's developing body means they may be interested in forming intimate relationships, but their brain needs time to catch up with all the new situations it finds itself in.

For children born with Jupiter in Capricorn, Jupiter will be transiting through the sign of Pisces as it had been during their second year. This is quite a crucial year as pupils tend to be considering their choices for exam subjects, a decision that will have a long term impact on their career choices. For some Jupiter in Capricorn students, the temptation would be to take easy options (at least as they might see it) rather than more challenging subjects such as extra Maths or Science. It is important for them to reflect on their ambitions and perhaps have some career guidance to help them make the right decisions for their future interests. Some time out away from the pressure may also help as the deadline for making choices approaches. A seaside or oceanic holiday can help them clear their heads and give them some space to decide what is really right for them.

The Saturn Opposition

The Saturn opposition begins some time during the fourteenth or fifteenth year (possibly earlier or later depending on individual cases) and marks the end of astrological adolescence. Parents and teachers usually notice that the adolescent begins to calm down and take a more mature approach to their academic progress. In the UK, this coincides with choosing academic subjects (as opposed to trying a little bit of everything), formal exam preparation and a marked change in mood. Depression, anxiety and their symptoms must be monitored and taken seriously. Schools will have access to support mechanisms for parents and carers, teachers will have been trained in how to identify potential difficulties and for parents who are home schooling, social services can be a sound source for help.

As they head towards their transiting Saturn opposition, Jupiter in Capricorn adolescents will also re-visit what they learned as transiting Jupiter once again passes through the signs of Aries and Taurus. This time can be like a shot of adrenaline as they mull over what is more important to them. It can be like an academic second wind.

The Second Jupiter Opposition

By the time a young adult finishes mandatory education, they will have a good idea of what they want to do with their lives and yet they still have time to re-take exams or re-train if they discover they want to do something else. The second Jupiter opposition is a time of making serious decisions: the young adult is no longer a child. The learner now knows there are consequences for undesirable behaviour and can no longer blame "the system" for their poor choices. Sadly, our prison services are filled with young people who have slipped through the net. As a collective whole, society could do with using a little astrology to help these young people get back on track. A more comprehensive mentoring service could be helpful.

Here are some ideas to help young adults focus on the rest of their adult lives:

Transiting Jupiter will be in Cancer as the young adult finishes their formal education at around the age of eighteen. Jupiter in Capricorn tends to be quite conservative when it comes to choosing a career. And they tend to make their choices with a future family (however they envisage this) in mind. With the odd exception, these learners are very sensible, hard working and even those who have been overlooked tend to knuckle-down and grow up fast once they commence their careers.

The Second and Subsequent Jupiter Returns

As a person continues to develop emotionally, physically and spiritually they will build on the lessons they learned in the formative years. Jupiter returns (roughly) at the ages of 24, 36, 48 and 60 (and beyond). The suggestions for activities can be modified to suit the developmental cycle for each Jupiter cycle. For example, a Jupiter in Capricorn learner experiencing a Jupiter in Pisces transit during their third year of life can be encouraged to listen to music or even play an instrument whilst following a simple rhythmic structure; during their fifteenth year, they may wish to try a different instrument or perhaps try a similar instrument but with cadences from a different culture; during their twenty-seventh year, they may wish to perform professionally. The key for all Jupiter returns is to choose a skill (or even one per year) and exercise the brain, all the way to the final years of life. As always, with Jupiter, the sky is the limit.

Jupiter returns at all ages should be celebrated and an experienced astrologer can help locate the exact moment of the return. New clothes to reflect a changing style, a good meal (with a magnificent dessert) with influential friends and maybe even a holiday to some exotic place are just a few ideas. To celebrate the ingress (entry) of Jupiter in a new sign, consult the table in the appendix. The Chinese culture does a wonderful job with celebrating, "The Year of the…". While theirs may be a different culture and system, the similarity of intention is still there.

Fine tuning the role of Jupiter:

Jupiter in Capricorn is ruled by Saturn, the planet of hard work and commitment. The combination of Jupiter and Saturn typically means steady progress. Saturn's position in the zodiac gives an indication as to how a person works towards his/her goals. Saturn also represents authority figures so parents and teachers need to be aware of the effects their discipline has on the children's minds.

Saturn in Aries: These pupils learn to work towards self-employment. Typically, they prefer their own company because they fear others will only hold them back. Group work situations can end with these pupils walking off in disgust and working on their own.

Saturn in Taurus: These pupils learn to work with sheer brute strength and the force of inertia because they never understand how strong they are. They can withstand long periods of isolation and study and often overdo it.

Saturn in Gemini: These pupils learn to work on using their minds efficiently. They doubt their intelligence and so doggedly plod their way through the educational system. Occasionally they give up completely. Teachers usually need to keep assuring them they are doing well even if it seems they are confident in what they are doing. Parents usually find these children don't say much but when they do, their words become solid household law.

Saturn in Cancer: These pupils work on preventing themselves from revealing too much. They are naturally protective of their true selves and take pains to conceal their emotions. They often need to be encouraged to care about their education.

Saturn in Leo: These pupils work on presenting their best face. They are often terrified of failing—though tempted to show off. They lack self-confidence but resent living in someone's shadows.

Saturn in Virgo: These pupils work on finding perfection in learning. Their minds work like highly tuned machines programmed to discard any problems. They are highly critical of themselves and others and never seem to take a break from their self-imposed duty of finding fault in everything.

Saturn in Libra: These pupils work towards learning to commit themselves to their studies. They learn early on that they can't do everything and therefore must pick and choose what is right for them. This can sometimes take a very long time and they may need some assistance with decision making processes.

Saturn in Scorpio: These pupils work towards controlling their learning. They will have an idea of what they want to do from an early age and will be very sure what they need to do to reach their goals because they have researched it so well.

Saturn in Sagittarius: These pupils work towards expanding their horizons. Quite spontaneously, these pupils understand they face insurmountable restrictions and will embark on any means necessary to remove any barriers they may face.

Saturn in Capricorn: These pupils work towards their goals without too much need for guidance. They are naturally at ease with hard work and will resist changes in the status quo.

Saturn in Aquarius: These pupils work towards being free of responsibilities. They can convince themselves they are mavericks but realise that even mavericks have their own codes of honour.

Saturn in Pisces: These pupils work towards securing their place in a world of chaos. They can see the world in all its unpredictability as a hostile environment waiting to swallow them up.

Case Studies

Lorde

Ella Marija Lani Yelich-O'Connor was born on 7 November 1996 at 10:00 a.m. (RR: A rating; Collector: Treindl) in Takapuna, New Zealand, with Jupiter in Capricorn and Saturn in Aries. With Jupiter right on her Ascendant, it is perhaps unsurprising that she would eventually be known as "Lorde".

Identified as a gifted child from the age of six—around the time of her first Jupiter opposition—Lorde was already excelling. While transiting Jupiter in Scorpio was conjunct her natal Mercury three times, she and her school teammates placed very highly (third and first) in national speech competitions in 2006 and 2007. As transiting Jupiter in Aquarius squared her natal Mercury in 2009, she and her team were runners-up in a global literature competition for children aged ten to fourteen. That same year, still under the influence of the Jupiter-Mercury square, she was signed to Universal Music Group for further development. In May of that year, her band placed third in the North Shore Battle of the Bands finals.

And this was all before she'd experienced her Jupiter and Uranus sextile transits.

In adolescence, she had her transiting Jupiter in Pisces sextile her natal Jupiter in Capricorn in 2010, about a year before transiting Uranus in Aries formed a sextile to her natal Uranus in Aquarius—indicating she is a truth seeker. Her avid reading habits are testament to this.

She performed original songs for the first time in November 2011, almost to the day of her final Uranus-Uranus sextile in adolescence. A year later, in November 2012, Lorde self-released her extended play 'The Love Club', eventually selling more than ten million units worldwide, as transiting Jupiter opposed her natal Mercury. And she was only sixteen years old. To top it off, she also won two Grammy Awards.

Lorde's debut studio album *Pure Heroine* was released in September 2013, just as transiting Jupiter in Cancer crossed her Ascendant and opposed her natal Jupiter three times. By November that year, she had signed a $2.5 million publishing deal, and a few weeks later she recorded a cover of 'Everybody Wants to Rule the World' for *The Hunger Games: Catching Fire*. That same year, she was listed in *Time* and *Forbes*, becoming

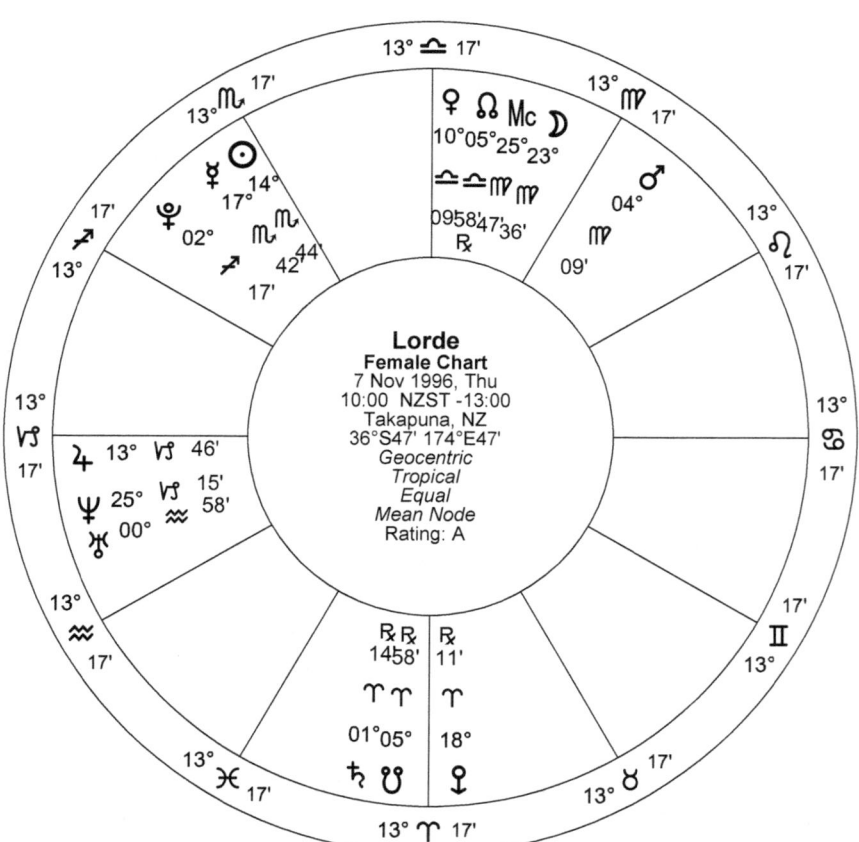

the youngest person ever to be featured on both lists. From 2014, she began a worldwide festival tour, including a performance with Nirvana at their Rock and Roll Hall of Fame induction.

Her second album, *Melodrama*, was released in March 2017 to great acclaim, as transiting Uranus in Aries opposed her natal Chiron. The maturity in her post-breakup lyrics was especially noted. Her third album, *Solar Power*, came six years later, released under a Uranus-in-Taurus opposition to her natal Mercury. Reviews, however, were mixed.

It's astonishing that someone so young has already achieved such a high level of success. As work begins on her fourth studio album, it's safe to assume that this driven Jupiter in Capricorn native will only continue to grow—and if not, she's achieved enough to retire before reaching her first Saturn return.

Prince Harry

Henry Charles Albert David, known affectionately as Prince Harry, was born on 15 September 1984 at 16:20 (RR: AA rating; Collector: Holliday) in London, UK. He has Jupiter in Capricorn, ruled by Saturn in Scorpio. From birth, he was referred to as "the spare," while his elder brother was "the heir". Despite this, the two brothers appeared close during their early years.

Tragically, his mother died the year after his first Jupiter return. During adolescence and this time of deep grief, Prince Harry experienced his transiting Jupiter in Pisces sextile his natal Jupiter in Capricorn just weeks before his transiting Uranus in Aquarius sextile his natal Uranus in Sagittarius—marking him as a truth seeker. Despite a privileged education, he chose a career in the military.

In 2001, during his second Jupiter opposition, Harry admitted to smoking cannabis and taking cocaine. His father encouraged him to visit a drug rehabilitation centre to witness the effects of addiction firsthand.

Like his grandfather, the Duke of Edinburgh, Harry was not immune to controversy. In January 2005, he referred to his Zimbabwean girlfriend as "not Black or anything, you know". Later that year, he was photographed wearing a Nazi uniform at a costume party. At the time, transiting Jupiter was making a series of three conjunctions to his natal Venus. In 2009, he made questionable comments about a Pakistani fellow officer cadet, following a Jupiter-Venus square a few months earlier. In August 2012, photos of a naked Harry and an unidentified woman were leaked to the press, just as transiting Jupiter in Gemini began a series of three oppositions to his natal Uranus in Sagittarius.

Harry began dating Meghan Markle in the early summer of 2016. In 2017, transiting Jupiter in Libra made three conjunctions to his natal Venus. That same year, Harry publicly acknowledged seeking therapy—encouraged by Meghan—to address PTSD and severe anxiety related to his mother's death. Their engagement was announced in November 2017, during a period when transiting Uranus in Aries had been opposing his natal Venus. Transiting Jupiter in Aries was also opposing Venus three times in the lead-up to their engagement. They married while Jupiter in Scorpio was opposing his natal Moon in Taurus.

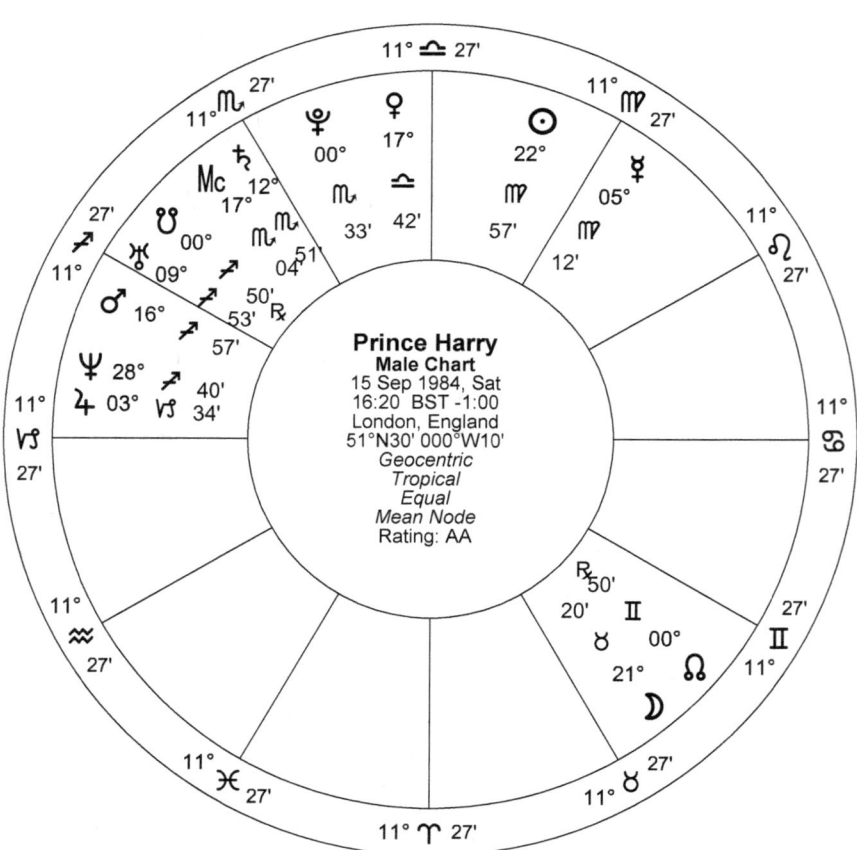

After his marriage, Harry's popularity briefly soared. However, following the couple's decision to step back from royal duties and their widely viewed interview with Oprah in March 2021, public opinion shifted. Just weeks after the interview, transiting Jupiter in Aquarius was opposite its natal position three times, magnifying the fallout as he and Meghan were metaphorically burnt at the stake by public opinion.

Harry's life exemplifies the long shadow that teenage trauma can cast. The loss of his mother in the public eye left a deep emotional scar. Though his call for privacy is complicated by continued public appearances and the use of royal funding, it's clear that this Jupiter in Capricorn native has chosen a more difficult—but more active—path. He could have lived a pampered, passive life, but instead, he has sought meaning through service, personal development, and global advocacy.

Jupiter in Aquarius

Aquarius is an air sign by element and a fixed sign by modality. Transiting squares and oppositions to its natal position will take place about every three years in the other fixed signs, Taurus, Leo and Scorpio. This pattern will repeat for the rest of the native's life, defining how a person learns, grows and develops a personal philosophy. Generally speaking, the fixed signs are resistant to change and for Aquarius, this usually manifests itself in unusual interests and a predilection for working and learning under their own terms. It can be very difficult to persuade Jupiter in Aquarius to move from a very carefully modified work space so they will need fair warning for any upcoming changes.

Jupiter transits through signs at a pace of about one sign per year. It is important to note that as children are taught by year group, they will learn alongside other children with Jupiter in Aquarius. Depending on the time of year they were born, they will also have classmates with either Jupiter in Capricorn or Jupiter in Pisces. This topic has been explored in depth in *Growing Pains: Astrology in Adolescence*.

Children with Jupiter in Aquarius learn through experimentation and invention. They like to tinker with instructions and they tend to modify even the most reliable of methods. More impatient authority figures might call them "rebellious" but if questioned about why they felt they needed to dismantle the toaster (for example), it may be discovered that they only did it because they saw a way of making it function better—even if they can't get the thing to work again. To them an act of love might very well be making someone's life a little easier with their futuristic thinking (kisses and cuddles are sooooo last century). Like the other signs of Jupiter, let's take a look at their phases of development.

The First Jupiter Square

All babies need the basics of adequate nutrition, a safe place to sleep, cleanliness and a comfortable environment. They also need the human touch in order to build trust and to feel their caregiver is responding to their signals for these necessities. Eye contact, talking/singing to the baby and providing a daily rhythm of sleep, cleaning, feeding and playing with age appropriate toys are essential for all babies, irrespective of the Jupiter signs. As the baby grows into a toddler, it is important caregivers have adequately "baby proofed" the child's environment. These essential needs are important all the way into old age. Once these needs are met consistently, a bit of astrology can help the caregivers find the learner's internal "beat" for development.

At some point during the first year of their life, the Jupiter in Aquarius learner will experience Jupiter transiting through the sign of Pisces. As the learner is a baby, the world is simply full of learning opportunities. Natally, the Jupiter in Aquarius learner may lean towards sweet foods but may have unusual tastes in general.

As their second year approaches Jupiter transits into Aries, and the child becomes more active, more mobile and, if it can be believed, even more independent. With strength and growth on their side, they are also faster. Because they tend to do things the unconventional way, they may have a few more bumps and tumbles than other toddlers. This can also include the way they express pain and discomfort: most children holler loudly if they get hurt. Jupiter in Aquarius learners may just rub their boo-boo with annoyance and get on with the task of tearing up any rule book in sight. They may good-naturedly tolerate any kisses to soothe said boo-boo but usually their reaction is to push the sympathiser aside and head to the nearest corner so they can cry in peace. They might not like it but they do need to let carers do their job by making sure there are no significant injuries that might need more professional attention. One of the great lessons of this stage is recognising that their heads are more than just battering rams.

Jupiter in Aquarius children will experience transiting Jupiter in Taurus some time during their third year. Like Aquarius, Taurus is a fixed sign which means the laws of inertia are very much in full swing: getting them to move when they're quiet and still is just as much a challenge as getting them to stop whatever it is they're doing and try something else. An activity they might enjoy is getting outside and enjoying the great outdoors. Much of this sense of wonder may stem from being curious about whether or not they can actually improve on Mother Nature. Getting them to paint about their experiences may give them the creative expression to experiment with different colours and textures. However, they may need to be monitored a bit more closely in the garden because what might not look good to anyone else might be a tempting snack for Jupiter in Aquarius children during this stage of development.

The first square is the Jupiter in Aquarius learner's first opportunity to make their impact on the world around them. It should be understood they operate from a position of really wanting to make the world a better place simply by doing things a little differently. Always guide them to safety but also allow them the autonomy to do things their way to see if it works. They have much to offer and the desire comes from the right place (even if they break something trying to make it better).

The First Jupiter Opposition

Between the ages of about three to six years old, most young children are preparing for formal education and socialisation. These are just some ideas to help Jupiter in Aquarius learners prepare for their first adventures away from their immediate care givers.

During their fourth year, Jupiter in Aquarius will experience transiting Jupiter in the sign of Gemini. At this stage of development, the world of verbal communication starts to become more accessible. They may recognise numbers and letters but have a slight variation to add when they try to write them on their own. They may be learning to speak but they like to invent new words, or pronounce them in their own unique way. This tends to be a passing phase because the Jupiter in Aquarius learner usually comes to realise that in order to get their message across, they have to be understood by others. As they become more adept at handling pencils or paintbrushes as their fine motor skills continue to develop, their designs become more intricate and perhaps themes begin to emerge such as favourite colours, topics (outer space is usually something that fascinates them) and even a rudimentary understanding of machines might be recognised. Toys that allow them to study movement could also be beneficial—along with an adult who can explain essential physics to them. They usually absorb scientific explanations with glee and, again with carers monitoring safety, they could build on these skills to form basic scientific testing.

Activities for enjoyment and learning outside of school: singing, synonyms for common words, giving names to unfamiliar items, becoming familiar with numbers and letters through simple calligraphy.

As their fifth year approaches with Jupiter transiting through the sign of Cancer, Jupiter in Aquarius learners may hit a bit of a bumpy patch as they embark on their formal education. Whereas they may have seemed ready for school before, they may suddenly prefer to be at home. This is quite logical: at school, there tend to be rigid rules but at home there is freedom to do as they please. School dinners may bear the brunt of their discontent (this can be easily fixed by allowing them to prepare their own nutritious lunches) but they are not likely to enjoy sitting at a table with other children either. Nor will they appreciate it when an adult tries to correct their interpretation of nature, their spellings or their letter formation. But they just may appreciate homework: working from home will allow them the independence and freedom that they can't have at school. With a bit of surreptitious guidance and home-school support, Jupiter in Aquarius learners can complete their tasks to the teacher's specifications (and get praise for it) as well as see school for what it is meant to be: a place where they can learn, demonstrate their knowledge and still maintain their autonomy.

Activities for enjoyment and learning outside of school: taking care of animals, singing (as a way to cope with negative emotions), helping with the cooking, taking responsibility for the management of one area of their living space, learning how to take care of their clothes and beds, visiting museums or investigating certain times in history.

Jupiter in Aquarius children will experience transiting Jupiter in Leo some time during their sixth year. If they were shy about presenting their new ideas for fear of being corrected the previous year, they may have got over it by this stage of development. Aquarius learners of this age will take pride in showing off their work and also working with their friends as part of a group project. They will probably need a bit of guidance to help them share the limelight (and credit) for their work. Around this stage, they will start to become aware of time: they are most likely aware of some sort of routine (like they usually have breakfast before lunch) but they may need to become more aware of taking turns. Classroom stopwatches could provide an opportunity to learn a new skill (how to manage a new machine) at the same time allowing them to learn the life skill of managing their time.

Activities for enjoyment and learning outside of school: stage play, making and wearing costumes and masks, dressing up to go to an event.

The first opposition can give Jupiter in Aquarius pupils ample opportunities to gain new insight from the variety of people they meet in the classroom. Whilst a school routine might seem stiff and rigid, these learners usually become adjusted to it and perhaps even find comfort in. After all, classroom routines are nothing if not time efficient, and these children will begin to understand that saving time equates to more time to do things the way they like at play time.

The Closing Jupiter Square

By this stage, children will have settled into a home/school routine and it is likely schools will begin to prepare students for the Scholastic Achievement Tests (or their equivalents). Debate rages as to whether these tests cause stress for the children but, drawing from personal experience, students tend not to get too upset if the adults around them don't behave as if the world is coming to an end. The purpose of these tests is to help identify strengths and weaknesses in the child's development. The results establish a baseline, not a final outcome. Here are some ways to help support the learners during these formative times:

During their seventh year, transiting Jupiter in Virgo with allow Jupiter in Aquarius pupils the opportunity to refine what they have learned. Using precision should become more important as during this year they will be learning how to read clocks to understand how to manage their time, use rulers to measure short distances and they will have more practical lessons to improve their Maths skills. Language, particularly more precise vocabulary and accurate use of grammar, will also become more important during this stage of development. As these learners become more fluent, it only stands to reason they will be able to get their messages across more efficiently. They will now also be preparing for their SATs and they will take to routines with more enthusiasm than they did when they were younger.

They may begin to see that routines eliminate the "fluff" from their lessons so they can get on with their own highly creative ideas.

Activities for enjoyment and learning outside of school: learning about the physical body of people or animals, learning about sickness and how to take care of someone (or a pet) who is not feeling well, understanding the basics of medicine. Learning to identify plants and different species of animals, learning to measure accurately with simple tools such as rulers.

As their eighth year approaches, Jupiter in Aquarius learners will experience transiting Jupiter in Libra. Working in groups can allow them the opportunity to share ideas and to investigate how other students learn. They may be very vocal (as both Libra and Aquarius are air signs) but they are revising in a manner that is not only fun but makes them think and balance their sometimes off the wall ideas with more grounded thought processes learned from the year before. For parents, holding "study parties" can make revision fun whilst preserving all the lessons Jupiter has brought them in previous years. Despite all the fun they seem to be having, they are also learning the all important social manners that they may not have been ready for when they were younger. They know polite words but during this transit, they can start to see that others respond positively and the idea of gratitude and courtesy can get them far.

Activities for enjoyment and learning outside of school: planning a themed party with a few friends (try themes based around *Horrible Histories* or their favourite kids' movies) and have "preparation parties" where all the invitees have to make their own party favours and costumes, plan their food and activities, etc.

Jupiter in Aquarius learners will have Jupiter transiting through the sign of Scorpio during their ninth year. With SATs out of the way, they can get to grips with the emotional intensity of human relationships. However, these pupils tend to find it difficult to immerse themselves in feelings and instead may try to imitate what they think other people expect them to do. It is very much like the thought is there but the genuine expression seems to fall short. They will dance to a popular song but it may seem contrived; they may like someone but they can't quite put themselves in the other person's shoes to get the notion of what this person actually enjoys doing. Another challenge may be that their interests fall on the side of morbidity: they can talk and write about death but it is from a detached point of view. It's almost like they have put up a barrier that stops them from being submerged completely in the human experience of grief and loss. Any real-life bereavement may see Jupiter in Aquarius children struggle to mourn, especially if it is in a public space. For these reasons, death is something that they should view as part of the circle of life and they should be allowed to express their grief in the manner they can understand rather than the manner in which society expects.

Activities for enjoyment and learning outside of school: mysteries and puzzles, being *gently* frightened (Halloween or cold, dark autumn nights are a good time to share simple ghost stories), nature walks so they can observe the cycle of life in plants and animals (NB: learners at this stage may take an interest in death and pregnancies so be prepared to explain).

This closing square gives Jupiter in Aquarius learners the opportunity to begin to see life as viewed from the perspective of other people. It can be a bit like watching swimmers without getting wet. At some point, whether they jump or are pushed, they eventually come to feel what it is like to truly walk in someone else's shoes.

The Jupiter Return

As the child heads towards their final years of primary school, they should be able to work more independently, understand the general rules of the classroom/playground and see home and school as two separate environments.

During their tenth year, Jupiter in Aquarius learners will experience transiting Jupiter in Sagittarius. This is a time for them to begin taking an interest in different languages and culture. Indeed, they may ask for holidays to far flung places or, if this is not physically possible, they may become the best armchair travellers in their school. They tend to enjoy experiences that are a little different. Encouraging them to study Geography and Religious Education are just two subjects that can allow teachers to indulge their interests. Other ways are taking them to food festivals or even encouraging parents to visit a range of different cuisines to help pique their interests.

Activities for enjoyment and learning outside of school: taking part in charity work, visiting places of worship, learning to discuss politics and identifying political leaders, learning about different countries (their map, geographical features, language, etc.).

As their eleventh year approaches, transiting Jupiter will enter into the sign of Capricorn. As they are drawing close to the end of primary school, these pupils may feel the need to pull out all the stops and really focus on getting off to the right start. Parents can help them feel prepared by getting them into a good, working routine that involves being aware of their activities in the calendar (it will only get more hectic in secondary school) and establishing habits that will serve them on a day-to-day basis as well. What is the best day to do the washing (probably the evening they have physical education)? Other chores such as washing their bed linen, keeping their room tidy (and smelly sock-free), ensuring they have what they need for their lunch and snacks and generally moving towards being more independent are all easy steps to shift a bit more responsibility from parent to child. If parents and carers do not help the Jupiter in Aquarius child work out a solid way of life as they head closer to their first Jupiter return, they can miss the opportunity to take control.

Activities for enjoyment and learning outside of school: hobbies that encourage one step at a time, like wool crafts, learning to do simple carpentry skills, learning to do "handyman/woman" jobs around the house, activities that encourage business skills.

Jupiter in Aquarius will return to its natal position some time during their twelfth year. By this time, secondary school will have started and, along with the other new starters of the academic year, everything can seem quite overwhelming. Pupils of this age tend to huddle together, staying in groups they are familiar with and often mourning their old friendship circles as new circles begin to form. However, Jupiter in Aquarius pupils seem to thrive on the new surroundings and they tend to make friends very easily. They quickly find others with common interests (even amongst the older children) and they usually thrive with all the learning opportunities secondary school can bring. As an academic group, they may excel at Information and Communication Technology (ICT) and they may understand social media even better than the adults around them (all the more reason to monitor them a bit more closely). They may find it challenging to understand the emotions of others but their communication skills can help bridge any gaps.

Activities for enjoyment and learning outside of school: leading/forming a new club and setting rules and expectations, simple science experiments (YouTube is full of ideas of home science experiments—ensure they have permission and understand they have to clean up), learning how to do simple tasks like changing light bulbs, fuses and understanding electrical circuits, recording and monitoring data accurately as part of an experiment.

The Jupiter return for Jupiter in Aquarius pupils brings the understanding that no one can exist without the help of other people. They may have unique ways of getting things done but they will understand the value of teamwork and good communication. Such skills will support their inventive spirit and will lead to many new and valuable innovations as they continue to learn.

When we return to a place have visited before, it is our nature to make comparisons to what has changed since the first time we were there. We may want to seek out the things we did before or perhaps try something completely different.

As almost all students will have had their first Jupiter return by the end of their first year of secondary school, schools could hold an end of year festival that would allow pupils to demonstrate their individual skills. Schools tend to hold sporting events during this time but how about a Science Fair? Students could be unleashed to experiment or research on any (ethical) topic of their choosing with the best ideas to be presented at a formal setting.

The Jupiter and Uranus Sextiles: In the Thick of Puberty

As noted in the Introduction, the thirteenth year of a child's life is usually when rebellion and defiance begin to become noticeable. Astrologically, transiting Jupiter forms a sextile aspect to its natal position at the same time Uranus, the planet of rebellion, will also make its first Ptolemaic aspect to its own natal position (also by sextile aspect). This combination quite literally means "big rebellion" and marks the time when adolescents (and their parents) begin the struggle to make that separation into adulthood.

Identifying when and how a young adolescent may struggle with the changing social rules they must face could be helpful for parents. For example, if an adolescent experiences the Uranus sextile before the Jupiter sextile, parents may view their child as needing more guidance for following the expectations of the home environment (which would include expectations in school). In the Case Studies section, subjects with this tendency are noted as "rebels". If an adolescent experiences the Jupiter sextile before the Uranus sextile, parents may view their child as needing more encouragement for academic work and possibly with social skills. In the Case Studies section, subjects with this tendency are noted as "truth seekers". There is no "good" or "bad" with these notations and they are only presented as starting points for understanding the life-long impact this stage of development has on learners as they continue their journey all the way into old age. To demonstrate how this particular stage of development can vary from person to person, there is a summary of the time frame for the subjects of the case studies on page 208.

Furthermore, an adolescent's developing body means they may be interested in forming intimate relationships but their brain needs time to catch up with all the new situations it finds itself in.

For children born with Jupiter in Aquarius, Jupiter will be transiting through the sign of Aries as it had been during their second year. This is a highly energetic year and students of this age tend to struggle with making sensible decisions. This may be especially so for Jupiter in Aquarius learners who find it difficult to understand the logic behind emotions and therefore override the advice of trusted adults in favour of the less than reliable advice of their friends. As a result, this academic group may need very clear rules and boundaries, especially if agreements have been breached. Trust must be earned and consequences must be followed through with or they may develop the idea that they don't have to take responsibility for their actions.

The Saturn Opposition

The Saturn opposition begins some time during the fourteenth or fifteenth year (possibly earlier or later depending on individual cases) and marks the end of astrological adolescence. Parents and teachers usually notice that the adolescent begins to calm down and take a more mature approach to their academic progress. In the UK, this coincides with choosing academic subjects (as opposed to trying a little bit of everything), formal exam preparation and a marked change in mood. Depression, anxiety and their symptoms must be monitored and taken seriously. Schools will have access to support mechanisms for parents and carers, teachers will have been trained in how to identify potential difficulties and for parents who are home schooling, social services can be a sound source for help.

As they head towards their transiting Saturn opposition, Jupiter in Aquarius children will also re-visit what they had learned as transiting Jupiter once again passes through the signs of Taurus and Gemini. They will tend to develop a sense of belonging and understanding what is important to them as well as experience in branching out with the range of academic interests. Reading and expressing themselves through the written word may take on a particular relevance (they may enjoy science fiction) as they strive to understand the world they live in. Re-visiting the appropriate stage of astrological development can be helpful to provide the right sort of help and support.

The Second Jupiter Opposition

By the time a young adult finishes mandatory education, they will have a good idea of what they want to do with their lives and yet they still have time to re-take exams or re-train if they discover they want to do something else. The second Jupiter opposition is a time of making serious decisions: the young adult is no longer a child. The learner now knows there are consequences for undesirable behaviour and can no longer blame "the system" for their poor choices. Sadly, our prison services are filled with young people who have slipped through the net. As a collective whole, society could do with using a little astrology to help these young people get back on track. A more comprehensive mentoring service could be helpful.

Here are some ideas to help young adults focus on the rest of their adult lives:

Transiting Jupiter will be in Leo as the young adult finishes their formal education at around the age of eighteen. These learners have been patiently sharing their achievements with others but they may crave a bit of credit for the work they have put into tasks like group projects. They may also feel ready to lead or manage groups and while such positions of responsibility can take some getting used to, they are usually very adept at getting others to listen to them because they have the strong belief that everyone should be treated fairly and have a good shot at being successful.

The Second and Subsequent Jupiter Returns

As a person continues to develop emotionally, physically and spiritually they will build on the lessons they learned in the formative years. Jupiter returns (roughly) at the ages of 24, 36, 48 and 60 (and beyond). For example, a Jupiter in Aquarius learner experiencing a Jupiter in Aries transit during their third year of life can be encouraged to take an interest in outer space or scientific themes; during their fifteenth year, they may wish to invent new computer games with their coding skills; during their twenty-seventh year, they may want to perfect their inventions to help create a better society.

The key for all Jupiter returns is to choose a skill (or even one per year) and exercise the brain, all the way to the final years of life. As always, with Jupiter, the sky is the limit.

Jupiter returns at all ages should be celebrated and an experienced astrologer can help locate the exact moment of the return. New clothes to reflect a changing style, a good meal (with a magnificent dessert) with influential friends and maybe even a holiday to some exotic place are just a few ideas. To celebrate the ingress (entry) of Jupiter in a new sign, consult the table in the appendix. The Chinese culture does a wonderful job with celebrating "The Year of the…". While theirs may be a different culture and system, there is a similarity of intention.

Fine tuning the role of Jupiter:

Jupiter in Aquarius is ruled by Saturn, the planet of responsibility and restriction. However, Aquarius is co-ruled by Uranus, the planet of experimentation and innovation (either or both planets can be used). It is often difficult to merge hard working Saturn with free-wheeling Uranus. It is important to note that Uranus works on a collective basis: it reaches and affects the masses. The interpretations below reflect how a person works towards personal freedom within the confines of society.

Saturn/Uranus in Aries: These pupils naturally work towards independence, perhaps sensing a strong urge to do something to change the status quo. Teachers and other authority figures may be prime targets of mistrust. Those who operate on the verge of society are trusted allies in the fight towards independence.

Saturn/Uranus in Taurus: These pupils naturally work towards stabilising major structures; perhaps sensing huge changes are imminent. Teachers and other authority figures may be relied upon to offer support during times of crisis. Banks and building societies may be viewed as catalysts for change.

Saturn/Uranus in Gemini: These pupils naturally work towards innovating communication systems, perhaps sensing it is imperative to communicate faster and more efficiently. Teachers and other authority figures may be seen as facilitators of this process. Friends and social groups are used to network and distribute information.

Saturn/Uranus in Cancer: These pupils work naturally towards reforming the way society views family values, perhaps sensing that this basic tradition is on the verge of revolution. Teachers and other authority figures are viewed as an intrinsic part of preventing change. Friends and social groups begin to take the place of family.

Saturn/Uranus in Leo: These pupils work naturally toward avant-garde creativity and self-expression, particularly through vehicles such as mass media. High technology begins to replace traditional authority figures. Youth starts to overtake experience.

Saturn/Uranus in Virgo: These pupils work naturally towards reforming work ethics and innovating health care. This generation, when they came of age, led the New Age into alternative medicines. Teachers and other authority figures are seen as "dirty" or "contaminated" and as such are rejected.

Saturn/Uranus in Libra: These pupils work naturally towards uniting people by equalising their status. Unusual marriages or new laws regarding marriages are more acceptable than traditional views. Teachers and other authority figures are seen as allies who try to enforce equality.

Saturn/Uranus in Scorpio: These pupils work naturally towards reforming attitudes towards sexuality and other forms of subtle power. Teachers and other authority figures are seen as if they were abusing their powers on a collective level.

Saturn/Uranus in Sagittarius: These pupils work naturally towards reforming attitudes towards religion, education and law. Teachers and other authority figures are seen as those who will not follow conventional law and order as accepted by society.

Saturn/Uranus in Capricorn: These pupils work naturally towards reforming business and government practices. Teachers and authority figures are viewed as those who prevent innovation from happening.

Saturn/Uranus in Aquarius: These pupils work towards changing society. Teachers and other authority figures are viewed as innovators and leaders towards change.

Saturn/Uranus in Pisces: these pupils work towards collectively accepting those who have been marginalised in society. Teachers and other authority figures may be viewed as unexpected martyrs to the harshness and unfairness of society.

Case Studies

Barack Obama

Barack Obama was born on August 4, 1961, at 7:24 PM (RR:AA rating; Collector: Taglilatelo) in Honolulu, Hawaii. He has Jupiter in Aquarius, ruled by Saturn in Capricorn.

Obama's parents divorced when he was just two years old. Soon afterwards, he and his mother moved from Hawaii to Seattle. Following his mother's remarriage, they returned to Hawaii, and from age six, Obama lived in Indonesia until shortly before his first Jupiter return. At the age of ten, he moved back to Hawaii to live with his grandparents until he graduated from high school. This unconventional upbringing, blending diverse cultures, locations, and generational influences, contributed to his unique perspective.

In 1973, Obama experienced his transiting Uranus in Libra sextile his natal Uranus in Leo, almost a year and a half before transiting Jupiter in Aries sextiled his natal Jupiter in Aquarius. During this time, his mother returned to Hawaii before moving back to Jakarta, while Obama chose to remain with his grandparents in Hawaii. This decision might reflect a desire for stability in his teenage years or the influence of older family members. It also provided the backdrop for his admitted experimentation with alcohol, marijuana, and cocaine during high school, an episode he later referred to as his greatest moral failure.

Years later, Obama's transiting Uranus trines in 1986–87 again preceded Jupiter trines. By then, he had lived with Sheila Miyoshi Jager and proposed marriage, though her parents objected. He later attended Harvard Law School, met Michelle Robinson before his Saturn return, and married her in 1992 during a series of Saturn oppositions to his Sun in Aquarius.

In 1995, shortly after Jupiter in Sagittarius opposed his Moon in Gemini, Obama published *Dreams from My Father*, a memoir that is essentially a love letter to his ethnically diverse upbringing and heritage. The book gained renewed attention after his senator's speech in 2004,

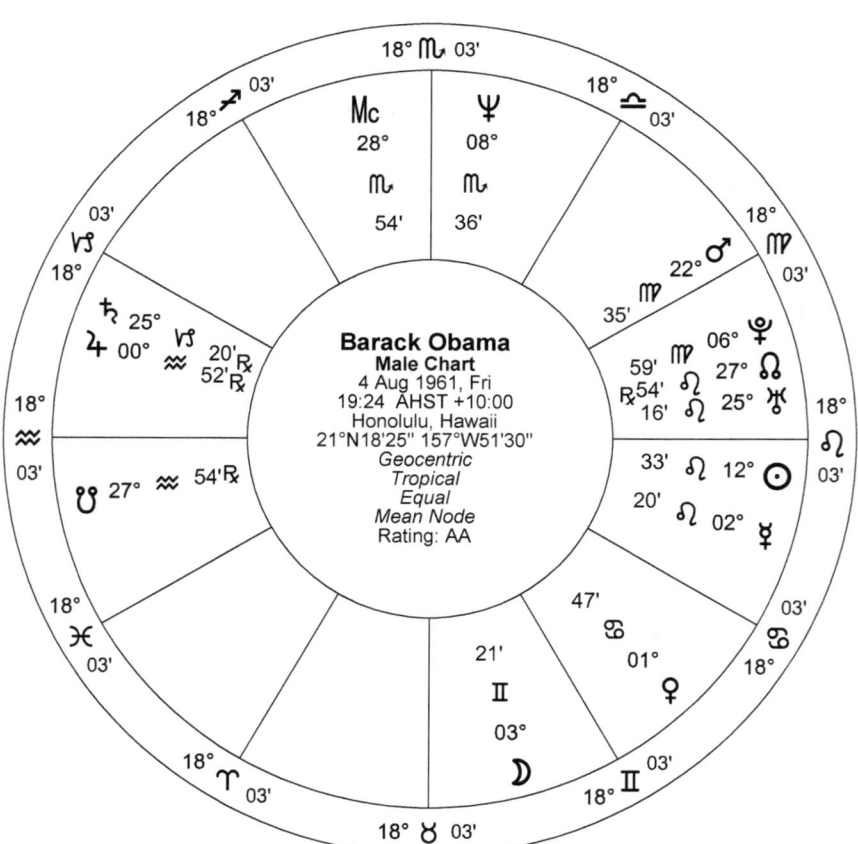

during a series of conjunctions from transiting Uranus in Pisces to his natal Chiron.

In February 2007, just after transiting Jupiter opposed his Moon, Obama announced his candidacy for President of the United States. By November 2008, a week before transiting Jupiter in Capricorn conjoined his natal Saturn, Obama won the election. His presidency included significant milestones, such as the Affordable Care Act, advancements in LGBTQ+ rights through the repeal of "Don't Ask, Don't Tell," and a Nobel Peace Prize in October 2009 after Jupiter's conjunction to his Aquarius Ascendant. He was re-elected in 2012 under Jupiter's conjunction to his Moon in Gemini and left office with a 60% approval rating.

Obama's natural diplomacy and vision for equality—hallmarks of Jupiter in Aquarius—helped him navigate political challenges and effect lasting change.

Meg Ryan

Meg Ryan was born on November 19, 1961, at 10:36 AM (RR:A rating) in Fairfield, Connecticut with Jupiter in Aquarius and Saturn in Capricorn.

While there is little documented about her adolescence, Ryan experienced her transiting Uranus in Scorpio sextile her natal Uranus in Virgo a couple of months before her Jupiter in Aries sextile her natal Jupiter in Aquarius, indicating her independent, rebellious streak.

Her first film role was in George Cukor's *Rich and Famous* (1981), during which transiting Uranus in Scorpio made three conjunctions to her natal Sun. This marked her entry into Hollywood, soon followed by a role on the soap opera *As the World Turns* (1982–1984) as Jupiter in Scorpio formed conjunctions with her natal planets.

Ryan gained wider recognition in the mid-1980s with appearances in *Top Gun* (1986) and *Innerspace* (1987), where she met her future husband, Dennis Quaid. During the filming of *When Harry Met Sally* (1989), transiting Jupiter in Taurus opposed her Sun in Scorpio, aligning with the film's thematic exploration of time, relationships, and maturity. And… funnily enough, given the transit… the famous coleslaw scene had to be shot over and over which meant Ryan had to fake her orgasms for hours. The line "I'll have what she's having" (delivered by director Rob Reiner's mother) is listed in the American Film Institute's list as one of the most memorable movie lines.

Her pairing with Tom Hanks in a series of romantic comedies—*Joe Versus the Volcano* (1990), *Sleepless in Seattle* (1993), and *You've Got Mail* (1998)—secured her reputation as a romantic comedy icon. This era began with Jupiter on her Descendant and ended with a square from Jupiter in Aries, reflecting her evolving career arc.

In 1995, as Ryan entered her third Jupiter return, she was described as "the current soul of romantic comedy". However, her career took a hit in 2000, when her affair with Russell Crowe during the filming of *Proof of Life* coincided with squares from both Jupiter and Saturn to her nodal axis. This led to a media backlash and her divorce from Dennis Quaid.

In 2001, Ryan found success again with *Kate and Leopold*. While the film generated buzz, it did not resonate with critics. It earned over $70

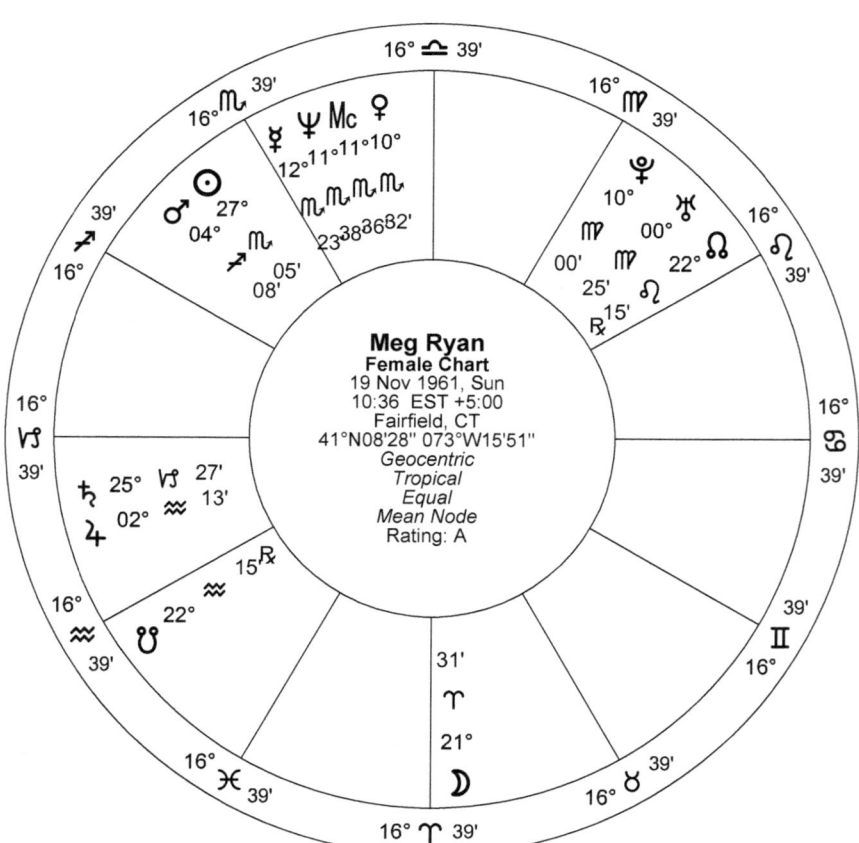

million and would become her highest grossing film of the early 2000s. Transiting Uranus had been on her South Node that year as she re-built her life without Quaid. In 2003, she completely broke away from being typecast by starring in Jane Campion's *Into the Cut*, an erotic thriller in which Ryan appeared nude in a lengthy love scene. The film did not please critics though it did earn the actress some media attention. Whilst promoting the film, Ryan gave a disastrous interview on *Parkinson* that continues to live on in infamy. Ryan, according to critics, appeared bored, rude and dismissive. That year transiting Jupiter was on her North Node in Leo. Just to prove the destruction Jupiter can bring, Ryan's star began to fall.

Ryan's career, while marked by iconic performances and critical acclaim, also demonstrates the complexities of a rebellious Jupiter in Aquarius. Though her star power faded, her willingness to break the mould solidifies her legacy as both a romantic comedy trailblazer and a boundary-pushing actor.

Jupiter in Pisces

Pisces is a water sign by element and a mutable sign by modality. Transiting squares and oppositions to its natal position will take place about every three years in the other mutable signs, Gemini, Virgo and Sagittarius. This pattern will repeat for the rest of the native's life, defining how a person learns, grows and develops a personal philosophy. Mutable signs are flexible, co-operative and interested in what goes on around them. They are usually very curious and collect and distribute information that passes their way. Jupiter in Pisces is extremely sensitive to the emotional charge found in any gathering and they tend to be guided by intuition and gut feelings rather than cold, hard logic.

Jupiter transits through signs at a pace of about one sign per year. It is important to note that as children are taught by year group, they will learn alongside other children with Jupiter in Pisces. Depending on the time of year they were born, they will also have classmates with either Jupiter in Aquarius or Jupiter in Aries. This topic has been explored in depth in *Growing Pains: Astrology in Adolescence.*

Children who have Jupiter in Pisces tend to learn through exercising their ability to sympathise with others, expressing themselves through the Arts (such as music and dance) and by using their imaginations. They are the dreamers, visionaries and healers. Motivated by the idea of eliminating the suffering in the world, they often instinctively know how they define success for themselves—and very rarely is that measured with money, power or the approval of other people.

The First Jupiter Square

All babies need the basics of adequate nutrition, a safe place to sleep, cleanliness and a comfortable environment. They also need the human touch in order to build trust and to feel the caregiver is responding to their signals for these necessities. Eye contact, talking/singing to the baby and providing a daily rhythm of sleep, cleaning, feeding and playing with age appropriate toys are essential for all babies, irrespective of their Jupiter sign. As the baby grows into a toddler, it is important caregivers have adequately "baby proofed" the child's environment. These essential needs are important all the way into old age. Once these needs are met consistently, a bit of astrology can help the caregivers find the learner's internal "beat" for development.

At some point during the first year of their life, the Jupiter in Pisces learner will experience Jupiter transiting through the sign of Aries. As the learner is a baby, the world is simply full of learning opportunities. Natally, the Jupiter in Pisces learner may lean towards sweet foods or have unusual food preferences.

As their second year approaches, Jupiter in Pisces learners will have Jupiter transiting through the sign of Taurus. As they slow down, their appetite may increase. They may have been on the thin side in their first year but this is their year for putting on a bit of weight. They may exhibit a sweet tooth or prefer the heavier, stodgier foods as they begin to express food preferences. At this stage of development, they may have to be encouraged to share their toys or the attention of their carers. Jupiter in Pisces children usually have their favourite possessions and playthings (usually cuddly toys) that they will hold onto well into adulthood. Because these children are so impressionable, they hold onto nostalgia too: they may start collections (encouraged by the adults around them). Music, in particular, may hold a place in their hearts but also items such as regalia from a favourite sports team. And Jupiter in Pisces at this stage of development usually loves to sing (even if it's not very tuneful, their enthusiasm will probably show through).

Jupiter in Pisces children will have transiting Jupiter in Gemini during their third year. Most children are able to use a few words but Jupiter in Pisces learners at this stage of development could just about be able to hold conversations. They may love the opportunity to learn new words (be careful about using bad word choices around them at this age as they will repeat everything they hear). Something for parents and carers to be careful about: these children tend to be very trusting, even if they have had a bad experience. And with Jupiter transiting through Gemini, they will talk to just about anyone. It's always a good idea to keep a watch on toddlers but be extra vigilant with these little ones: they tend to wander, they are insatiably curious and they tend not to have favourite adults (they just like everyone).

During the first Jupiter square, Jupiter in Pisces learners begin understanding the world through understanding themselves. This is an important step for self-preservation and learning how to take care of themselves before they can take on the care of others. Though they may not be able to verbalise it (although they may try), they can accept they are inexperienced and physically immature (though their hearts are huge). And yet, they can still inspire others and pull on the heartstrings like no others.

The First Jupiter Opposition

Between the ages of about three and six years old, most young children are preparing for formal education and socialisation. These are just some ideas to help Jupiter in Pisces learners prepare to begin the process of their first adventures away from their immediate care givers.

During their fourth year they will experience transiting Jupiter through the sign of Cancer. Young children will often be wary of strangers and although Jupiter in Pisces learners may not have done so before, there will most likely be signs that they want to play it safe. Home is where they want to be and they will probably like to be involved in taking care of the family in some way. They can do small tasks that might make a bit more work for the caregivers but with practice, these little homemakers get better and better. No child is too young for chores (bearing in mind safety issues) and establishing a routine can really help them find order in what can be a chaotic world from their viewpoint.

Activities for enjoyment and learning outside of school: taking care of animals, singing (as a way to cope with negative emotions), helping with the cooking, taking responsibility for the management of one area of their living space, learning how to take care of their clothes and beds, visiting museums or investigating certain times in history.

As their fifth year approaches for Jupiter in Pisces learners, transiting Jupiter will be in the sign of Leo. Children of this age love to create but there is usually something very special about what Jupiter in Pisces learners can come up with. Toy musical instruments will likely be worn out, the paint sets will be empty and, if parents and carers are not vigilant, their clean walls and furniture could become the canvases for these young Van Goghs. Young artists need guidelines and careful rules for expressing their creativity. However, if there is a blank wall somewhere in the home, why not turn it into a long term project for young Jupiter in Pisces artists? This would be a wonderful opportunity to teach them about different-sized paintbrushes, how to use different brushstrokes for effect and even experiment with colour. Once the project is finished, Jupiter in Pisces learners at this stage of development would love nothing more than an exhibition in front of loved ones.

Activities for enjoyment and learning outside of school: stage play, making and wearing costumes and masks, dressing up to go to an event.

Jupiter in Pisces learners during their sixth year will have Jupiter transiting through Virgo. This is a time for refining the artistic skills they have learned and it is also a great time to introduce the works of other artists, be it musicians, painters or dancers. At this stage of their development, they will be preparing to start school where there are more resources and more children they can explore their imaginations with. And they will have plenty to share. The make-believe world is something that tends to leave us a couple of years after this stage of development. Allowing them to indulge their imaginary friends, to tell you about their dreams and to dress up in a different outfit every other minute can really help these young learners to have faith in their imaginations and to feel accepted for thinking a little differently. Jupiter in Pisces learners at this age tend to like to make up their own secret languages. They may share it with others or parents and teachers may just catch little bits of words that sound suspiciously like their mother tongue but yet have their own meaning and nuance.

Activities for enjoyment and learning outside of school: learning about the physical body of people or animals, learning about sickness and how to take care of someone (or a pet) who is not feeling well, understanding the basics of medicine. Learning to identify plants and different species of animals, learning to measure accurately with simple tools such as rulers.

The first Jupiter opposition appears to allow Jupiter in Pisces learners the opportunity to create without worrying about the critical judgment that can come from peers at school or from teachers (no matter how well intended they are). If parents and carers can support the creative process, the child will gain valuable confidence and perhaps take an interest in other artistic techniques and mediums.

The Closing Jupiter Square

By this stage, children will have settled into a home/school routine and it is likely schools will begin to prepare students for the Scholastic Achievement Tests (or their equivalents). Debate rages as to whether these tests cause stress for the children but, drawing from personal experience, students tend not to get too upset if the adults around them don't behave as if the world is coming to an end. The purpose of these tests is to help identify strengths and weaknesses in the child's development. The results establish a baseline, not a final outcome. Here are some ways to help support the learners during these formative times:

During their seventh year, Jupiter in Pisces learners are usually in formal education and are starting the process of reading and writing alongside other learners of a similar age. Generally speaking, it is a time for learning how to socialise with others but also how to stand up for what they think is right rather than just accepting that the other person is right. This is a very tall order because Jupiter in Pisces learners almost always take the road of least resistance (this tends to mean they prefer not to say or do anything). Furthermore, the sign of Libra would also rather keep the peace. The result could be a very silent standoff between silently stewing pupils with the adults in charge wondering why everyone is being so quiet. The trick, of course, is to ensure that conflicts are resolved as soon as they crop up. Disagreements should be aired and, if apologies and handshakes are needed, then they should be done before the next playground break. No one can declare a war—silent or otherwise—like signs that are ruled (Libra) or exalted (Pisces) by Venus. To add to the challenge, Jupiter in Pisces pupils will most likely be preparing for their SATs so they really should be encouraged to keep their focus on their studies.

Activities for enjoyment and learning outside of school: planning a themed party with a few friends (try themes based around *Horrible Histories* or their favourite kids' movies) and have "preparation parties" where all the invitees have to make their own party favours and costumes, plan their food and activities, etc.

As their eighth year approaches Jupiter in Pisces learners will experience transiting Jupiter in Scorpio. If you thought Jupiter in Pisces learners went quiet when angry as Jupiter transited through Libra, just wait until transiting Jupiter in Scorpio takes hold. Not only are Jupiter in Pisces learners quiet when angry, they almost always find a way to secretly avenge themselves. And they can be creative about it too—and probably make themselves look like the victim to boot. For these reasons, teachers should be aware of "silent wars" when it appears that a child has been suddenly ostracised. It is fortunate that learners of this age do not have access to social media but keep an eye out for problems between parents. If it all sounds like cloak and dagger stuff, it is. Jupiter in Pisces children are very intuitive and they know how to hurt and make it look like an accident. They really do need "circle time" at the end of each day so they can be given the opportunity to express their hurt feelings, receive their apologies or explanations for any misunderstandings so they can move on and forgive or call on more support to help them resolve the conflict.

Activities for enjoyment and learning outside of school: mysteries and puzzles, being *gently* frightened (Halloween or cold, dark autumn nights are a good time to share simple ghost stories), nature walks so they can observe the cycle of life in plants and animals (NB: learners at this stage may take an interest in death and pregnancies so be prepared to explain).

Jupiter in Pisces learners will have Jupiter transiting through the sign of Sagittarius during their ninth year. Having learned how to work through conflicts, they are usually eager to show others how to keep the peace. They are patient listeners, highly intuitive and have the knack of saying and doing the right things at the best possible time. However, sometimes they can't help but use the information they have gleaned to find a way to benefit themselves: two warring factions couldn't possibly notice if a Jupiter in Pisces snuck into their places in the lunchtime queue for example. And the funny thing is, Jupiter in Pisces can get away with it.

Activities for enjoyment and learning outside of school: taking part in charity work, visiting places of worship, learning to discuss politics and identifying political leaders, learning about different countries (their map, geographical features, language, etc.).

Pisces is, on the surface, a quiet, peaceful sign that would rather stick their head in their palette of paints than step into the middle of an argument. However, they do need to be able to stand up for themselves and employ a bit of self-protection when they are in danger of being taken advantage of. The closing Jupiter square will give the Jupiter in Pisces child the opportunity to understand their boundaries and help them to determine what they can and cannot tolerate.

The Jupiter Return

As the learner heads towards their final years of primary school, they should be able to work more independently, understand the general rules of the classroom/playground and see home and school as two separate environments.

During their tenth year, Jupiter in Pisces learners will experience Jupiter as it transits through the sign of Capricorn. Capricorn is no-nonsense, hardworking sign and Jupiter in Pisces learners may struggle with the do-or-die approach of a Saturn-ruled sign. What could be helpful to them is a general, back-to-basics approach to learning. These learners need to set their tender feelings aside (with all due respect, the world needs more sensitivity but there are limits) and just for a few months, focus on academic expectations. Some questions to consider are: what are the routines needed to be successful in the bigger school? What expectations do others have and how will they know if they have met them? Generally speaking, this is a good opportunity to have a clear out of their personal space. By this age, there will be many toys, clothes and general memorabilia that they simply have no use for anymore. Parents can help them clear their space, refresh the decor and make way for new opportunities.

Activities for enjoyment and learning outside of school: hobbies that encourage one step at a time, like wool crafts, learning to do simple carpentry skills, learning to do "handyman/woman" jobs around the house, activities that encourage business skills.

As their eleventh year approaches, Jupiter in Pisces learners will begin preparing for the transition into a bigger school. For some, a fresh start is exactly what they need but for others, the thought of starting all over again can make them feel as if they were lost at sea. They will need to be assured that there really are "safe spaces" or people they can rely on even if everything is very new. Introducing new staff from their allocated secondary school as early as possible as well as visiting their new school can really help these students orientate themselves to this brand new life. They will need help getting their heads around the new rules, uniforms (if they have to wear one) and any new policies that might be coming their way. It is important to ensure Jupiter in Pisces learners understand the bigger picture of secondary school and its purpose before they begin looking for ways to get around the ground rules that have already been accepted by their parents and themselves.

Activities for enjoyment and learning outside of school: leading/forming a new club and setting rules and expectations, simple science experiments (YouTube is full of ideas of home science experiments—ensure they have permission and understand they have to clean up), learning how to do simple tasks like changing light bulbs, fuses and understanding electrical circuits, recording and monitoring data accurately as part of an experiment.

Jupiter in Pisces learners will reach their first Jupiter return sometime during their twelfth year, and with the new resources found in their new school, will often dive head first into the mess and look the part. Getting used to a new routine can feel like a whole different life to them. However, if they are struggling to keep things together, they need adult intervention even if they don't ask for it. For parents, this can mean they spend a few minutes in the evening helping their child to pack their bags for the next day and then helping them unpack their bags when then come home after school. With positive reinforcement and persistence, Jupiter in Pisces will understand how important it is to not let little jobs pile up to become unmanageable. This may be a lesson they have to learn again and again but if they can understand this concept during adolescence, the good habits established at this time will serve them for the rest of their lives.

Activities for enjoyment and learning outside of school: Music lessons, art projects not found in school like pottery courses that allow the learner to complete a project all the way to the end, studying a particular artist and their work medium (painting, sculpture, carving, etc.).

When we return to a place have visited before, it is our nature to make comparisons to what has changed since the first time we were there. We may want to seek out the things we did before or perhaps try something completely different.

As almost all students will have had their first Jupiter return by the end of their first year of secondary school, schools could hold an end of year festival that would allow pupils to demonstrate their individual skills.

Schools tend to hold sporting events during this time but how about an Art and Music exhibition? Students could create their own Artwork/Music or invite artists to come to their school to perform.

The Jupiter and Uranus Sextiles: In the Thick of Puberty

As noted in the Introduction, the thirteenth year of a child's life is usually when rebellion and defiance begin to become noticeable. Astrologically, transiting Jupiter forms a sextile aspect to its natal position at the same time Uranus, the planet of rebellion, will also make its first Ptolemaic aspect to its own natal position (also by sextile aspect). This combination quite literally means "big rebellion" and marks the time when adolescents (and their parents) begin the struggle to make that separation into adulthood.

Identifying when and how a young adolescent may struggle with the changing social rules they must face could be helpful for parents. For example, if an adolescent experiences the Uranus sextile before the Jupiter sextile, parents may view their child as needing more guidance for following the expectations of the home environment (which would include expectations in school). In the Case Studies section, subjects with this tendency are noted as "rebels". If an adolescent experiences the Jupiter sextile before the Uranus sextile, parents may view their child as needing more encouragement for academic work and possibly with social skills. In the Case Studies section, subjects with this tendency are noted as "truth seekers". There is no "good" or "bad" with these notations and they are only presented as starting points for understanding the life-long impact this stage of development has on learners as they continue their journey all the way into old age. To demonstrate how this particular stage of development can vary from person to person, there is a summary of the time frame for the subjects of the case studies on page 208.

Furthermore, an adolescent's developing body means they may be interested in forming intimate relationships but their brain needs time to catch up with all the new situations it finds itself in.

For children born with Jupiter in Pisces, Jupiter will be transiting through the sign of Taurus as it had been during their second year. At this stage, the young adolescents can be quite possessive of the things or people they like and find it difficult to share with others. They may have collections as well that could potentially swell into being unmanageable. A major theme of Jupiter in Pisces is learning how to manage clutter—even if they claim their junk is spelled J-U-N-Q-U-E.

The Saturn Opposition

The Saturn opposition begins some time during the fourteenth or fifteenth year (possibly earlier or later depending on individual cases) and marks the end of astrological adolescence. Parents and teachers usually notice that the adolescent begins to calm down and take a more mature approach to their academic progress. In the UK, this coincides with choosing academic subjects (as opposed to trying a little bit of everything), formal exam preparation and a marked change in mood. Depression, anxiety and their symptoms must be monitored and taken seriously. Schools will have access to support mechanisms for parents and carers, teachers will have been trained in how to identify potential difficulties and for parents who are home schooling, social services can be a sound source for help.

As they head towards their transiting Saturn opposition, Jupiter in Pisces children will also re-visit what they had learned as transiting Jupiter once again passes through the signs of Gemini and Cancer. At this stage of learning, they may show a talent for information recall such as is required for formal examinations with multiple choice answers. However, pulling together cohesive essays may be a skill they need to practise. Fortunately, Jupiter transiting through the sign of Cancer can bequeath them a good working memory and the ability to write intuitively and sensitively, a real advantage.

The Second Jupiter Opposition

By the time a young adult finishes mandatory education, they will have a good idea of what they want to do with their lives and yet they still have time to re-take exams or re-train if they discover they want to do something else. The second Jupiter opposition is a time of making serious decisions: the young adult is no longer a child. The learner now knows there are consequences for undesirable behaviour and can no longer blame "the system" for their poor choices. Sadly, our prison services are filled with young people who have slipped through the net. As a collective whole, society could do with using a little astrology to help these young people get back on track. A more comprehensive mentoring service could be helpful.

Here are some ideas to help young adults focus on the rest of their adult lives:

Transiting Jupiter will be in Virgo as the young adult finishes their formal education at around the age of eighteen. By this stage of maturity, Jupiter in Pisces students have essentially outgrown their messy ways of doing things and they tend to embrace a more organised approach to learning. They will understand that their notes should be kept organised and will have most likely developed a way of critical thinking that can help them sift through (and dispose of) information that only serves to clutter and confuse them. Conversely, if they haven't been encouraged to keep on top of the disorder that seems to follow them, they may become overwhelmed, and not be able to decide what is important and what needs to be disposed of. Again, they may need a bit of help keeping things in order—or a very tidy roommate who will have no problem letting them know when it's time to empty the trash.

The Second and Subsequent Jupiter Returns

As a person continues to develop emotionally, physically and spiritually they will build on the lessons they learned in the formative years. Jupiter returns (roughly) at the ages of 24, 36, 48 and 60 (and beyond).

The suggestions for activities can be modified to suit the developmental cycle for each Jupiter cycle. For example, a Jupiter in Pisces learner experiencing a Jupiter in Taurus transit during their third year of life can be encouraged to practise their building skills (with toys such as Lego or similar) to help them understand structure; during their fifteenth year, they may wish to try applying these skills to artistic endeavours such as painting or music; during their twenty-seventh year, they may want to teach some of these ideas on a voluntary basis to those less fortunate.

The key for all Jupiter returns is to choose a skill (or even one per year) and exercise the brain, all the way to the final years of life. As always, with Jupiter, the sky is the limit.

Jupiter returns at all ages should be celebrated and an experienced astrologer can help locate the exact moment of the return. New clothes to reflect a changing style, a good meal (with a magnificent dessert) with influential friends and maybe even a holiday to some exotic place are just a few ideas. To celebrate the ingress (entry) of Jupiter in a new sign, consult the table in the appendix. The Chinese culture does a wonderful job with celebrating "The Year of the…". While theirs may be a different culture and system, the similarity of intention is still there.

Fine tuning the role of Jupiter:

Jupiter in Pisces is ruled by Neptune and co-ruled by Jupiter. In mythology, Jupiter was god of the heavens whilst Neptune was god of the sea. This combination of rulers makes for a grand kingdom in which it is easy to become overwhelmed, sucked in or lost altogether. Neptune influences are said to be addictive. Like Uranus, Neptune works collectively, affecting many people at once and may not become apparent until the collective group matures enough to have an effect on society.

Jupiter/Neptune in Aries: These pupils may idealise learning independently and/or the need for teamwork is sacrificed for greater efficiency. Mass media may be the teachers and authority figures. There may be an addiction to speed and immediate action.

Jupiter/Neptune in Taurus: These pupils may idealise education for the material gain it brings. Personal power may be sacrificed for greater stability in society. Mother Nature may be the teachers and authority figures. There may be an addiction to material goods and property.

Jupiter/Neptune in Gemini: These pupils may idealise education for the improvement it brings to communication. Philosophies may be sacrificed for simplified codes. Symbols may be used to teach or to exert authority. There may be an addiction to communicating on a more psychic level.

Jupiter/Neptune in Cancer: These pupils may idealise education because it unites the family. Social status may be sacrificed for emotional freedom. Mother figures may replace traditional authority figures. There may be an addiction to the traditional family occasion or its surrogate.

Jupiter/Neptune in Leo: These pupils may idealise glamour. Friendship and social groups may be sacrificed for youth and beauty. Young people become authority figures. There may be an addiction to entertainment.

Jupiter/Neptune in Virgo: These pupils may idealise human health. The use of imagination may be sacrificed for natural products. The search for perfection becomes the authority figure. There may be an addiction to work and order.

Jupiter/Neptune in Libra: These pupils may idealise human relationships. The need for independent thought is sacrificed for the yearning for teamwork. Couples or pairs are seen as authority figures. There may be an addiction to search for beauty and harmony.

Jupiter/Neptune in Scorpio: These pupils may idealise power. The need for stability may be sacrificed for the urge to make profound changes in society. The occult may be seen as having ultimate power. There may be an addiction to the dark side of society.

Jupiter/Neptune in Sagittarius: These pupils may idealise foreign policies, philosophies or religions. Casual conversation may be sacrificed for profound spiritual growth. Authority figures may come from foreign lands or religions. There may be an addiction to holding unusual beliefs.

Jupiter/Neptune in Capricorn: These pupils may idealise control and order. The status quo may be sacrificed to bring family structure. Authority figures may have more global powers. There may be an addiction to maintaining traditional values.

Jupiter/Neptune in Aquarius: These pupils may idealise equality. The rights of the individual may be sacrificed for the rights of the collective. Authority figures may search for alternatives to the truth. There may be an addiction to the unusual or unexpected.

Jupiter/Neptune in Pisces: These pupils may idealise sacrifice. Perfection may be sacrificed for chaos. Authority figures may be imaginary. There may be an addiction to what is perceived and accepted as the ideal.

Case Studies

Emilia Clarke

Emilia Clarke was born on 23 October 1986 (time unknown, source: Wikipedia) in London, UK. With Jupiter in Pisces and Neptune in Capricorn, Clarke embodies the imaginative and sensitive qualities associated with her Jupiter placement, balanced by the disciplined and structured influence of Neptune in Capricorn. Her early interest in acting emerged at the age of three, during a Jupiter square, and she participated in her first West End audition at age ten. By then, transiting Jupiter in Capricorn was sextile her natal Jupiter in Pisces, closely followed by a sextile from transiting Uranus in Aquarius to her natal Uranus in Sagittarius—an aspect that often reflects a seeker of deeper truths.

Clarke's first significant professional role came with the 2010 television film *Triassic Attack*, coinciding with her second Jupiter return. Although the film itself received mixed reviews, it marked the beginning of a career that would soon skyrocket. Later that year, she was cast as Daenerys Targaryen in *Game of Thrones,* a role that would define her career and earn her recognition as one of television's highest-paid actors. By the end of the series' eight-season run, transiting Jupiter was in the closing square of its cycle, reflecting a culmination of her journey with this character.

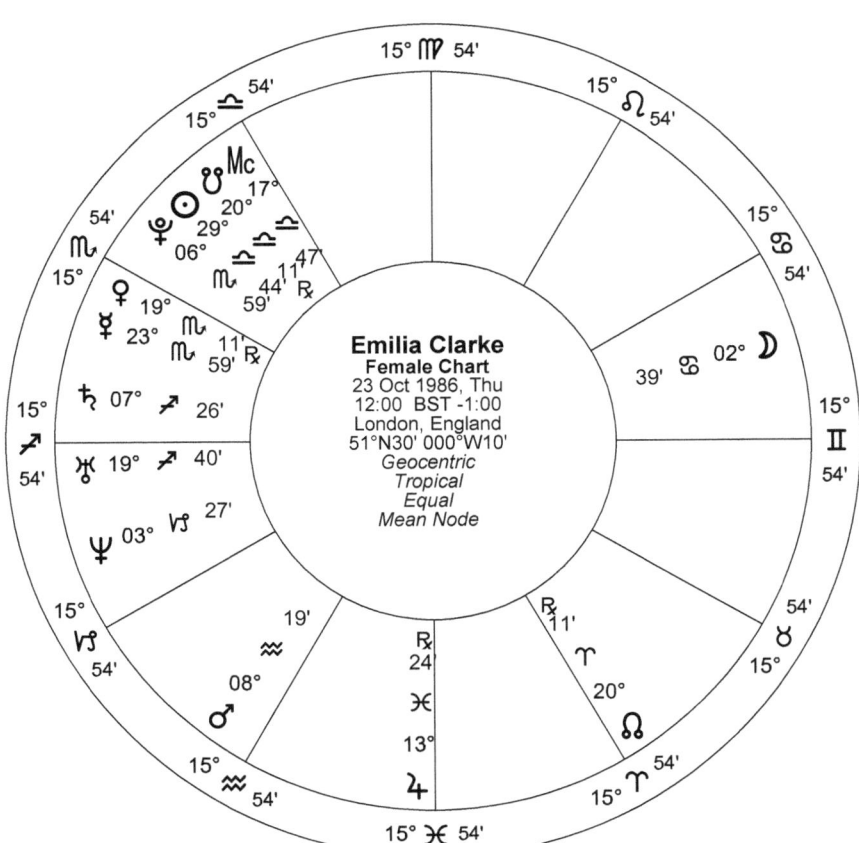

In 2016, as transiting Jupiter opposed her natal position in Pisces, Clarke took on the role of a caregiver in *Me Before You*, a heartfelt drama that earned the MTV Tearjerker Award. This opposition reflected the poignant and deeply emotional nature of the film. She followed this role with *Voice from the Stone*, where she played a nurse—again emphasising the compassionate and supportive qualities of Jupiter in Pisces. Around this time, Jupiter in Aries conjunct her South Node further highlighted themes of nurturing and healing.

Beyond her acting accolades, Clarke has demonstrated the charitable and idealistic tendencies often associated with Jupiter in Pisces. Following two brain aneurysms she suffered in 2011 and 2013, she launched her own charity, SameYou, aimed at improving neurorehabilitation for young people. Her charitable efforts earned her and her mother the title of Members of the Order of the British Empire in 2024. She was officially recognised that February, as transiting Jupiter opposed her natal Pluto in Scorpio—underscoring her transformational impact on society.

Amber Heard

Amber Heard was born on 22 April 1986 (time unknown, source: Wikipedia) in Austin, Texas, also with Jupiter in Pisces and Neptune in Capricorn. While her early career showed promise, it is her personal life—especially her tumultuous relationship with Johnny Depp—that has garnered the most attention.

As a teenager, Heard experienced a Jupiter sextile to its natal position in Pisces, followed by a sextile from Uranus in Pisces to Uranus in Sagittarius—indications of a naturally inquisitive and truth-seeking disposition. These aspects coincided with her early appearances in music videos and television roles, laying the groundwork for her career.

In 2008, Heard gained wider recognition with roles in *Pineapple Express* and *Never Back Down*. That year, Jupiter was conjunct her natal Neptune in Capricorn, reflecting her rising star and the beginning of her more prominent public presence. However, the combination of Neptune's influence and the idealism of Jupiter in Pisces suggests that her ascent also brought challenges in distinguishing reality from perception.

The release of *The Rum Diary* in 2011 marked another significant moment in Heard's life. Although the film was not a commercial success, it led to her relationship with Depp. In 2015, during a Jupiter opposition, the couple's legal battles and allegations of abuse became public. The opposition's tension was reflected in the highly publicised court case surrounding their attempt to bring dogs into Australia, eventually resulting in a good behaviour bond for Heard and a public apology from the couple.

The legal disputes, culminating in a trial that concluded during Heard's third Jupiter return in 2022, overshadowed much of her career. As of 2025, it appears that she has not yet resumed her acting career. Despite her early promise, Heard's Jupiter in Pisces journey highlights the dual-edged nature of idealism—its potential to inspire and its capacity to cloud judgment.

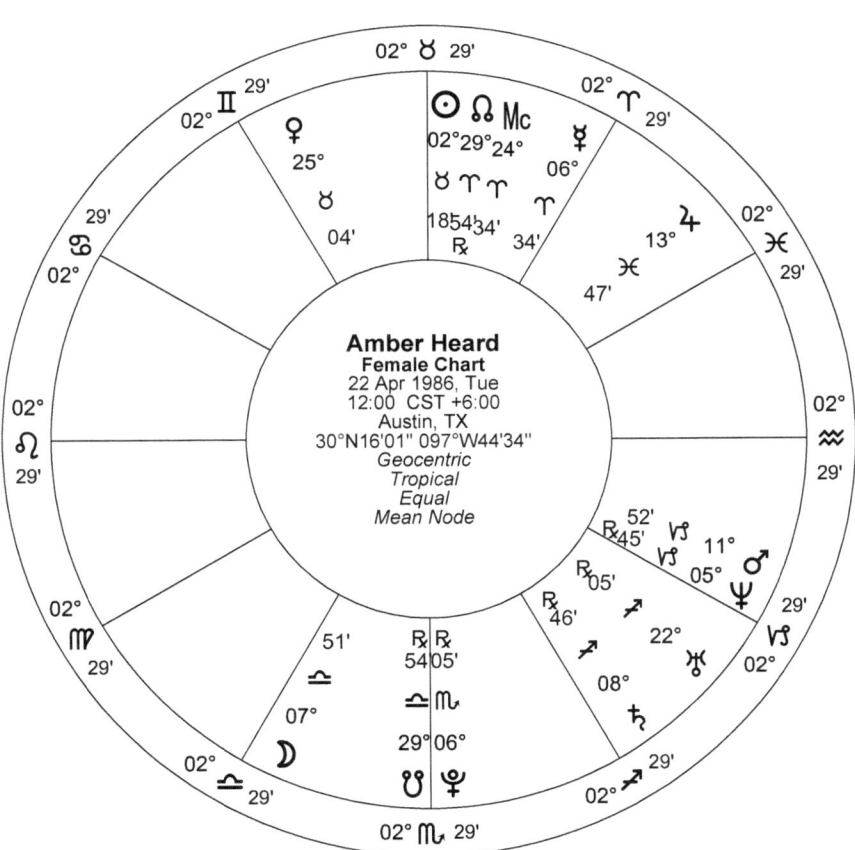

Conclusion

As we come to the end of this journey through Jupiter's twelve signs, it's clear that astrology offers more than just a lens for understanding personality. It provides a rich, layered framework for guiding personal growth, shaping educational approaches, and nurturing the unique strengths within each individual. By exploring Jupiter's placement in the natal chart, we gain valuable insights into learning styles, developmental milestones, and the kinds of experiences that foster wisdom and resilience.

Throughout these chapters, we have seen that every Jupiter sign holds its own promise. Each one represents a distinct way of engaging with the world, building knowledge, and finding meaning. By understanding these placements, parents, educators, and astrologers alike can tailor their guidance to suit the individual—fostering confidence, encouraging curiosity, and helping people rise to meet their own potential.

Ultimately, astrology is a tool of empowerment. It helps us recognise the natural cycles of growth, accept the challenges that come with change, and embrace the wisdom that emerges from life's experiences. By applying the insights from this book, we can not only support the development of those we teach or care for, but also inspire them to discover their own truth, expand their horizons, and contribute their unique gifts to the world.

Jupiter Sign Changes (Ingresses) from 1900 to 2050 (Eastern Time)

Courtesy of Astrocafé

Jan 19, 1901 3:33 AM   Jupiter enters Capricorn
Feb 6, 1902 2:30 PM   Jupiter enters Aquarius
Feb 20, 1903 3:34 AM   Jupiter enters Pisces
Feb 29, 1904 9:59 PM   Jupiter enters Aries
Aug 8, 1904 3:06 PM   Jupiter enters Taurus
Aug 31, 1904 8:58 AM   Jupiter Rx enters Aries
Mar 7, 1905 1:27 PM   Jupiter enters Taurus
Jul 20, 1905 7:22 PM   Jupiter enters Gemini
Dec 4, 1905 5:32 PM   Jupiter Rx enters Taurus
Mar 9, 1906 4:47 PM   Jupiter enters Gemini
Jul 30, 1906 6:12 PM   Jupiter enters Cancer
Aug 18, 1907 6:14 PM   Jupiter enters Leo
Sep 12, 1908 5:01 AM   Jupiter enters Virgo
Oct 11, 1909 6:33 PM   Jupiter enters Libra
Nov 11, 1910 12:04 PM   Jupiter enters Scorpio
Dec 10, 1911 6:35 AM   Jupiter enters Sagittarius
Jan 2, 1913 2:45 PM   Jupiter enters Capricorn
Jan 21, 1914 10:13 AM   Jupiter enters Aquarius
Feb 3, 1915 7:43 PM   Jupiter enters Pisces
Feb 12, 1916 2:10 AM   Jupiter enters Aries
Jun 25, 1916 8:31 PM   Jupiter enters Taurus
Oct 26, 1916 9:54 AM   Jupiter Rx enters Aries
Feb 12, 1917 10:57 AM   Jupiter enters Taurus
1 Jun 29, 1917 6:51 PM   Jupiter enters Gemini
    *** Daylight Saving Time begins ***
Jul 13, 1918 1:53 AM   Jupiter enters Cancer
Aug 2, 1919 4:38 AM   Jupiter enters Leo
Aug 27, 1920 1:29 AM   Jupiter enters Virgo
Sep 25, 1921 7:10 PM   Jupiter enters Libra
    *** Daylight Saving Time ends ***
Oct 26, 1922 2:16 PM   Jupiter enters Scorpio
Nov 24, 1923 12:31 PM   Jupiter enters Sagittarius

Dec 18, 1924 1:25 AM   Jupiter enters Capricorn
Jan 5, 1926 8:00 PM   Jupiter enters Aquarius
Jan 18, 1927 6:43 AM   Jupiter enters Pisces
   *** Daylight Saving Time begins ***
Jun 6, 1927 6:13 AM   Jupiter enters Aries
Sep 10, 1927 11:44 PM   Jupiter Rx enters Pisces
   *** Daylight Saving Time ends ***
Jan 22, 1928 9:54 PM   Jupiter enters Aries
   *** Daylight Saving Time begins ***
Jun 4, 1928 12:50 AM   Jupiter enters Taurus
Jun 12, 1929 8:20 AM   Jupiter enters Gemini
Jun 26, 1930 6:41 PM   Jupiter enters Cancer
Jul 17, 1931 3:51 AM   Jupiter enters Leo
Aug 11, 1932 3:16 AM   Jupiter enters Virgo
Sep 10, 1933 1:10 AM   Jupiter enters Libra
   *** Daylight Saving Time ends ***
Oct 10, 1934 11:55 PM   Jupiter enters Scorpio
Nov 8, 1935 9:55 PM   Jupiter enters Sagittarius
Dec 2, 1936 3:38 AM   Jupiter enters Capricorn
Dec 19, 1937 11:05 PM   Jupiter enters Aquarius
   *** Daylight Saving Time begins ***
May 14, 1938 3:45 AM   Jupiter enters Pisces
Jul 29, 1938 11:02 PM   Jupiter Rx enters Aquarius
   *** Daylight Saving Time ends ***
Dec 29, 1938 1:34 PM   Jupiter enters Pisces
   *** Daylight Saving Time begins ***
May 11, 1939 10:08 AM   Jupiter enters Aries
   *** Daylight Saving Time ends ***
Oct 29, 1939 7:46 PM   Jupiter Rx enters Pisces
Dec 20, 1939 12:02 PM   Jupiter enters Aries
   *** Daylight Saving Time begins ***
May 16, 1940 3:54 AM   Jupiter enters Taurus
May 26, 1941 8:48 AM   Jupiter enters Gemini
Jun 10, 1942 6:36 AM   Jupiter enters Cancer
Jun 30, 1943 5:45 PM   Jupiter enters Leo
Jul 25, 1944 9:03 PM   Jupiter enters Virgo
Aug 25, 1945 2:05 AM   Jupiter enters Libra
Sep 25, 1946 6:19 AM   Jupiter enters Scorpio
   *** Daylight Saving Time ends ***
3 Oct 23, 1947 9:59 PM   Jupiter enters Sagittarius
Nov 15, 1948 5:38 AM   Jupiter enters Capricorn

Apr 12, 1949 2:17 PM	Jupiter enters Aquarius
*** Daylight Saving Time begins ***	
Jun 27, 1949 2:30 PM	Jupiter Rx enters Capricorn
*** Daylight Saving Time ends ***	
Nov 30, 1949 3:07 PM	Jupiter enters Aquarius
Apr 15, 1950 3:58 AM	Jupiter enters Pisces
*** Daylight Saving Time begins ***	
Sep 14, 1950 10:23 PM	Jupiter Rx enters Aquarius
*** Daylight Saving Time ends ***	
Dec 1, 1950 2:56 PM	Jupiter enters Pisces
Apr 21, 1951 9:57 AM	Jupiter enters Aries
*** Daylight Saving Time begins ***	
Apr 28, 1952 4:50 PM	Jupiter enters Taurus
May 9, 1953 11:33 AM	Jupiter enters Gemini
May 24, 1954 12:43 AM	Jupiter enters Cancer
Jun 12, 1955 8:06 PM	Jupiter enters Leo
*** Daylight Saving Time ends ***	
Nov 16, 1955 10:58 PM	Jupiter enters Virgo
Jan 17, 1956 9:04 PM	Jupiter Rx enters Leo
*** Daylight Saving Time begins ***	
Jul 7, 1956 3:01 PM	Jupiter enters Virgo
*** Daylight Saving Time ends ***	
4 Dec 12, 1956 9:17 PM	Jupiter enters Libra
Feb 19, 1957 10:38 AM	Jupiter Rx enters Virgo
*** Daylight Saving Time begins ***	
Aug 6, 1957 10:11 PM	Jupiter enters Libra
*** Daylight Saving Time ends ***	
Jan 13, 1958 7:51 AM	Jupiter enters Scorpio
Mar 20, 1958 2:14 PM	Jupiter Rx enters Libra
*** Daylight Saving Time begins ***	
Sep 7, 1958 4:52 AM	Jupiter enters Scorpio
*** Daylight Saving Time ends ***	
Feb 10, 1959 8:45 AM	Jupiter enters Sagittarius
Apr 24, 1959 9:11 AM	Jupiter Rx enters Scorpio
*** Daylight Saving Time begins ***	
Oct 5, 1959 10:39 AM	Jupiter enters Sagittarius
*** Daylight Saving Time ends ***	
Mar 1, 1960 8:10 AM	Jupiter enters Capricorn
*** Daylight Saving Time begins ***	
June 9, 1960 9:53 PM	Jupiter Rx enters Sagittarius
Oct 25, 1960 11:00 PM	Jupiter enters Capricorn

*** Daylight Saving Time ends ***
Mar 15, 1961 3:01 AM   Jupiter enters Aquarius
*** Daylight Saving Time begins ***
Aug 12, 1961 4:54 AM   Jupiter Rx enters Capricorn
*** Daylight Saving Time ends ***
5 Nov 3, 1961 9:49 PM   Jupiter enters Aquarius
Mar 25, 1962 5:07 PM   Jupiter enters Pisces
Apr 3, 1963 10:19 PM   Jupiter enters Aries
Apr 12, 1964 1:52 AM   Jupiter enters Taurus
Apr 22, 1965 9:32 AM   Jupiter enters Gemini
*** Daylight Saving Time begins ***
*** Daylight Saving Time ends ***
Sep 20, 1965 11:39 PM   Jupiter enters Cancer
Nov 16, 1965 10:08 PM   Jupiter Rx enters Gemini
*** Daylight Saving Time begins ***
May 5, 1966 10:52 AM   Jupiter enters Cancer
Sep 27, 1966 9:19 AM   Jupiter enters Leo
*** Daylight Saving Time ends ***
Jan 15, 1967 10:50 PM   Jupiter Rx enters Cancer
*** Daylight Saving Time begins ***
May 23, 1967 4:20 AM   Jupiter enters Leo
Oct 19, 1967 6:51 AM   Jupiter enters Virgo
*** Daylight Saving Time ends ***
Feb 26, 1968 10:33 PM   Jupiter Rx enters Leo
*** Daylight Saving Time begins ***
Jun 15, 1968 10:43 AM   Jupiter enters Virgo
*** Daylight Saving Time ends ***
Nov 15, 1968 5:44 PM   Jupiter enters Libra
Mar 30, 1969 4:36 PM   Jupiter Rx enters Virgo
*** Daylight Saving Time begins ***
Jul 15, 1969 9:30 AM   Jupiter enters Libra
*** Daylight Saving Time ends ***
Dec 16, 1969 10:55 AM   Jupiter enters Scorpio
*** Daylight Saving Time begins ***
Apr 30, 1970 2:44 AM   Jupiter Rx enters Libra
Aug 15, 1970 1:57 PM   Jupiter enters Scorpio
*** Daylight Saving Time ends ***
Jan 14, 1971 3:49 AM   Jupiter enters Sagittarius
*** Daylight Saving Time begins ***
Jun 4, 1971 10:12 PM   Jupiter Rx enters Scorpio
Sep 11, 1971 11:33 AM   Jupiter enters Sagittarius

*** Daylight Saving Time ends ***
Feb 6, 1972 2:36 PM   Jupiter enters Capricorn
*** Daylight Saving Time begins ***
Jul 24, 1972 12:43 PM   Jupiter Rx enters Sagittarius
Sep 25, 1972 2:19 PM   Jupiter enters Capricorn
*** Daylight Saving Time ends ***
Feb 23, 1973 4:28 AM   Jupiter enters Aquarius
Mar 8, 1974 6:11 AM   Jupiter enters Pisces
Mar 18, 1975 11:47 AM   Jupiter enters Aries
Mar 26, 1976 5:25 AM   Jupiter enters Taurus
*** Daylight Saving Time begins ***
Aug 23, 1976 6:24 AM   Jupiter enters Gemini
7 Oct 16, 1976 4:24 PM   Jupiter Rx enters Taurus
*** Daylight Saving Time ends ***
Apr 3, 1977 10:42 AM   Jupiter enters Gemini
*** Daylight Saving Time begins ***
Aug 20, 1977 8:42 AM   Jupiter enters Cancer
*** Daylight Saving Time ends ***
Dec 30, 1977 6:50 PM   Jupiter Rx enters Gemini
Apr 11, 1978 7:12 PM   Jupiter enters Cancer
*** Daylight Saving Time begins ***
Sep 5, 1978 4:30 AM   Jupiter enters Leo
*** Daylight Saving Time ends ***
Feb 28, 1979 6:35 PM   Jupiter Rx enters Cancer
Apr 20, 1979 3:29 AM   Jupiter enters Leo
*** Daylight Saving Time begins ***
Sep 29, 1979 6:23 AM   Jupiter enters Virgo
*** Daylight Saving Time ends ***
Oct 27, 1980 5:10 AM   Jupiter enters Libra
Nov 26, 1981 9:19 PM   Jupiter enters Scorpio
Dec 25, 1982 8:57 PM   Jupiter enters Sagittarius
Jan 19, 1984 10:04 AM   Jupiter enters Capricorn
Feb 6, 1985 10:35 AM   Jupiter enters Aquarius
Feb 20, 1986 11:05 AM   Jupiter enters Pisces
Mar 2, 1987 1:41 PM   Jupiter enters Aries
Mar 8, 1988 10:44 AM   Jupiter enters Taurus
*** Daylight Saving Time begins ***
Jul 21, 1988 8:00 PM   Jupiter enters Gemini
*** Daylight Saving Time ends ***
Nov 30, 1988 3:53 PM   Jupiter Rx enters Taurus
Mar 10, 1989 10:26 PM   Jupiter enters Gemini

Jupiter Sign Changes (Ingresses) from 1900 to 2050 (Eastern Time)

 *** Daylight Saving Time begins ***
Jul 30, 1989 7:50 PM Jupiter enters Cancer
Aug 18, 1990 3:30 AM Jupiter enters Leo
Sep 12, 1991 2:00 AM Jupiter enters Virgo
Oct 10, 1992 9:26 AM Jupiter enters Libra
 *** Daylight Saving Time ends ***
Nov 10, 1993 3:15 AM Jupiter enters Scorpio
Dec 9, 1994 5:54 AM Jupiter enters Sagittarius
Jan 3, 1996 2:22 AM Jupiter enters Capricorn
Jan 21, 1997 10:13 AM Jupiter enters Aquarius
Feb 4, 1998 5:52 AM Jupiter enters Pisces
Feb 12, 1999 8:23 PM Jupiter enters Aries
 *** Daylight Saving Time begins ***
Jun 28, 1999 5:29 AM Jupiter enters Taurus
Oct 23, 1999 1:48 AM Jupiter Rx enters Aries
 *** Daylight Saving Time ends ***
Feb 14, 2000 4:40 PM Jupiter enters Taurus
 *** Daylight Saving Time begins ***
Jun 30, 2000 3:35 AM Jupiter enters Gemini
9 Jul 12, 2001 8:03 PM Jupiter enters Cancer
Aug 1, 2002 1:20 PM Jupiter enters Leo
Aug 27, 2003 5:26 AM Jupiter enters Virgo
Sep 24, 2004 11:23 PM Jupiter enters Libra
Oct 25, 2005 10:52 PM Jupiter enters Scorpio
 *** Daylight Saving Time ends ***
Nov 23, 2006 11:43 PM Jupiter enters Sagittarius
Dec 18, 2007 3:11 PM Jupiter enters Capricorn
Jan 5, 2009 10:41 AM Jupiter enters Aquarius
Jan 17, 2010 9:10 PM Jupiter enters Pisces
 *** Daylight Saving Time begins ***
Jun 6, 2010 2:28 AM Jupiter enters Aries
Sep 9, 2010 12:49 AM Jupiter Rx enters Pisces
 *** Daylight Saving Time ends ***
Jan 22, 2011 12:11 PM Jupiter enters Aries
 *** Daylight Saving Time begins ***
Jun 4, 2011 9:56 AM Jupiter enters Taurus
Jun 11, 2012 1:22 PM Jupiter enters Gemini
Jun 25, 2013 9:40 PM Jupiter enters Cancer
Jul 16, 2014 6:31 AM Jupiter enters Leo
Aug 11, 2015 7:11 AM Jupiter enters Virgo
Sep 9, 2016 7:18 AM Jupiter enters Libra
Oct 10, 2017 9:20 AM Jupiter enters Scorpio

*** Daylight Saving Time ends ***
10 Nov 8, 2018 7:39 AM   Jupiter enters Sagittarius
Dec 2, 2019 1:20 PM   Jupiter enters Capricorn
Dec 19, 2020 8:07 AM   Jupiter enters Aquarius
   *** Daylight Saving Time begins ***
May 13, 2021 6:36 PM   Jupiter enters Pisces
Jul 28, 2021 8:42 AM   Jupiter Rx enters Aquarius
   *** Daylight Saving Time ends ***
Dec 28, 2021 11:09 PM   Jupiter enters Pisces
   *** Daylight Saving Time begins ***
May 10, 2022 7:22 PM   Jupiter enters Aries
Oct 28, 2022 1:10 AM   Jupiter Rx enters Pisces
   *** Daylight Saving Time ends ***
Dec 20, 2022 9:32 AM   Jupiter enters Aries
   *** Daylight Saving Time begins ***
May 16, 2023 1:20 PM   Jupiter enters Taurus
May 25, 2024 7:15 PM   Jupiter enters Gemini
Jun 9, 2025 5:02 PM   Jupiter enters Cancer
Jun 30, 2026 1:52 AM   Jupiter enters Leo
Jul 26, 2027 12:49 AM   Jupiter enters Virgo
Aug 24, 2028 1:08 AM   Jupiter enters Libra
Sep 24, 2029 2:24 AM   Jupiter enters Scorpio
Oct 22, 2030 7:14 PM   Jupiter enters Sagittarius
   *** Daylight Saving Time ends ***
Nov 15, 2031 5:29 AM   Jupiter enters Capricorn
   *** Daylight Saving Time begins ***
Apr 11, 2032 8:58 PM   Jupiter enters Aquarius
Jun 26, 2032 8:56 AM   Jupiter Rx enters Capricorn
   *** Daylight Saving Time ends ***
Nov 29, 2032 10:31 PM   Jupiter enters Aquarius
   *** Daylight Saving Time begins ***
Apr 14, 2033 6:44 PM   Jupiter enters Pisces
Sep 12, 2033 6:27 PM   Jupiter Rx enters Aquarius
   *** Daylight Saving Time ends ***
Dec 1, 2033 5:34 PM   Jupiter enters Pisces
   *** Daylight Saving Time begins ***
Apr 21, 2034 5:39 AM   Jupiter enters Aries
Apr 29, 2035 2:57 PM   Jupiter enters Taurus
May 9, 2036 10:52 AM   Jupiter enters Gemini
May 23, 2037 10:12 PM   Jupiter enters Cancer
Jun 12, 2038 11:25 AM   Jupiter enters Leo

*** Daylight Saving Time ends ***
Nov 16, 2038 4:20 PM   Jupiter enters Virgo
Jan 16, 2039 9:54 AM   Jupiter Rx enters Leo
    *** Daylight Saving Time begins ***
Jul 7, 2039 8:24 PM   Jupiter enters Virgo
    *** Daylight Saving Time ends ***
Dec 12, 2039 5:05 PM   Jupiter enters Libra
Feb 20, 2040 12:35 AM   Jupiter Rx enters Virgo
    *** Daylight Saving Time begins ***
Aug 5, 2040 6:03 PM   Jupiter enters Libra
    *** Daylight Saving Time ends ***
Jan 11, 2041 2:33 PM   Jupiter enters Scorpio
    *** Daylight Saving Time begins ***
Mar 20, 2041 8:01 PM   Jupiter Rx enters Libra
Sep 5, 2041 8:12 PM   Jupiter enters Scorpio
    *** Daylight Saving Time ends ***
Feb 8, 2042 6:52 PM   Jupiter enters Sagittarius
    *** Daylight Saving Time begins ***
Apr 24, 2042 8:40 AM   Jupiter Rx enters Scorpio
Oct 4, 2042 5:59 AM   Jupiter enters Sagittarius
    *** Daylight Saving Time ends ***
Mar 1, 2043 12:05 PM   Jupiter enters Capricorn
    *** Daylight Saving Time begins ***
Jun 9, 2043 5:41 PM   Jupiter Rx enters Sagittarius
Oct 26, 2043 7:30 AM   Jupiter enters Capricorn
Mar 15, 2044 12:27 AM   Jupiter enters Aquarius
Aug 9, 2044 8:41 AM   Jupiter Rx enters Capricorn
Nov 4, 2044 1:32 PM   Jupiter enters Aquarius
Mar 26, 2045 1:08 AM   Jupiter enters Pisces
Apr 4, 2046 12:10 PM   Jupiter enters Aries
Apr 13, 2047 5:03 PM   Jupiter enters Taurus
Apr 22, 2048 9:43 PM   Jupiter enters Gemini
13 Sep 23, 2048 8:57 AM   Jupiter enters Cancer
    *** Daylight Saving Time ends ***
Nov 12, 2048 9:05 AM   Jupiter Rx enters Gemini
    *** Daylight Saving Time begins ***
May 5, 2049 2:12 PM   Jupiter enters Cancer
Sep 27, 2049 6:28 AM   Jupiter enters Leo
    *** Daylight Saving Time ends ***

Summary of the Adolescence of Case Studies

Celebrity Name	First Jupiter return	Uranus/ Jupiter sextiles	Rebel or Truth Seeker?	Final Saturn opposition	Span of time between Jupiter return and Saturn opposition
Sting	May 1963	Ur: Nov 1964-Aug 65 Ju: 1 Jun 65	Rebel	May 67-Jun 67	4y 1 mo
Nicholas Cage	May 1975	Ur: Dec 76-Sep 77 Ju: May 77	Rebel	Aug 77	3y 3 mo
Liam Neeson	May 1964	Ur: Oct 64-July 65 Ju: Jun 66	Rebel	Feb 68	4y 9 mo
Dana Plato	July 76	Ur: Dec 77 Ju: Aug 78	Rebel	10 Jul 78	2y 0mo
Emma Stone	Jul 00-Mar 01	Ur: Ma 02-Feb 03 Ju: Aug 02	Rebel	Jun 03	2y 11mo
Charlie Sheen	Aug 77-Apr 78	Ur: Jan 78 Ju: Sep 79	Rebel	Aug 79	2y 0mo
Margot Robbie	Jun 02	Ju: Aug 04 Ur: Ma-Dec 05	Truth Seeker	Aug 04-Jun 05	3y 0mo
Mike Tyson	Jun 78	Ur: Jan 78-Nov 78 Ju: Aug 80	Rebel	Sep 80	2y 3mo
Gordon Ramsay	Sep 78-May 79	Ur: Sep 79-Oct 80 Ju: Nov 80-Jul 81	Rebel	Oct 79-Jul 80	1y 10mo
Gary Busey	Oct 55-Jun 56	Ur: Oct 57 Ju: Dec 57	Rebel	Jan-Oct 59	4y 0mo

Summary of the Adolescence of Case Studies 209

Julia Roberts	Oct 79	Ju: Dec 81-Jul 82 Ur: Dec 80-Sep 81	Truth Seeker	Nov 80-Aug 81	1 y 10mo
Will Smith	Ju: Sep 80	Ur: Feb-Nov 81 Ju: Nov 82	Rebel	Oct 82	2y 1mo
Beyonce Knowles	Dec 92-Aug 93	Ur: Jan 95 Ju: Feb-Oct 95	Rebel	Mar 97	4y 3mo
Judy Garland	Oct 33	Ju: Dec 35 Aug 37-Mar 38	Truth Seeker	May 1937-Jan 1938	4y 8mo
Stephen King	Dec-58 - Aug 59	Ju: Feb 1961 Ur: Aug 1961	Truth Seeker	Mar-Dec 63	5y 0mo
Kevin Spacey	Dec 70	Ur: Nov 71-Aug 72 Ju: Jan 73	Rebel	Aug 73-May 74	3y 5mo
Timothee Chalamet	Dec 2007	Ju: Jan 10 Ur: May 10-Feb 11	Truth Seeker	Nov 08-Aug 09	1y 7mo
Dua Lipo	Dec 06	Ju: Feb 09 Ur: Mar 10-Jan 11	Truth Seeker	Sep 09	2y 9mo
Lorde	Feb-Oct 08	Ju: Mar 10 Ur: Apr 10-Jan 11	Truth Seeker	Jul 10	2y 5mo
Prince Harry	Jan 96	Ju: Feb 98 Ur: Feb-Dec 98	Truth Seeker	Jun 99-Mar 00	4y 2mo
Barack Obama	Feb 73	Ju: Mar 75 Ur: Nov 73-Aug 74	Truth Seeker	Aug 75	2y 6mo
Meg Ryan	Mar 73	Ju: Mar 75 Ur: Nov 74-Sep 75	Truth Seeker	Aug 75	2y 5mo
Emilia Clarke	Apr 98	Ju: Jun 99-Apr 00 Ur: Apr 00-Jan 01	Truth Seeker	Jun 01	3y 2mo
Amber Heard	Apr 98	Ju: Jun 99-Apr 00 Ur: Mar 01-Jan 02	Truth Seeker	Jul 01-Mar 02	3y 11mo

How to calculate the Jupiter and Uranus Sextiles

Transiting Jupiter to its natal position and transiting Uranus to its natal position (in reference to "Truth Seeker" or "Rebel" have been referenced throughout this book. Here is how to use Solar Fire to find the exact time of these transits.

Using the graphic ephemeris from Solar Fire, a few adjustments need to made to examine the sextiles of Jupiter and Uranus. It is highly recommended that these next steps are followed with patience.

1) On Solar Fire, go to the graphic ephemeris "Selection"

2) Adjust the modulus angle to 60 degrees (the default is 45 degrees)

3) From the point selection (to the far right), select the transits. A menu will appear.

4) From the menus, select "create" and choose Jupiter and Uranus

5) Repeat the previous step for the Radix (under the transits) in the point selection

What is created is a much easier way to locate sextiles for Jupiter and Uranus. This can be done manually but the process is much more arduous.

www.ingramcontent.com/pod-product-compliance
Lightning Source LLC
Chambersburg PA
CBHW062026220426
43662CB00010B/1490